2001
Yearbook of
Astronomy

2001 Yearbook of Astronomy

edited by
Patrick Moore

MACMILLAN

First published 2000 by Macmillan
an imprint of Macmillan Publishers Ltd
25 Eccleston Place, London SW1W 9NF
Basingstoke and Oxford
Associated companies throughout the world
www.macmillan.com

ISBN 0 333 78183 X

9 8 7 6 5 4 3 2

Typeset by Rowland Phototypesetting Ltd,
Bury St Edmunds, Suffolk
Printed and bound in Great Britain by
Mackays of Chatham plc, Chatham, Kent

Contents

Part III
Miscellaneous

Editor's Foreword

The first *Yearbook* of the new millennium follows the usual pattern; there seems no reason to change it. As always, Gordon Taylor has provided the material for the monthly notes; we also have contributions from our regular authors, such as Paul Murdin, Iain Nicolson and Fred Watson, as well as some welcome newcomers. We hope that the result will be acceptable – and regarded as worthy of ushering in the twenty-first century.

PATRICK MOORE
Selsey, April 2000

Preface

New readers will find that all the information in this *Yearbook* is given in diagrammatic or descriptive form; the positions of the planets may easily be found from the specially designed star charts, while the monthly notes describe the movements of the planets and give details of other astronomical phenomena visible in both the northern and southern hemispheres. Two sets of star charts are provided. The **Northern Charts** (pp. 16 to 41) are designed for use at latitude 52°N, but may be used without alteration throughout the British Isles, and (except in the case of eclipses and occultations) in other countries of similar northerly latitude. The **Southern Charts** (pp. 42 to 67) are drawn for latitude 35°S, and are suitable for use in South Africa, Australia and New Zealand, and other locations in approximately the same southerly latitude. The reader who needs more detailed information will find *Norton's Star Atlas* an invaluable guide, while more precise positions of the planets and their satellites, together with predictions of occultations, meteor showers and periodic comets, may be found in the *Handbook* of the British Astronomical Association. Readers will also find details of forthcoming events given in the American magazine *Sky & Telescope* and the British monthly *Modern Astronomer*.

Important note
The times given on the star charts and in the Monthly Notes are generally given as local times, using the 24-hour clock, the day beginning at midnight. All the dates, and the times of a few events (e.g. eclipses), are given in Greenwich Mean Time (GMT), which is related to local time by the formula

Local Mean Time = GMT – west longitude

In practice, small differences in longitude are ignored, and the observer will use local clock time, which will be the appropriate Standard (or Zone) Time. As the formula indicates, places in west longitude will have a Standard Time slow on GMT, while places in east longitude will have a Standard Time fast on GMT. As examples we have:

Standard Time in

New Zealand	GMT + 12 hours
Victoria; NSW	GMT + 10 hours
Western Australia	GMT + 8 hours
South Africa	GMT + 2 hours
British Isles	GMT
Eastern ST	GMT − 5 hours
Central ST	GMT − 6 hours, etc.

If Summer Time is in use, the clocks will have been advanced by one hour, and this hour must be subtracted from the clock time to give Standard Time.

Part I

Monthly Charts and Astronomical Phenomena

Notes on the Star Charts

The stars, together with the Sun, Moon and planets, seem to be set on the surface of the celestial sphere, which appears to rotate about the Earth from east to west. Since it is impossible to represent a curved surface accurately on a plane, any kind of star map is bound to contain some form of distortion. But it is well known that the eye can endure some kinds of distortion better than others, and it is particularly true that the eye is most sensitive to deviations from the vertical and horizontal. For this reason the star charts given in this volume have been designed to give a true representation of vertical and horizontal lines, whatever may be the resulting distortion in the shape of a constellation figure. It will be found that the amount of distortion is, in general, quite small, and is obvious only in the case of large constellations such as Leo and Pegasus, when these appear at the top of a chart and so are elongated sideways.

The charts show all stars down to the fourth magnitude, together with a number of fainter stars which are necessary to define the shapes of constellations. There is no standard system for representing the outlines of the constellations, and triangles and other simple figures have been used to give outlines which are easy to trace with the naked eye. The names of the constellations are given, together with the proper names of the brighter stars. The apparent magnitudes of the stars are indicated roughly by using four different sizes of dot, the larger dots representing the brighter stars.

The two sets of star charts are similar in design. At each opening there is a group of four charts which give a complete coverage of the sky up to an altitude of 62½°; there are twelve such groups to cover the entire year. In the **Northern Charts** (for 52°N) the upper two charts show the southern sky, south being at the centre and east on the left. The coverage is from 10° north of east (top left) to 10° north of west (top right). The two lower charts show the northern sky from 10° south of west (lower left) to 10° south of east (lower right). There is thus an overlap east and west.

Conversely, in the **Southern Charts** (for 35°S) the upper two charts show the northern sky, with north at the centre and east on the right. The two lower charts show the southern sky, with south at the centre and east on the left. The coverage and overlap are the same on both sets of charts.

Because the sidereal day is shorter than the solar day, the stars appear to rise and set about four minutes earlier each day, and this amounts to two hours in a month. Hence the twelve groups of charts in each set are sufficient to give the appearance of the sky throughout the day at intervals of two hours, or at the same time of night at monthly intervals throughout the year. The actual range of dates and times when the stars on the charts are visible is indicated at the top of each page. Each group is numbered in bold type, and the number to be used for any given month and time may be found from the following table:

Local Time	18h	20h	22h	0h	2h	4h	6h
January	11	12	1	2	3	4	5
February	12	1	2	3	4	5	6
March	1	2	3	4	5	6	7
April	2	3	4	5	6	7	8
May	3	4	5	6	7	8	9
June	4	5	6	7	8	9	10
July	5	6	7	8	9	10	11
August	6	7	8	9	10	11	12
September	7	8	9	10	11	12	1
October	8	9	10	11	12	1	2
November	9	10	11	12	1	2	3
December	10	11	12	1	2	3	4

The charts are drawn to scale, the horizontal measurements, marked at every 10°, giving the azimuths (or true bearings) measured from the north round through east (90°), south (180°) and west (270°). The vertical measurements, similarly marked, give the altitudes of the stars up to 62½°. Estimates of altitude and azimuth made from these charts will necessarily be mere approximations, since no observer will be exactly at the particular latitude, or at the stated time, but they will serve for the identification of stars and planets.

The ecliptic is drawn as a broken line on which longitude is marked every 10°; the positions of the planets are then easily found by reference to the table on p. 74. It will be noticed that on the Southern Charts the *ecliptic* may reach an altitude in excess of 62½° on star charts 5 to 9. The continuations of the broken line will be found on the charts of overhead stars.

There is a curious illusion that stars at an altitude of 60° or more are actually overhead, and beginners may often feel that they are leaning over backwards in trying to see them. These overhead stars are given separately on the pages immediately following the main star charts. The entire year is covered at one opening, each of the four maps showing the overhead stars at times which correspond to those for three of the main star charts. The position of the zenith is indicated by a cross, and this cross marks the centre of a circle which is 35° from the zenith; there is thus a small overlap with the main charts.

The broken line leading from the north (on the Northern Charts) or from the south (on the Southern Charts) is numbered to indicate the corresponding main chart. Thus on p. 40 the N–S line numbered 6 is to be regarded as an extension of the centre (south) line of chart 6 on pp. 26 and 27, and at the top of these pages are printed the dates and times which are appropriate. Similarly, on p. 67 the S–N line numbered 10 connects with the north line of the upper charts on pp. 60 and 61.

The overhead stars are plotted as maps on a conical projection, and the scale is rather smaller than that of the main charts.

1L

October 6 at 5ʰ   October 21 at 4ʰ
November 6 at 3ʰ   November 21 at 2ʰ
December 6 at 1ʰ   December 21 at midnight
January 6 at 23ʰ   January 21 at 22ʰ
February 6 at 21ʰ   February 21 at 20ʰ

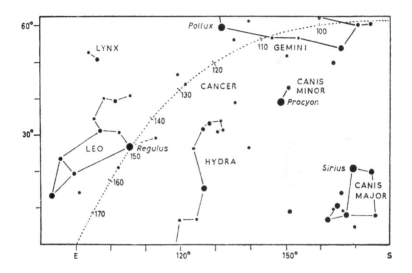

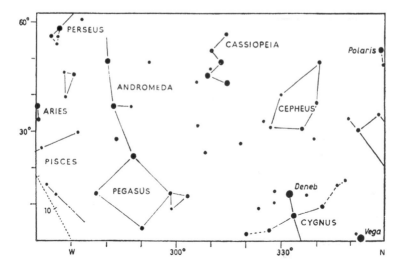

October 6 at 5ʰ	October 21 at 4ʰ
November 6 at 3ʰ	November 21 at 2ʰ
December 6 at 1ʰ	December 21 at midnight
January 6 at 23ʰ	January 21 at 22ʰ
February 6 at 21ʰ	February 21 at 20ʰ

1R

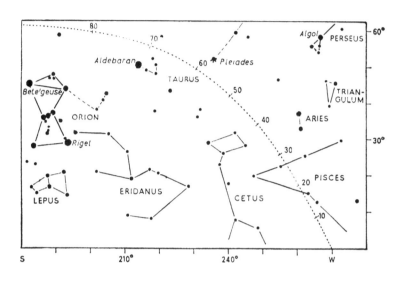

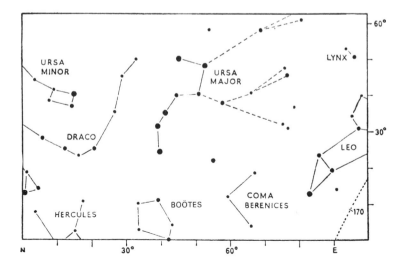

2L

November 6 at 5ʰ   November 21 at   4ʰ
December 6 at 3ʰ   December 21 at   2ʰ
January 6 at 1ʰ   January 21 at midnight
February 6 at 23ʰ   February 21 at   22ʰ
March 6 at 21ʰ   March 21 at   20ʰ

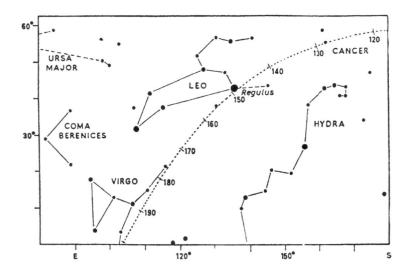

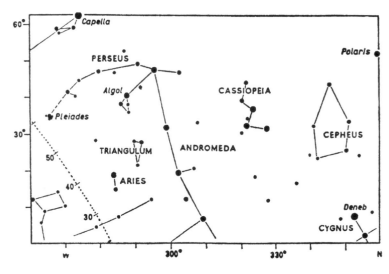

November 6 at 5ʰ	November 21 at 4ʰ	**2R**
December 6 at 3ʰ	December 21 at 2ʰ	
January 6 at 1ʰ	January 21 at midnight	
February 6 at 23ʰ	February 21 at 22ʰ	
March 6 at 21ʰ	March 21 at 20ʰ	

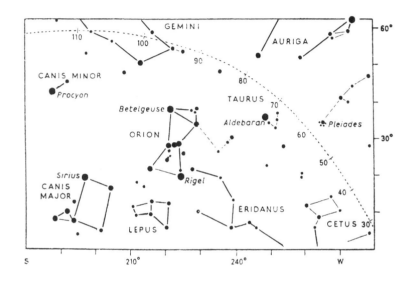

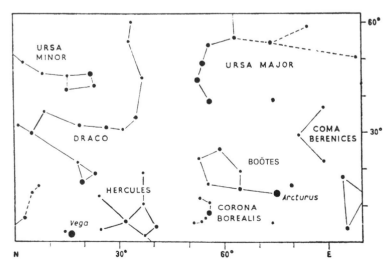

3L

December 6 at	5ʰ	December 21 at	4ʰ
January 6 at	3ʰ	January 21 at	2ʰ
February 6 at	1ʰ	February 21 at	midnight
March 6 at	23ʰ	March 21 at	22ʰ
April 6 at	21ʰ	April 21 at	20ʰ

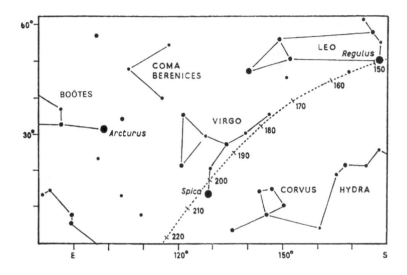

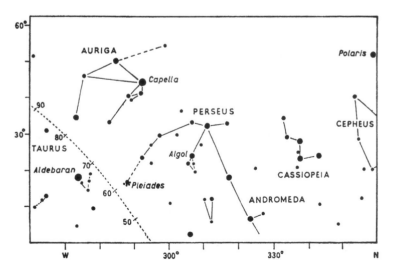

December 6 at 5ʰ	December 21 at 4ʰ	**3R**
January 6 at 3ʰ	January 21 at 2ʰ	
February 6 at 1ʰ	February 21 at midnight	
March 6 at 23ʰ	March 21 at 22ʰ	
April 6 at 21ʰ	April 21 at 20ʰ	

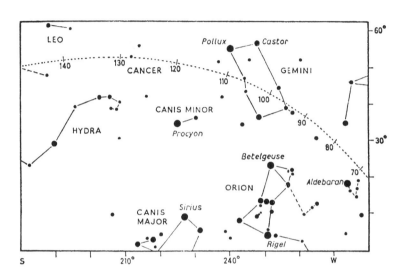

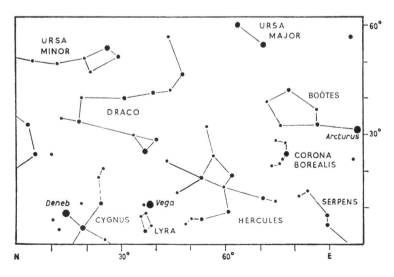

4L

January 6 at	5ʰ	January 21 at	4ʰ
February 6 at	3ʰ	February 21 at	2ʰ
March 6 at	1ʰ	March 21 at midnight	
April 6 at	23ʰ	April 21 at	22ʰ
May 6 at	21ʰ	May 21 at	20ʰ

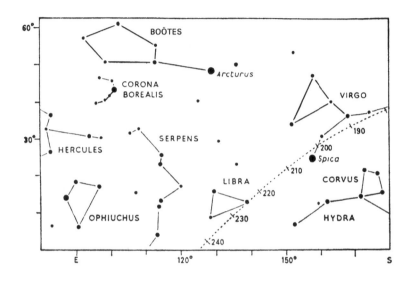

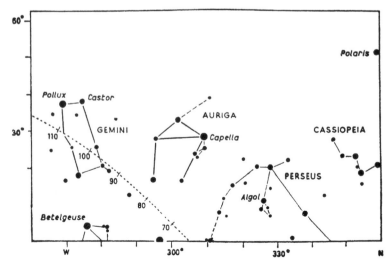

January 6 at 5ʰ	January 21 at 4ʰ
February 6 at 3ʰ	February 21 at 2ʰ
March 6 at 1ʰ	March 21 at midnight
April 6 at 23ʰ	April 21 at 22ʰ
May 6 at 21ʰ	May 21 at 20ʰ

4R

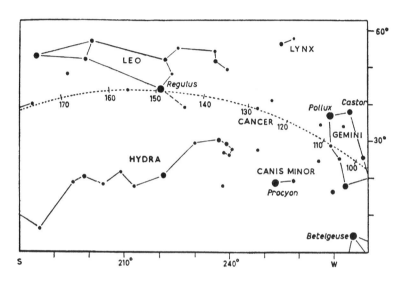

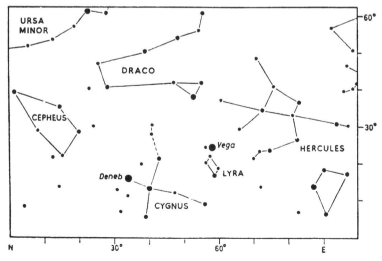

5L

January 6 at	7ʰ	January 21 at	6ʰ
February 6 at	5ʰ	February 21 at	4ʰ
March 6 at	3ʰ	March 21 at	2ʰ
April 6 at	1ʰ	April 21 at midnight	
May 6 at	23ʰ	May 21 at	22ʰ

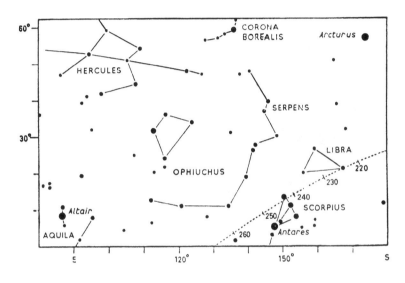

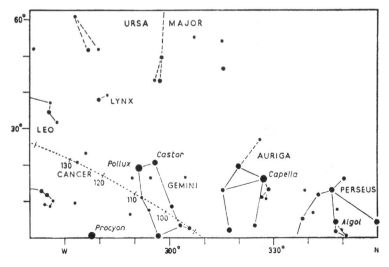

January 6 at 7ʰ January 21 at 6ʰ
February 6 at 5ʰ February 21 at 4ʰ
March 6 at 3ʰ March 21 at 2ʰ
April 6 at 1ʰ April 21 at midnight
May 6 at 23ʰ May 21 at 22ʰ

5R

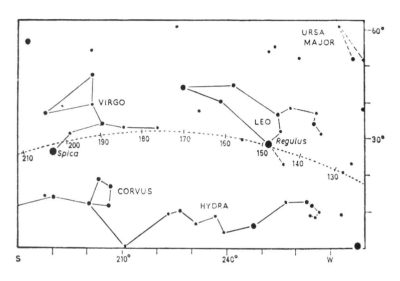

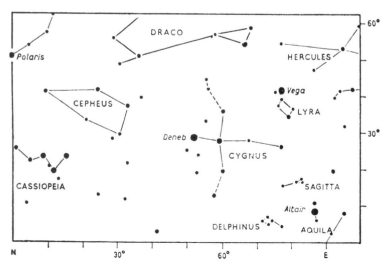

6L

March 6 at 5ʰ	March 21 at 4ʰ
April 6 at 3ʰ	April 21 at 2ʰ
May 6 at 1ʰ	May 21 at midnight
June 6 at 23ʰ	June 21 at 22ʰ
July 6 at 21ʰ	July 21 at 20ʰ

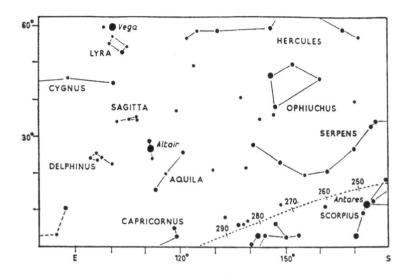

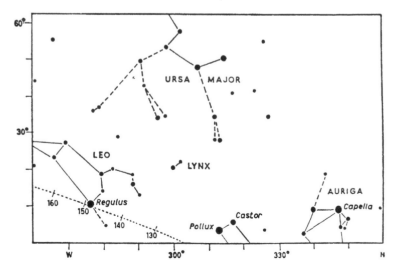

March 6 at 5ʰ	March 21 at 4ʰ
April 6 at 3ʰ	April 21 at 2ʰ
May 6 at 1ʰ	May 21 at midnight
June 6 at 23ʰ	June 21 at 22ʰ
July 6 at 21ʰ	July 21 at 20ʰ

6R

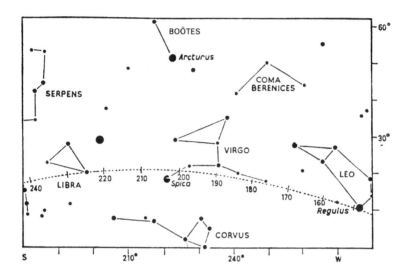

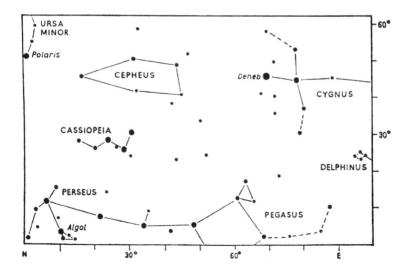

7L

May 6 at 3ʰ	May 21 at 2ʰ
June 6 at 1ʰ	June 21 at midnight
July 6 at 23ʰ	July 21 at 22ʰ
August 6 at 21ʰ	August 21 at 20ʰ
September 6 at 19ʰ	September 21 at 18ʰ

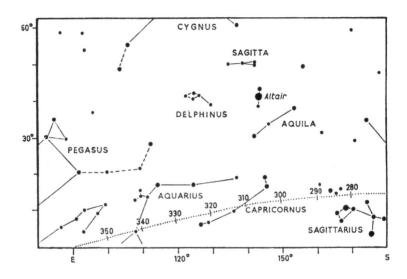

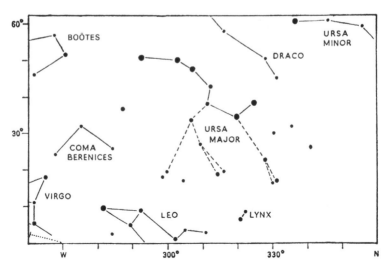

May 6 at 3ʰ   May 21 at   2ʰ
June 6 at 1ʰ   June 21 at midnight
July 6 at 23ʰ   July 21 at   22ʰ
August 6 at 21ʰ   August 21 at   20ʰ
September 6 at 19ʰ   September 21 at   18ʰ

7R

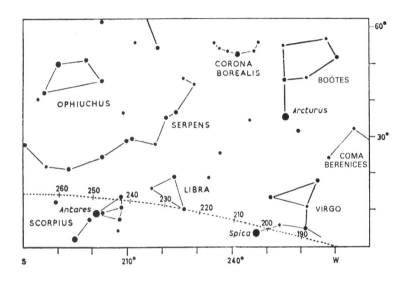

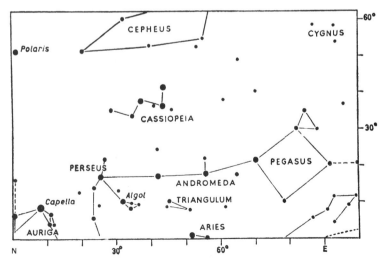

8L

July 6 at 1ʰ	July 21 at midnight
August 6 at 23ʰ	August 21 at 22ʰ
September 6 at 21ʰ	September 21 at 20ʰ
October 6 at 19ʰ	October 21 at 18ʰ
November 6 at 17ʰ	November 21 at 16ʰ

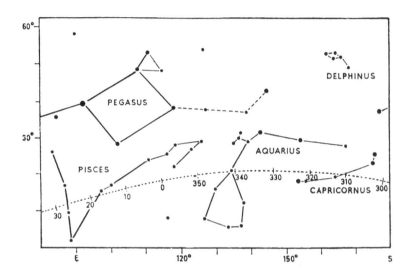

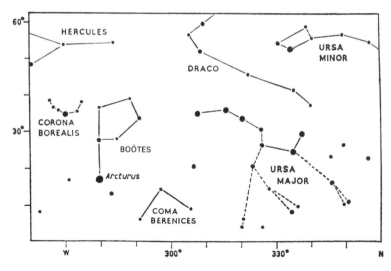

July 6 at 1h	July 21 at midnight
August 6 at 23h	August 21 at 22h
September 6 at 21h	September 21 at 20h
October 6 at 19h	October 21 at 18h
November 6 at 17h	November 21 at 16h

8R

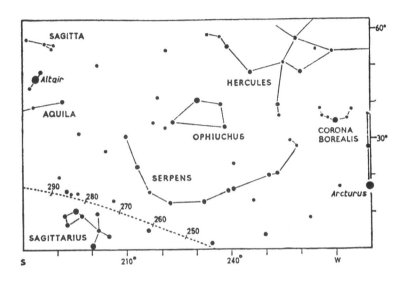

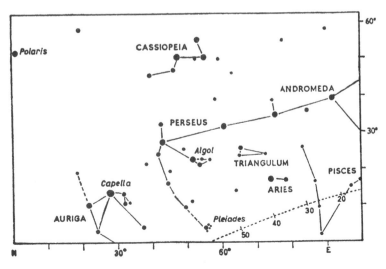

9L

August 6 at 1ʰ	August 21 at midnight
September 6 at 23ʰ	September 21 at 22ʰ
October 6 at 21ʰ	October 21 at 20ʰ
November 6 at 19ʰ	November 21 at 18ʰ
December 6 at 17ʰ	December 21 at 16ʰ

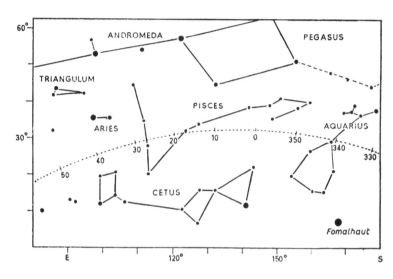

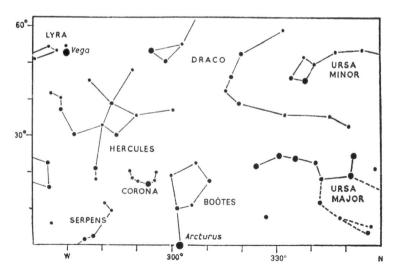

August 6 at   1ʰ   August 21 at midnight
September 6 at 23ʰ   September 21 at   22ʰ
October 6 at 21ʰ   October 21 at   20ʰ
November 6 at 19ʰ   November 21 at   18ʰ
December 6 at 17ʰ   December 21 at   16ʰ

9R

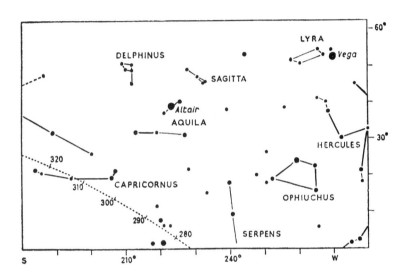

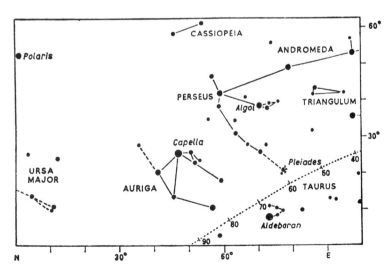

10L

August 6 at 3ʰ	August 21 at 2ʰ
September 6 at 1ʰ	September 21 at midnight
October 6 at 23ʰ	October 21 at 22ʰ
November 6 at 21ʰ	November 21 at 20ʰ
December 6 at 19ʰ	December 21 at 18ʰ

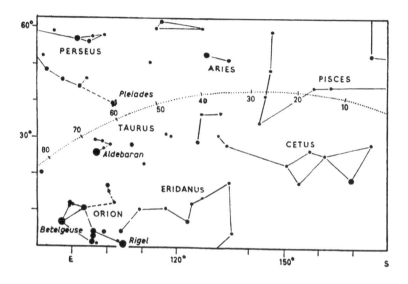

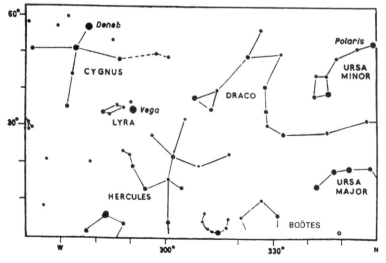

August 6 at 3ʰ	August 21 at 2ʰ
September 6 at 1ʰ	September 21 at midnight
October 6 at 23ʰ	October 21 at 22ʰ
November 6 at 21ʰ	November 21 at 20ʰ
December 6 at 19ʰ	December 21 at 18ʰ

10R

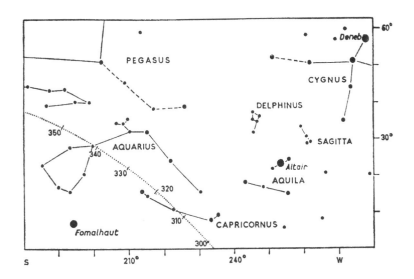

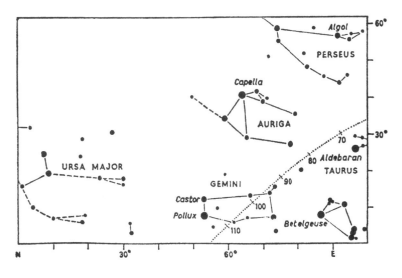

11L

September 6 at 3h	September 21 at 2h
October 6 at 1h	October 21 at midnight
November 6 at 23h	November 21 at 22h
December 6 at 21h	December 21 at 20h
January 6 at 19h	January 21 at 18h

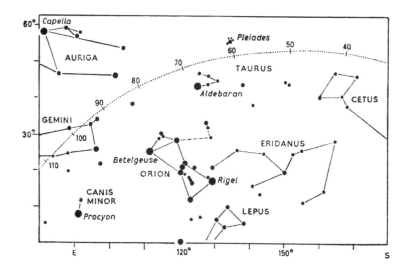

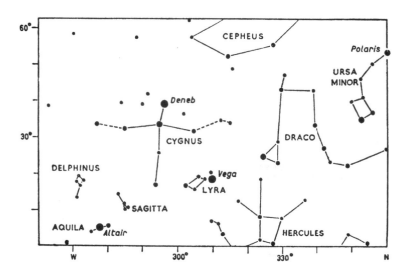

September 6 at   3ʰ   September 21 at   2ʰ
October 6 at   1ʰ   October 21 at midnight
November 6 at 23ʰ   November 21 at   22ʰ
December 6 at 21ʰ   December 21 at   20ʰ
January 6 at 19ʰ   January 21 at   18ʰ

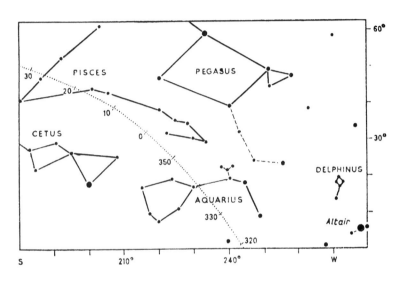

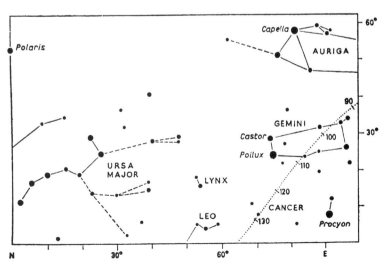

12L

October 6 at	3ʰ	October 21 at	2ʰ
November 6 at	1ʰ	November 21 at midnight
December 6 at	23ʰ	December 21 at	22ʰ
January 6 at	21ʰ	January 21 at	20ʰ
February 6 at	19ʰ	February 21 at	18ʰ

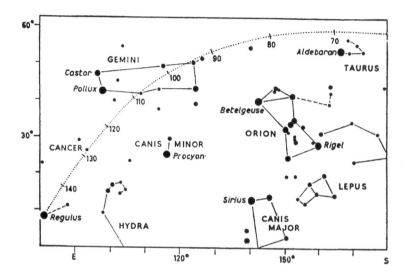

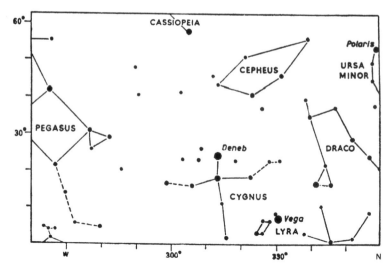

October 6 at 3ʰ   October 21 at 2ʰ
November 6 at 1ʰ   November 21 at midnight
December 6 at 23ʰ   December 21 at 22ʰ
January 6 at 21ʰ   January 21 at 20ʰ
February 6 at 19ʰ   February 21 at 18ʰ

12R

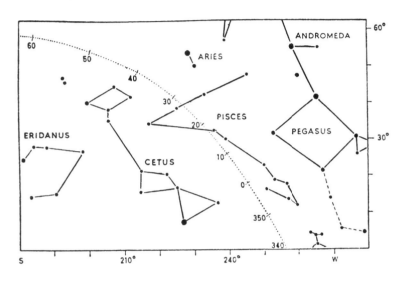

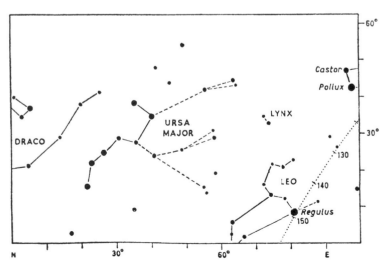

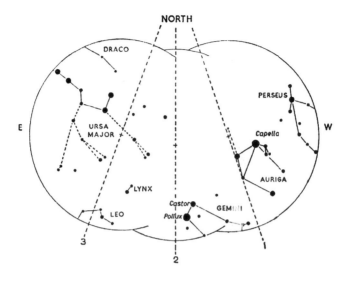

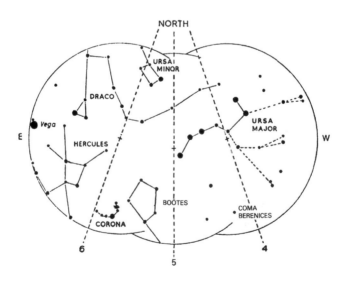

Northern Hemisphere Overhead Stars

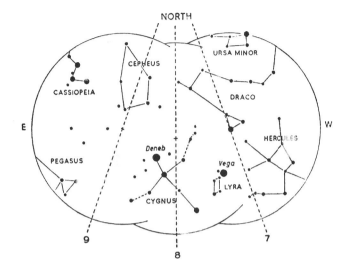

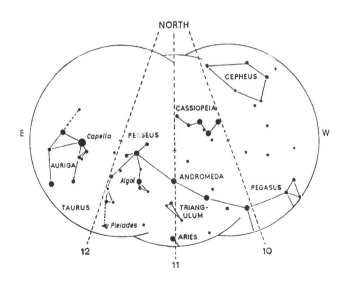

Northern Hemisphere Overhead Stars

1L

October 6 at 5ʰ	October 21 at 4ʰ
November 6 at 3ʰ	November 21 at 2ʰ
December 6 at 1ʰ	December 21 at midnight
January 6 at 23ʰ	January 21 at 22ʰ
February 6 at 21ʰ	February 21 at 20ʰ

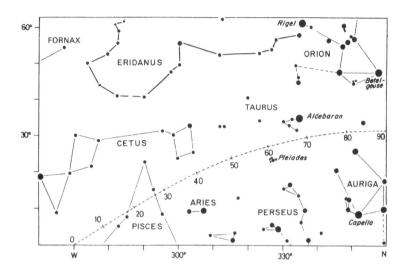

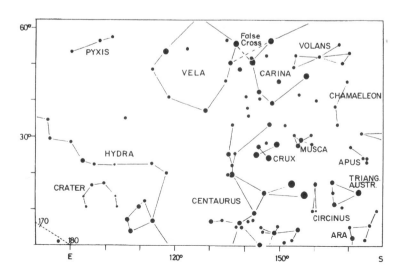

October 6 at 5ʰ   October 21 at 4ʰ
November 6 at 3ʰ   November 21 at 2ʰ
December 6 at 1ʰ   December 21 at midnight
January 6 at 23ʰ   January 21 at 22ʰ
February 6 at 21ʰ   February 21 at 20ʰ

1R

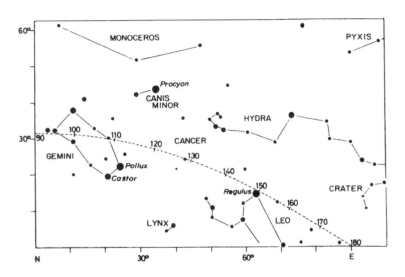

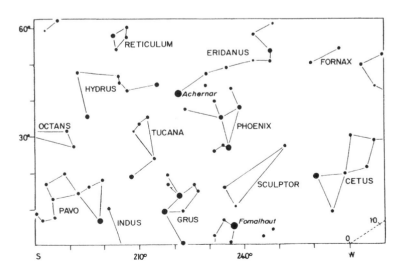

2L

November 6 at 5ʰ	November 21 at 4ʰ
December 6 at 3ʰ	December 21 at 2ʰ
January 6 at 1ʰ	January 21 at midnight
February 6 at 23ʰ	February 21 at 22ʰ
March 6 at 21ʰ	March 21 at 20ʰ

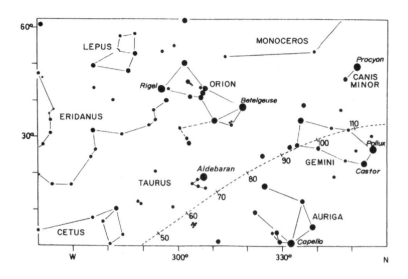

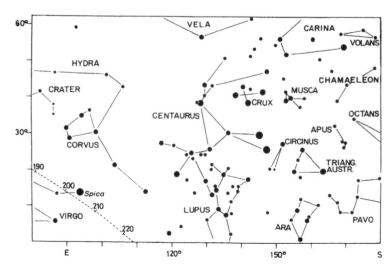

November 6 at 5ʰ	November 21 at 4ʰ
December 6 at 3ʰ	December 21 at 2ʰ
January 6 at 1ʰ	January 21 at midnight
February 6 at 23ʰ	February 21 at 22ʰ
March 6 at 21ʰ	March 21 at 20ʰ

2R

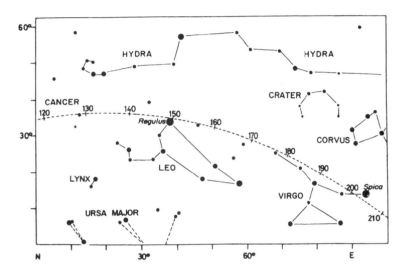

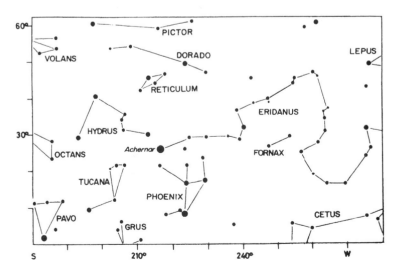

3L

January 6 at 3ʰ	January 21 at 2ʰ
February 6 at 1ʰ	February 21 at midnight
March 6 at 23ʰ	March 21 at 22ʰ
April 6 at 21ʰ	April 21 at 20ʰ
May 6 at 19ʰ	May 21 at 18ʰ

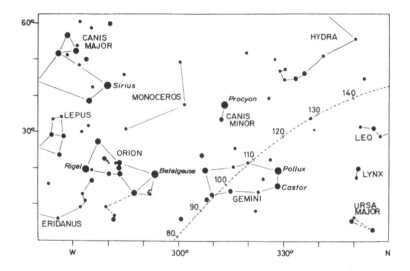

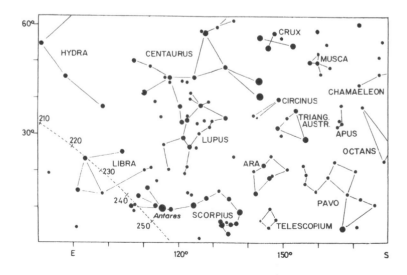

January 6 at 3ʰ	January 21 at 2ʰ
February 6 at 1ʰ	February 21 at midnight
March 6 at 23ʰ	March 21 at 22ʰ
April 6 at 21ʰ	April 21 at 20ʰ
May 6 at 19ʰ	May 21 at 18ʰ

3R

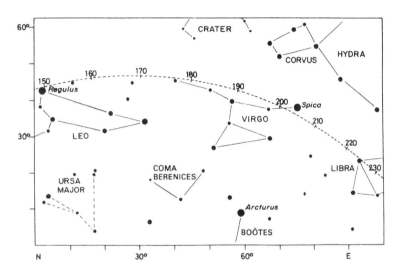

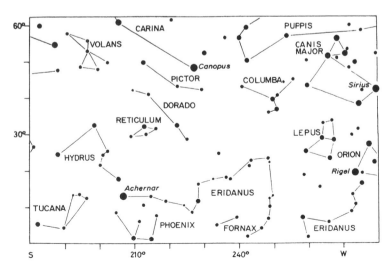

4L

February 6 at 3ʰ	February 21 at 2ʰ
March 6 at 1ʰ	March 21 at midnight
April 6 at 23ʰ	April 21 at 22ʰ
May 6 at 21ʰ	May 21 at 20ʰ
June 6 at 19ʰ	June 21 at 18ʰ

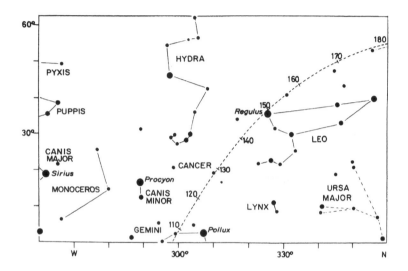

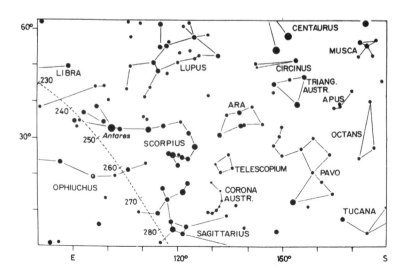

February 6 at 3ʰ	February 21 at 2ʰ
March 6 at 1ʰ	March 21 at midnight
April 6 at 23ʰ	April 21 at 22ʰ
May 6 at 21ʰ	May 21 at 20ʰ
June 6 at 19ʰ	June 21 at 18ʰ

4R

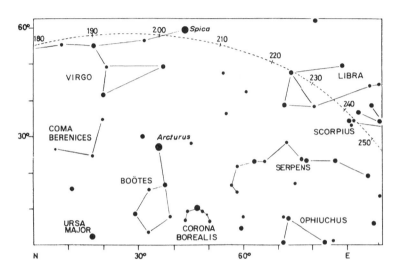

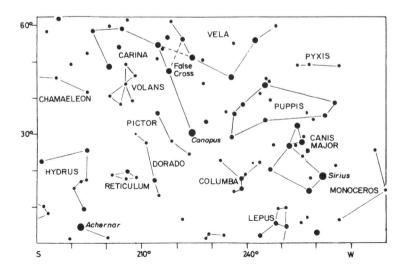

5L

March 6 at	3ʰ	March 21 at	2ʰ
April 6 at	1ʰ	April 21 at midnight	
May 6 at	23ʰ	May 21 at	22ʰ
June 6 at	21ʰ	June 21 at	20ʰ
July 6 at	19ʰ	July 21 at	18ʰ

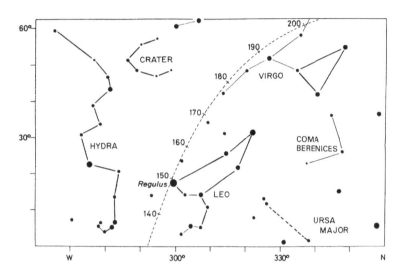

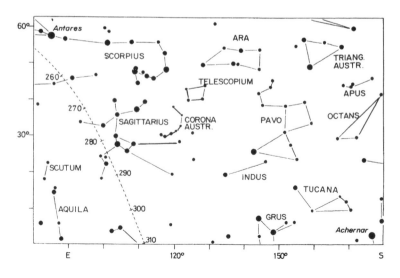

March 6 at 3ʰ	March 21 at 2ʰ
April 6 at 1ʰ	April 21 at midnight
May 6 at 23ʰ	May 21 at 22ʰ
June 6 at 21ʰ	June 21 at 20ʰ
July 6 at 19ʰ	July 21 at 18ʰ

5R

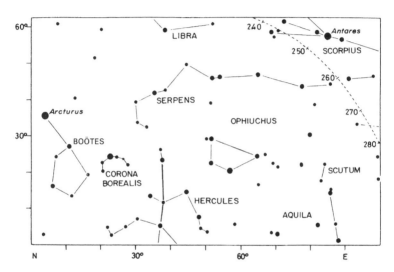

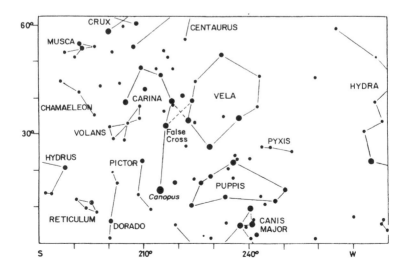

6L

March 6 at 5ʰ	March 21 at 4ʰ
April 6 at 3ʰ	April 21 at 2ʰ
May 6 at 1ʰ	May 21 at midnight
June 6 at 23ʰ	June 21 at 22ʰ
July 6 at 21ʰ	July 21 at 20ʰ

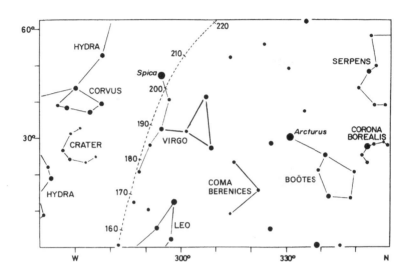

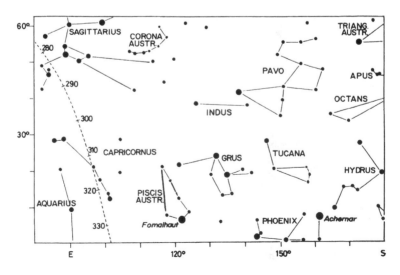

March 6 at	5ʰ	March 21 at	4ʰ
April 6 at	3ʰ	April 21 at	2ʰ
May 6 at	1ʰ	May 21 at midnight	
June 6 at	23ʰ	June 21 at	22ʰ
July 6 at	21ʰ	July 21 at	20ʰ

6R

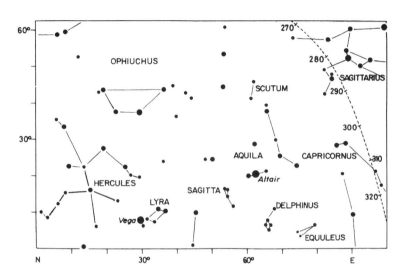

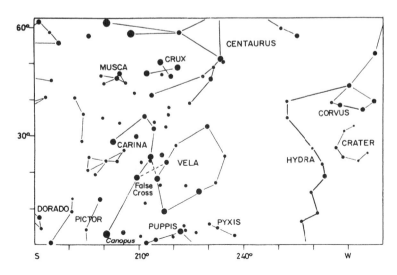

7L

April 6 at 5ʰ	April 21 at 4ʰ
May 6 at 3ʰ	May 21 at 2ʰ
June 6 at 1ʰ	June 21 at midnight
July 6 at 23ʰ	July 21 at 22ʰ
August 6 at 21ʰ	August 21 at 20ʰ

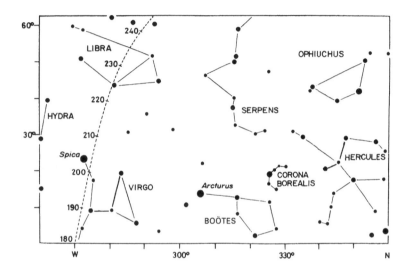

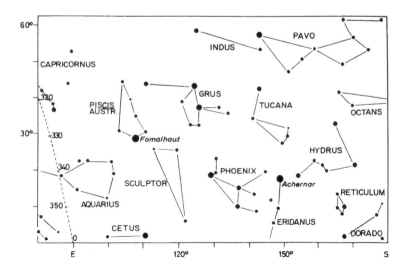

April 6 at 5ʰ	April 21 at 4ʰ
May 6 at 3ʰ	May 21 at 2ʰ
June 6 at 1ʰ	June 21 at midnight
July 6 at 23ʰ	July 21 at 22ʰ
August 6 at 21ʰ	August 21 at 20ʰ

7R

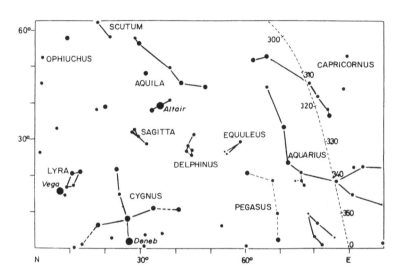

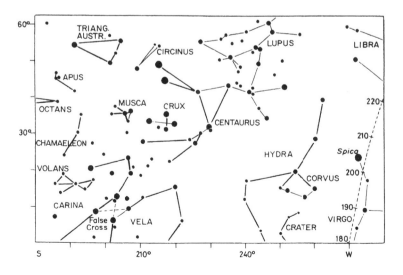

8L

May 6 at 5ʰ	May 21 at 4ʰ
June 6 at 3ʰ	June 21 at 2ʰ
July 6 at 1ʰ	July 21 at midnight
August 6 at 23ʰ	August 21 at 22ʰ
September 6 at 21ʰ	September 21 at 20ʰ

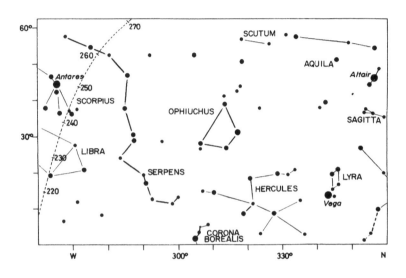

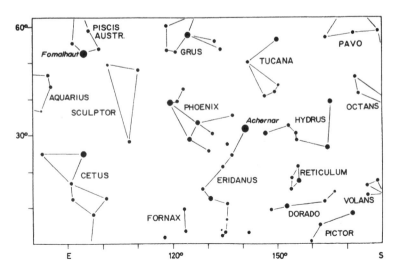

May 6 at 5ʰ   May 21 at   4ʰ
June 6 at 3ʰ   June 21 at   2ʰ
July 6 at 1ʰ   July 21 at midnight
August 6 at 23ʰ   August 21 at   22ʰ
September 6 at 21ʰ   September 21 at   20ʰ

8R

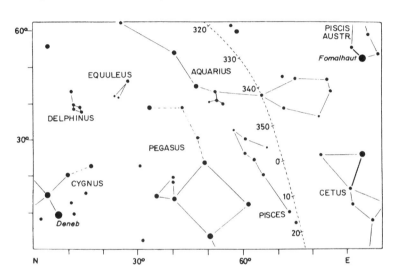

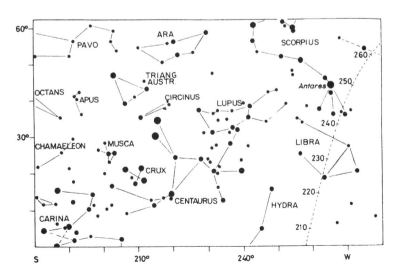

9L

June 6 at 5ʰ	June 21 at 4ʰ
July 6 at 3ʰ	July 21 at 2ʰ
August 6 at 1ʰ	August 21 at midnight
September 6 at 23ʰ	September 21 at 22ʰ
October 6 at 21ʰ	October 21 at 20ʰ

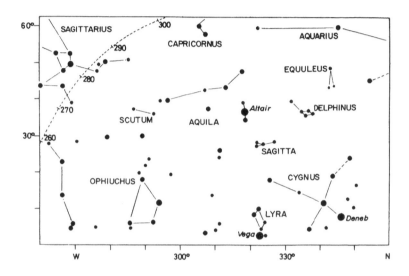

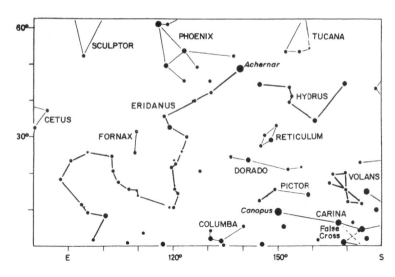

June 6 at 5ʰ	June 21 at 4ʰ
July 6 at 3ʰ	July 21 at 2ʰ
August 6 at 1ʰ	August 21 at midnight
September 6 at 23ʰ	September 21 at 22ʰ
October 6 at 21ʰ	October 21 at 20ʰ

9R

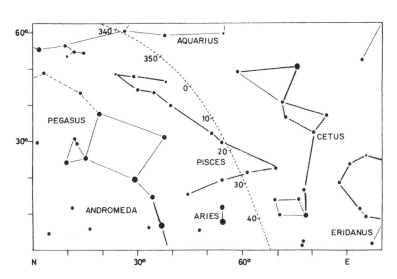

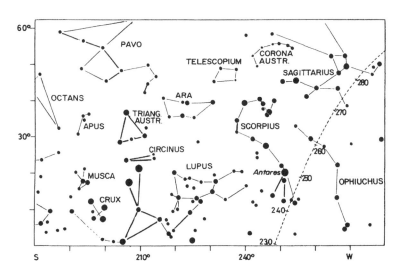

10L

July 6 at	5h	July 21 at	4h
August 6 at	3h	August 21 at	2h
September 6 at	1h	September 21 at midnight	
October 6 at	23h	October 21 at	22h
November 6 at	21h	November 21 at	20h

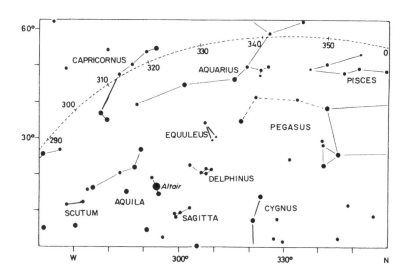

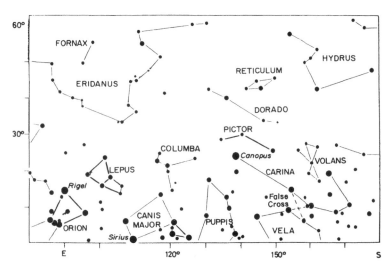

July 6 at 5ʰ   July 21 at   4ʰ
August 6 at 3ʰ   August 21 at   2ʰ
September 6 at 1ʰ   September 21 at midnight
October 6 at 23ʰ   October 21 at   22ʰ
November 6 at 21ʰ   November 21 at   20ʰ

10R

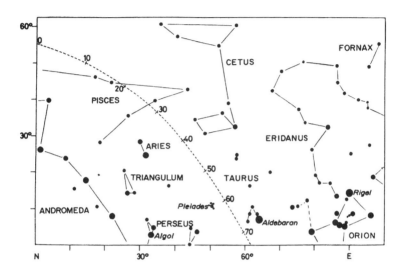

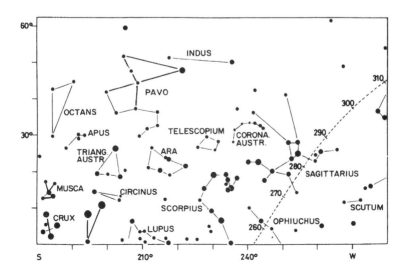

11L

August 6 at 5ʰ	August 21 at 4ʰ
September 6 at 3ʰ	September 21 at 2ʰ
October 6 at 1ʰ	October 21 at midnight
November 6 at 23ʰ	November 21 at 22ʰ
December 6 at 21ʰ	December 21 at 20ʰ

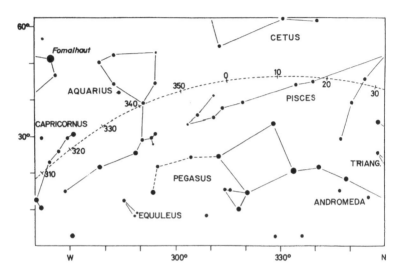

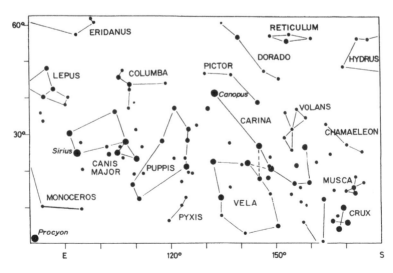

August 6 at 5ʰ	August 21 at 4ʰ
September 6 at 3ʰ	September 21 at 2ʰ
October 6 at 1ʰ	October 21 at midnight
November 6 at 23ʰ	November 21 at 22ʰ
December 6 at 21ʰ	December 21 at 20ʰ

11R

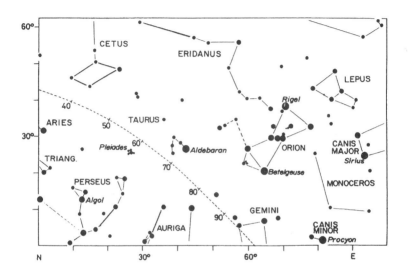

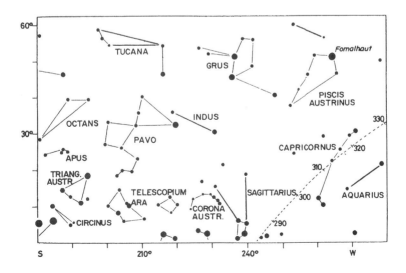

12L

September 6 at 5ʰ	September 21 at 4ʰ
October 6 at 3ʰ	October 21 at 2ʰ
November 6 at 1ʰ	November 21 at midnight
December 6 at 23ʰ	December 21 at 22ʰ
January 6 at 21ʰ	January 21 at 20ʰ

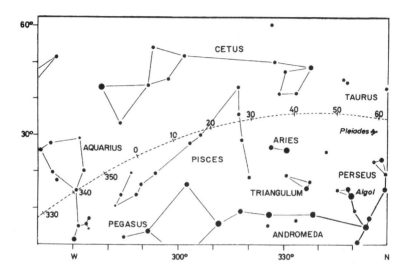

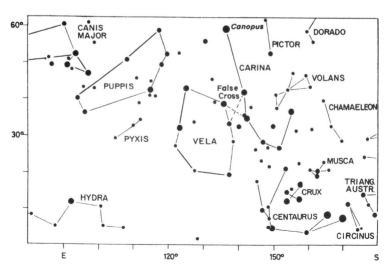

September 6 at   5ʰ   September 21 at   4ʰ
October 6 at   3ʰ   October 21 at   2ʰ
November 6 at   1ʰ   November 21 at midnight
December 6 at 23ʰ   December 21 at   22ʰ
January 6 at 21ʰ   January 21 at   20ʰ

12R

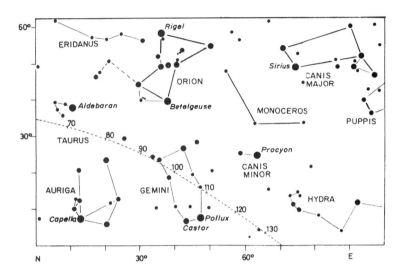

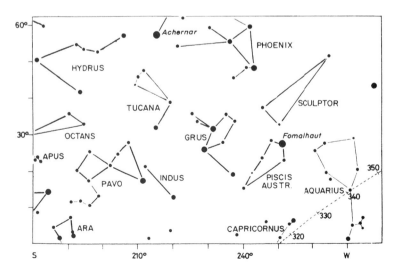

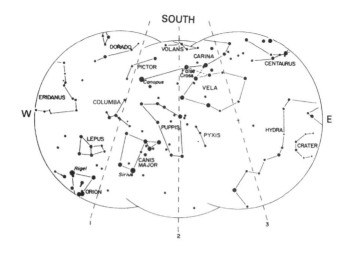

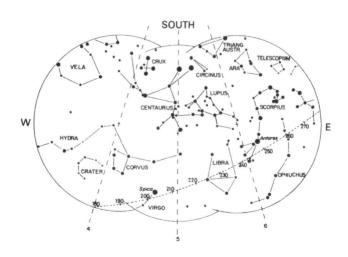

Southern Hemisphere Overhead Stars

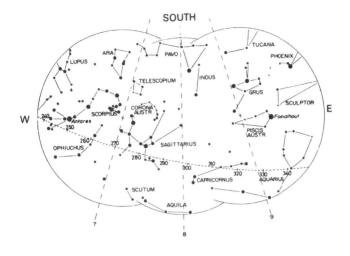

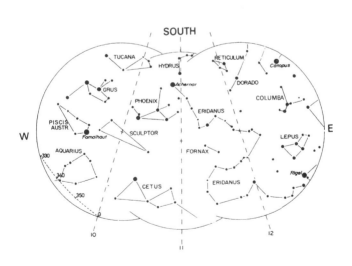

Southern Hemisphere Overhead Stars

The Planets and the Ecliptic

The paths of the planets about the Sun all lie close to the plane of the ecliptic, which is marked for us in the sky by the apparent path of the Sun among the stars, and is shown on the star charts by a broken line. The Moon and naked-eye planets will always be found close to this line, never departing from it by more than about 7°. Thus the planets are most favourably placed for observation when the ecliptic is well displayed, and this means that it should be as high in the sky as possible. This avoids the difficulty of finding a clear horizon, and also overcomes the problem of atmospheric absorption, which greatly reduces the light of the stars. Thus a star at an altitude of 10° suffers a loss of 60 per cent of its light, which corresponds to a whole magnitude; at an altitude of only 4°, the loss may amount to two magnitudes.

The position of the ecliptic in the sky is therefore of great importance, and since it is tilted at about 23½° to the equator, it is only at certain times of the day or year that it is displayed to the best advantage. It will be realized that the Sun (and therefore the ecliptic) is at its highest in the sky at noon in midsummer, and at its lowest at noon in midwinter. Allowing for the daily motion of the sky, it follows that the ecliptic is highest at midnight in winter, at sunset in the spring, at noon in summer and at sunrise in the autumn. Hence these are the best times to see the planets. Thus, if Venus is an evening object in the western sky after sunset, it will be seen to best advantage if this occurs in the spring, when the ecliptic is high in the sky and slopes down steeply to the horizon. Thus means that the planet is not only higher in the sky, but will remain for a much longer period above the horizon. For similar reasons, a morning object will be seen at its best on autumn mornings before sunrise, when the ecliptic is high in the east. The outer planets, which can come to opposition (i.e. opposite the Sun), are best seen when opposition occurs in the winter months, when the ecliptic is high in the sky at midnight.

The seasons are reversed in the Southern Hemisphere, spring beginning at the September Equinox, when the Sun crosses the Equator on its way south, summer beginning at the December Solstice, when the

Sun is highest in the southern sky, and so on. Thus, the times when the ecliptic is highest in the sky, and therefore best placed for observing the planets, may be summarized as follows:

	Midnight	Sunrise	Noon	Sunset
Northern latitudes	December	September	June	March
Southern latitudes	June	March	December	September

In addition to the daily rotation of the celestial sphere from east to west, the planets have a motion of their own among the stars. The apparent movement is generally *direct*, i.e. to the east, in the direction of increasing longitude, but for a certain period (which depends on the distance of the planet) this apparent motion is reversed. With the outer planets this *retrograde* motion occurs about the time of opposition. Owing to the different inclination of the orbits of these planets, the actual effect is to cause the apparent path to form a loop, or sometimes an S-shaped curve. The same effect is present in the motion of the inferior planets, Mercury and Venus, but it is not so obvious, since it always occurs at the time of inferior conjunction.

The *inferior planets*, Mercury and Venus, move in smaller orbits than that of the Earth, and so are always seen near the Sun. They are most obvious at the times of greatest angular distance from the Sun (greatest elongation), which may reach 28° for Mercury, and 47° for Venus. They are seen as evening objects in the western sky after sunset (at eastern elongations) or as morning objects in the eastern sky before sunrise (at western elongations). The succession of phenomena, conjunctions and elongations, always follows the same order, but the intervals between them are not equal. Thus, if either planet is moving round the far side of its orbit its motion will be to the east, in the same direction in which the Sun appears to be moving. It therefore takes much longer for the planet to overtake the Sun – that is, to come to superior conjunction – than it does when moving round to inferior conjunction, between Sun and Earth. The intervals given in the table at the top of p. 70 are average values; they remain fairly constant in the case of Venus, which travels in an almost circular orbit. In the case of Mercury, however, conditions vary widely because of the great eccentricity and inclination of the planet's orbit.

			Mercury	**Venus**
Inferior Conjunction	to	Elongation West	22 days	72 days
Elongation West	to	Superior Conjunction	36 days	220 days
Superior Conjunction	to	Elongation East	36 days	220 days
Elongation East	to	Inferior Conjunction	22 days	72 days

The greatest brilliancy of Venus always occurs about 36 days before or after inferior conjunction. This will be about a month *after* greatest eastern elongation (as an evening object), or a month *before* greatest western elongation (as a morning object). No such rule can be given for Mercury, because its distances from the Earth and the Sun can vary over a wide range.

Mercury is not likely to be seen unless a clear horizon is available. It is seldom as much as 10° above the horizon in the twilight sky in northern temperate latitudes, but this figure is often exceeded in the Southern Hemisphere. This favourable condition arises because the maximum elongation of 28° can occur only when the planet is at aphelion (farthest from the Sun), and it then lies well south of the equator. Northern observers must be content with smaller elongations, which may be as little as 18° at perihelion. In general, it may be said that the most favourable times for seeing Mercury as an evening object will be in spring, some days before greatest eastern elongation; in autumn, it may be seen as a morning object some days after greatest western elongation.

Venus is the brightest of the planets and may be seen on occasions in broad daylight. Like Mercury, it is alternately a morning and an evening object, and it will be highest in the sky when it is a morning object in autumn, or an evening object in spring. Venus is to be seen at its best as an evening object in northern latitudes when eastern elongation occurs in June. The planet is then well north of the Sun in the preceding spring months, and is a brilliant object in the evening sky over a long period. In the Southern Hemisphere a November elongation is best. For similar reasons, Venus gives a prolonged display as a morning object in the months following western elongation in October (in northern latitudes) or in June (in the Southern Hemisphere).

The *superior planets*, which travel in orbits larger than that of the Earth, differ from Mercury and Venus in that they can be seen opposite the Sun in the sky. The superior planets are morning objects after conjunction with the Sun, rising earlier each day until they come to opposition. They will then be nearest to the Earth (and therefore at their brightest), and will be on the meridian at midnight, due south in northern latitudes, but due north in the Southern Hemisphere. After opposition they are evening objects, setting earlier each evening until they set in the west with the Sun at the next conjunction. The difference in brightness from one opposition to another is most noticeable in the case of Mars, whose distance from Earth can vary considerably and rapidly. The other superior planets are at such great distances that there is very little change in brightness from one opposition to the next. The effect of altitude is, however, of some importance, for at a December opposition in northern latitudes the planets will be among the stars of Taurus or Gemini, and can then be at an altitude of more than 60° in southern England. At a summer opposition, when the planet is in Sagittarius, it may only rise to about 15° above the southern horizon, and so makes a less impressive appearance. In the Southern Hemisphere the reverse conditions apply, a June opposition being the best, with the planet in Sagittarius at an altitude which can reach 80° above the northern horizon for observers in South Africa.

Mars, whose orbit is appreciably eccentric, comes nearest to the Earth at oppositions at the end of August. It may then be brighter even than Jupiter, but rather low in the sky in Aquarius for northern observers, though very well placed for those in southern latitudes. These favourable oppositions occur every fifteen or seventeen years (e.g. in 1988, 2003, 2018), but in the Northern Hemisphere the planet is probably better seen at oppositions in the autumn or winter months, when it is higher in the sky. Oppositions of Mars occur at an average interval of 780 days, and during this time the planet makes a complete circuit of the sky.

Jupiter is always a bright planet, and comes to opposition a month later each year, having moved, roughly speaking, from one Zodiacal constellation to the next.

Saturn moves much more slowly than Jupiter, and may remain in the same constellation for several years. The brightness of Saturn depends on the aspects of its rings, as well as on the distance from Earth and Sun. The Earth passed through the plane of Saturn's rings in 1995 and 1996, when they appeared edge-on; we shall next see them at maximum opening, and Saturn at its brightest, around 2002. The rings will next appear edge-on in 2009.

Uranus, Neptune and *Pluto* are hardly likely to attract the attention of observers without adequate instruments.

Phases of the Moon in 2001

New Moon				First Quarter				Full Moon				Last Quarter			
	d	h	m		d	h	m		d	h	m		d	h	m
				Jan.	2	22	31	Jan.	9	20	24	Jan.	16	12	35
Jan.	24	13	07	Feb.	1	14	02	Feb.	8	07	12	Feb.	15	03	24
Feb.	23	08	21	Mar.	3	02	03	Mar.	9	17	23	Mar.	16	20	45
Mar.	25	01	21	Apr.	1	10	49	Apr.	8	03	22	Apr.	15	15	31
Apr.	23	15	26	Apr.	30	17	08	May	7	13	53	May	15	10	11
May	23	02	46	May	29	22	09	June	6	01	29	June	14	03	28
June	21	11	58	June	28	03	19	July	5	15	04	July	13	18	45
July	20	19	44	July	27	10	08	Aug.	4	05	56	Aug.	12	07	53
Aug.	19	02	55	Aug.	25	19	55	Sept.	2	21	43	Sept.	10	19	00
Sept.	17	10	27	Sept.	24	09	31	Oct.	2	13	49	Oct.	10	04	20
Oct.	16	19	23	Oct.	24	02	58	Nov.	1	05	41	Nov.	8	12	21
Nov.	15	06	40	Nov.	22	23	21	Nov.	30	20	49	Dec.	7	19	52
Dec.	14	20	47	Dec.	22	20	56	Dec.	30	10	40				

All times are GMT

Longitudes of the Sun, Moon and Planets in 2001

		Sun °	Moon °	Venus °	Mars °	Jupiter °	Saturn °
January	6	286	53	332	218	62	54
	21	301	263	348	226	61	54
February	6	317	105	3	235	61	54
	21	332	307	13	243	62	55
March	6	345	114	18	250	64	56
	21	0	315	15	256	66	57
April	6	16	167	5	262	69	58
	21	31	0	1	267	71	60
May	6	46	205	6	269	75	62
	21	60	34	16	268	78	64
June	6	75	255	30	265	82	66
	21	90	83	44	260	85	68
July	6	104	288	60	256	88	70
	21	118	121	77	255	92	71
August	6	134	333	95	257	95	73
	21	148	175	113	262	98	74
September	6	163	18	132	269	101	75
	21	178	227	150	277	103	75
October	6	193	52	168	286	104	75
	21	208	262	187	295	105	74
November	6	224	101	207	306	106	74
	21	239	307	226	317	105	72
December	6	254	140	244	328	104	71
	21	269	339	263	339	102	70

Longitude of *Uranus* 322°
Neptune 307°

Moon: Longitude of ascending node
Jan. 1: 106°   Dec. 31: 86°

Mercury moves so quickly among the stars that it is not possible to indicate its position on the star charts at convenient intervals. The monthly notes must be consulted for the best times at which the planet may be seen.

The positions of the other planets are given in the table on p. 74. This gives the apparent longitudes on dates which correspond to those of the star charts, and the position of the planet may at once be found near the ecliptic at the given longitude.

EXAMPLE

In the Northern Hemisphere two planets are seen in the south-western sky in the evenings, in early February. Identify them.

The Northern Star Chart 12R shows the south-western sky on February 6 at 19^h and shows longitudes 340° to 62°. Reference to the table on p. 74 gives the longitude of Jupiter as 61° and that of Saturn as 54°. Thus these planets are to be found in the south-western sky, and the brighter one is Jupiter.

The positions of the Sun and Moon can be plotted on the star maps in the same manner as for the planets. The average daily motion of the Sun is 1°, and of the Moon 13°. For the Moon an indication of its position relative to the ecliptic may be obtained from a consideration of its longitude relative to that of the ascending node. The latter changes only slowly during the year, as will be seen from the values given on p. 74. Let us denote by d the difference in longitude between the Moon and its ascending node. Then if $d = 0°$, 180° or 360°, the Moon is on the ecliptic. If $d = 90°$ the Moon is 5° north of the ecliptic, and if $d = 270°$ the Moon is 5° south of the ecliptic.

On August 21 the Moon's longitude is given in the table on p. 74 as 175°, and the longitude of the node is found by interpolation to be about 93°. Thus $d = 82°$, and the Moon is about 5° north of the ecliptic. Its position may be plotted on Northern Star Charts 1L, 2L, 3L, 4R, 5R and 6R, and on Southern Star Charts 1R, 2R, 3R, 4L, 5L and 6L.

Some Events in 2001

ECLIPSES

There will be four eclipses, two of the Sun and two of the Moon.

January 9: total eclipse of the Moon – Australia, Africa, Europe, eastern part of the Americas.

June 21: total eclipse of the Sun – South America, Africa.

July 5: partial eclipse of the Moon – Australasia, Asia, Africa.

December 14: annular eclipse of the Sun – the Americas.

THE PLANETS

Mercury may be seen more easily from northern latitudes in the evenings about the time of greatest eastern elongation (May 22) and in the mornings around greatest western elongation (October 29). In the Southern Hemisphere the corresponding most favourable dates are around March 11 (mornings) and September 18 (evenings).

Venus is visible in the evenings until the last week of March, and in the mornings from mid-April to early December.

Mars is at opposition on June 21.

Jupiter does not come to opposition in 2001.

Saturn is at opposition on December 3.

Uranus is at opposition on August 15.

Neptune is at opposition on July 30.

Pluto is at opposition on June 4.

Monthly Notes 2001

January

New Moon: January 24   *Full Moon*: January 9

EARTH is at perihelion (nearest to the Sun) on January 4, at a distance of 147 million kilometres (91.4 million miles).

MERCURY attains its greatest eastern elongation (18°) from the Sun on January 28. For the last ten days of the month it is visible as an evening object to observers in the latitudes of the British Isles, its magnitude ranging from –0.9 to 0.0. This elusive planet may only be seen low above the south-western horizon at the end of evening civil twilight. Observers near the equator are best placed since they should be able to detect the planet after about January 10. Observers in southern temperate latitutes are not so well placed as the planet is only 5° or 6° above the east-by-south horizon at the end of evening civil twilight: they are unlikely to see it during the last few days of the month.

VENUS attains its greatest eastern elongation (47°) on January 17. Thus it is a magnificent object, magnitude –4.4, completely dominating the western evening sky for several hours after sunset.

MARS is visible throughout the year. It is a morning object in January, magnitude +1.2, in the south-eastern quadrant of the sky. Early in the month Mars moves eastwards from Virgo into Libra. The path of Mars among the stars from January to the end of August is shown in Figure 1.

JUPITER is a brilliant evening object, magnitude –2.6, and visible long after midnight in the western sky. Jupiter is moving slowly retrograde in the constellation of Taurus, roughly halfway between the Pleiades and the Hyades, reaching its second stationary point on January 25. The path of Jupiter among the stars is shown in Figure 2, accompanying the notes for February. Jupiter is now east of Saturn, the two planets being only 8° apart at the beginning of the year. On January 6 the gibbous Moon passes about 3° or 4° south of both planets.

SATURN is an evening object, magnitude 0.0. The planet is moving slowly retrograde in the constellation of Taurus and reaches its second stationary point on January 25, the same day that Jupiter does. Observers in the British Isles will see the planet cross the meridian during the early part of the evening, and its northerly declination means that it remains visible until the early hours of the morning. The path of Saturn among the stars is shown in Figure 2, accompanying the notes for February.

The new millennium. For the very last time, let us return to the question of when the new millennium starts. There can be no doubt about this: the correct date is January 1, 2001. There was no year 0, since at that time the zero had not been invented. Thus 1 BC was followed immediately by AD 1, and the first day of that millennium was the first day of AD 1. Not that it has any significance in any case, for all our time scales of that period are very uncertain. At least we can be sure that Christ was not born on December 25, AD 1!

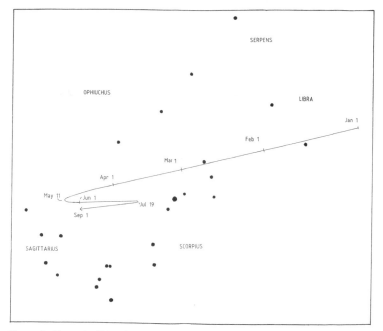

Figure 1. The path of Mars from January to August 2001.

Earth at perihelion. Our world is at its closest to the Sun on January 4 – appreciably closer than it will be in the northern summer. Our seasons have very little to do with the Earth's changing distance from the Sun; they are due to the 23½° tilt of the rotational axis. Theoretically, the Southern Hemisphere should have slightly shorter, hotter summers and slightly longer, colder winters, but this is masked by the greater amount of ocean south of the equator, which tends to stabilize the temperature.

The Earth's orbit does not depart greatly from the circular form, but this is not true of some of the other planets, so their seasons are different. Mars is a case in point. Its axial tilt is much the same as ours, but its distance from the Sun ranges between 206.8 and 248.6 million kilometres, which makes quite a difference – particularly as there are no oceans. The southern climate there is much more extreme than the northern, and this shows up in the behaviour of the polar caps. The southern cap can become larger than its northern counterpart, and is of a different constitution: recent results indicate that the northern residual cap is water ice, while the southern cap is a mixture of water ice and carbon dioxide ice.

Jupiter, with an axial tilt of only 3° to the orbital perpendicular, has no comparable 'seasons'; its distance from the Sun ranges between 740 and 816 million kilometres. The seasons on Uranus are indeed peculiar; the axial tilt is 98°, so that during each Uranian 'year', 84 times as long as ours, each pole has a 'night' lasting for 21 Earth years! But the changing distance from the Sun is most marked in the case of Pluto, the orbit of which is much more eccentric. The perihelion distance is 4450 million kilometres – closer in than Neptune – while at aphelion Pluto recedes to 7375 million kilometres. The last perihelion passage was in 1989, and in 1999 Pluto became once more 'the outermost planet' (assuming that it is still classed as a bona fide planet). As Pluto swings outwards, the surface temperature drops, and the thin atmosphere freezes out onto the surface. For part of its 'year' (248 Earth years) there will be no atmosphere at all. This is one reason why we are anxious to send a probe there before the atmosphere disappears.

The Hubble Space Telescope has shown a certain amount of surface detail on Pluto, but obviously we do not yet know much about the features there. Pluto is not of planetary size; it is smaller than the Moon, and also smaller than Triton, the senior satellite of Neptune.

February

MERCURY, for the first few days of the month, is a difficult evening object for observes near the equator and farther north, and may be glimpsed low above the south-western horizon at the end of civil twilight. Mercury passes through inferior conjunction on February 13. For the last few days of the month it becomes visible as a morning object, low above the south-eastern horizon, though its magnitude, +0.8, makes it difficult to detect. It is not visible to observers in northern temperate latitudes. Observers nearer the equator and in southern latitudes should consult Figure 4, accompanying the notes for March.

VENUS continues to be visible as a magnificent object in the western evening sky. It attains its greatest brilliancy, magnitude −4.6, on February 22. Now is a good time to look for Venus in daylight, in the late afternoon, *provided you shield your eyes from direct sunlight* and know exactly where to look − Venus is 46° from the Sun at the beginning of February, and 37° at the end.

MARS, magnitude +0.8, continues to be visible as a morning object in the south-eastern sky. The planet is moving rapidly eastwards, passing from Libra into Scorpius and then, at the end of the month, into Ophiuchus.

JUPITER, magnitude −2.4, continues to be visible as a brilliant evening object in the constellation Taurus. Observers in the latitudes of the British Isles will be able to see it from sunset until shortly after midnight, even by the end of the month. As we noted in January, the Moon again passes south of both Saturn and Jupiter, this time on February 2. The path of Jupiter among the stars is shown in Figure 2.

SATURN, magnitude +0.1, continues to be visible as an evening object in the western sky. Like Jupiter, Saturn is in the constellation of Taurus.

Venus at its brightest. Venus reaches its maximum brightness this month. This may seem curious, because the phase is now well below half. In fact, the decrease in phase balances the lesser distance from Earth – Venus is always at its best when a crescent. Keen-sighted people can see it with the naked eye in broad daylight. Sweeping for it with binoculars is not to be recommended; it is only too easy to look at the Sun by mistake, with disastrous consequences for your eyesight.

No telescope will show much on Venus; all that can be made out are very vague cloudy features. Before the space age, Venus was often called 'the planet of mystery', and it was generally believed that there might be oceans there. Yet nothing could be further from the truth: Venus is overwhelmingly hostile.

Capella and the Kids. During January evenings, as seen from the latitude of Britain, the brilliant yellow star Capella is almost overhead. It is

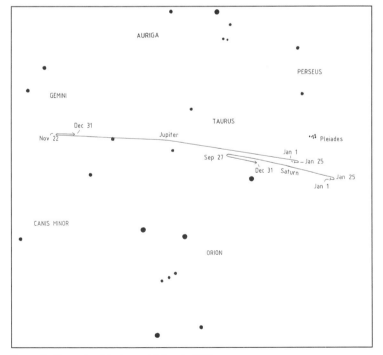

Figure 2. The paths of Jupiter and Saturn in 2001.

in fact a close binary, but to the naked eye, and in ordinary telescopes, it appears single. It is 42 light-years away; of its two components, one is 90 times as luminous as the Sun and the other 70 times.

Close by Capella are three much fainter stars forming a triangle; these are often known as the Haedi, or Kids (Figure 3). One of them, Eta Aurigae, is an ordinary star, 450 light-years away and 200 times as powerful as the Sun, but the other two are remarkable eclipsing binaries. Epsilon Aurigae (it does have a proper name, Almaaz, which is however seldom used), a very powerful yellow supergiant, 4600 light-years away, is periodically eclipsed by an invisible companion which is probably a smaller, hot star with an opaque shell of material around it. Eclipses happen only once in 27 years, so that for most of the time the brightness is steady.

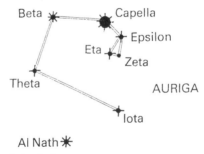

Figure 3. The constellation Auriga.

The third Kid, Zeta Aurigae (Sadatoni), is also an eclipsing binary, but less extreme: the period is 972 days. There is no connection between these two eclipsing binaries; Zeta is only 520 light-years away.

As well as Capella, the constellation of Auriga (the Charioteer) contains other bright stars: Beta or Menkarina (magnitude 1.9), Theta (2.6) and Iota (2.7); Iota is decidedly orange. The star Al Nath (magnitude 1.6) was once included in Auriga, as Gamma Aurigae, but has been transferred to Taurus, and is now officially known as Beta Tauri.

March

New Moon: March 25   *Full Moon*: March 9

Equinox: March 20

Summer Time in Great Britain and Northern Ireland commences on March 25.

MERCURY, for observers in the latitudes of the British Isles, is too close to the Sun for observation throughout March, but for observers farther south this is the most favourable morning apparition of the year. Figure 4 shows, for observers in latitude S.35°, the changes in the azimuth (the true bearing from north, through east, south and west) and altitude of Mercury on successive evenings when the Sun is 6° below the horizon. This position of the Sun is known as the beginning of morning civil twilight, and in this latitude and at this time of year it occurs about 30 minutes before sunrise. The changes in the brightness of the planet are indicated in Figure 4 by the relative sizes of the circles, which mark Mercury's position at five-day intervals. Mercury is at its brightest after it reaches greatest western elongation (27°) on March 11.

VENUS, magnitude –4.3, continues to be visible as a brilliant evening object in the western sky. However, observers will notice that the period available for observation shortens appreciably as Venus appears to move rapidly in towards the Sun, reaching inferior conjunction on the last day of the month. Such a situation favours observers in higher northern latitudes, since Venus reaches its maximum northern ecliptic latitude towards the end of March. Thus observers in the British Isles will have the rare opportunity of seeing Venus as a morning object, low in the east-north-east before sunrise, as well as being seen low in the west just after sunset for several days before it passes through inferior conjunction. The optimum dates are March 21–31.

MARS continues to be visible in the early mornings in the south-eastern sky. During the month its magnitude brightens from +0.5 to –0.1. Mars is actually in the constellation of Ophiuchus, but passes 5° north of Antares, in Scorpius, on March 4

JUPITER is still visible as a brilliant evening object in the western sky after sunset, magnitude –2.2. The monthly spectacle of the Moon, now as a crescent, passing south of Jupiter continues, occurring during the nights of March 1 and March 29.

SATURN, magnitude +0.2, is moving closer to the Sun but continues to remain visible in the western sky in the evenings, though lost to view long before midnight.

The Great Bear. As seen from Britain, Ursa Major (the Great Bear) is very high up during March evenings. It never sets over these latitudes,

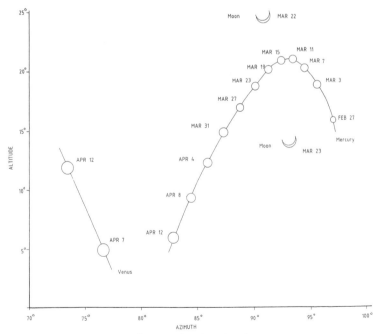

Figure 4. Morning apparition of Mercury, from latitude 35°S.

and so can always be found whenever the sky is sufficiently clear and dark. Seven of its stars make up the famous pattern known as the Plough, Charles's Wain or (in America) the Big Dipper (Figure 5). In fact, the Plough is only part of the larger constellation of Ursa Major.

Of the Plough stars, five are genuinely associated, and make up what is termed a moving cluster; the remaining two (Alkaid and Dubhe) are actually moving in an opposite direction, so that eventually the pattern will become distorted. According to the authoritative Cambridge catalogue, the Plough stars are listed as follows:

Star	Proper name	Luminosity, Sun = 1	Distance, light-years
Alpha	Dubhe	60	75
Beta	Merak	28	62
Gamma	Phad	50	75
Delta	Megrez	17	65
Epsilon	Alioth	60	62
Zeta	Mizar	56 + 11	59
Eta	Alkaid	450	108

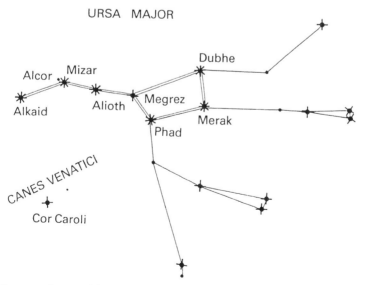

Figure 5. The stars of the Plough, in Ursa Major.

Alkaid (also sometimes called Benetnasch) is therefore the most luminous of the seven; Megrez is the least powerful. There has been a suggestion that Megrez has decreased in brightness since ancient times, but the evidence is, at best, very slender.

Dubhe is an orange star of spectral type K; the others are white. Mizar is, of course, the celebrated double; its companion, Alcor, is an easy naked-eye object. Telescopically, Mizar is itself an easy double, and each component is a spectroscopic binary, so that the whole system is decidedly complicated. A small telescope will show another star between Alcor and the main Mizar pair, but this is not a member of the system, and lies 'in the background'.

Mythologically, Ursa Major represents Callisto, daughter of King Lycaon of Arcadia, who was changed into a bear by the goddess Juno. There is also a Little Bear, marked by Polaris, the Pole Star; this can be found by following a line through the 'Pointers', Merak and Dubhe. Polaris lies within a degree of the north celestial pole, and has always been of immense help to air and sea navigators. There is no comparable south polar star; the nearest naked-eye object to the south celestial pole is the obscure Sigma Octantis.

April

New Moon: April 23   *Full Moon*: April 8

MERCURY continues to be visible as a morning object for the first ten or twelve days of the month for observers in equatorial and southern latitudes (and they should consult the diagram given with the notes for March). Thereafter Mercury is too close to the Sun for observation as it passes through superior conjunction on April 23. For observers in the latitudes of the British Isles it remains unsuitably placed for observation throughout April.

VENUS, magnitude –4.5, is already a brilliant morning object low in the eastern sky before dawn for observers in the British Isles. After the first couple of days of April even observers at southern temperate latitudes will have the same opportunity.

MARS is still a morning object and by the end of the month it is crossing the meridian shortly after 0.3^h. Its magnitude is now brightening considerably and by the end of the month it is –1.0. Mars is in the constellation of Ophiuchus but crosses into Sagittarius at the end of the month.

JUPITER, magnitude –2.0, continues to be visible as a brilliant evening object in the western sky after dusk. Both Jupiter and Saturn are moving directly in Taurus, and the distance between the two bodies, is increasing, and has now increased to about 10°.

SATURN is still visible low in the western sky in the early evenings but will be lost to view in the gathering twilight by the end of April. Its magnitude is +0.2.

Arcturus. Arcturus (Alpha Boötis) is the brightest star in the Northern Hemisphere of the sky; it is marginally superior to Vega and Capella, and is outshone only by the southern Sirius, Canopus and Alpha

Centauri. It is easy to find: simply follow round the 'tail' of the Great Bear (Figure 6). Its declination is +19°, so that it can be seen from every inhabited country; only some Antarctic penguins will lose it.

Arcturus actually has a negative magnitude, –0.04. It is 36 light-years away, and 115 times as luminous as the Sun. It is classified as a red giant, though it seems puny compared with red supergiants such as Betelgeuse and Antares. Its real diameter is probably about 30 million kilometres, so that if its centre lay in the same position as the centre of the Sun, it would more than half-fill the orbit of Mercury.

The star has a relatively large proper motion: 2.28 seconds of arc per year. In 1718 Edmond Halley found that it had shifted appreciably since Ptolemy wrote his *Almagest* in or around AD 150; since then it has crawled across the sky, covering a distance more than twice the apparent diameter of the full moon. Halley also found shifts for two other bright stars, Sirius and Aldebaran, and he concluded that these three stars must be the closest known; in fact this is not so, though Sirius, at 8.6 light-years, is certainly one of our nearest neighbours.

Arcturus has been approaching us for the past half million years, and is now as close as it will be; in the future it will recede from us, dropping below naked-eye visibility about 500,000 years from now.

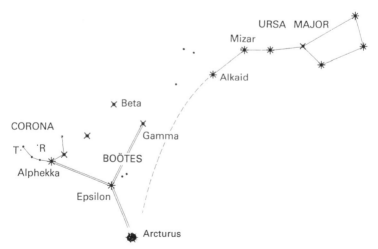

Figure 6. The star Arcturus in the constellation Boötes.

The brightest stars in the Northern Hemisphere of the sky are:

Star	Designation	Magnitude
Arcturus	α Boötis	−0.04
Vega	α Lyrae	0.03
Capelia	α Aurigae	0.08
Procyon	α Canis Minoris	0.38
Betelgeuse	α Orionis	0.4 var
Altair	α Aquilae	0.76
Aldebaran	α Tauri	0.87
Pollux	β Geminorum	1.14
Deneb	α Cygni	1.25
Regulus	α Leonis	1.36
Castor	α Geminorum	1.58
Bellatrix	γ Orionis	1.64
Al Nath	β Tauri	1.65
Dubhe	α Ursae Majoris	1.81
Mirphak	α Persei	1.80
Alkaid	η Ursae Majoris	1.85
Menkalinan	β Aurigae	1.93
Alhena	γ Geminorum	1.93
Algieba	γ Leonis	1.99
Polaris	α Ursae Minoris	1.99
Hamal	α Arietis	2.00
Mirach	β Andromedae	2.06
Alpheratz	α Andromedae	2.06
Kochab	β Ursae Minoris	2.08
Rasalhague	α Ophiuchi	2.08
Mizar	ζ Ursae Majoris	2.09

May

MERCURY is at greatest eastern elongation (22°) on May 22. It does not become visible to observers in the Southern Hemisphere until almost the middle of the month, but farther north it is visible much earlier. For observers in northern temperate latitudes this will be the most favourable evening apparition of the year. Figure 7 shows, for observers in latitude 52°N, the changes in the azimuth (the true bearing from north, through east, south and west) and altitude of Mercury on successive evenings when the Sun is 6° below the horizon. This position of the Sun is known as the end of evening civil twilight, and at this latitude and at this time of year occurs about 35 minutes after sunset. The changes in the brightness of the planet are indicated in Figure 7 by the relative sizes of the circles, which mark Mercury's position at five-day intervals. Mercury is at its brightest before it reaches greatest eastern elongation. Jupiter, about two magnitudes brighter than Mercury, may be used as a guide to locating the fainter planet, around April 16. From the British Isles Mercury will be seen passing below Jupiter, as shown in Figure 7, while from latitude 35°S it will be seen below and to the right of Jupiter.

VENUS is a magnificent object in the eastern sky before dawn, attaining its greatest brilliancy with a magnitude of −4.5 on May 4. For observers in the latitudes of the British Isles it is never visible for more than about an hour before sunrise.

MARS is now a prominent object in the night sky, its magnitude brightening from −1.1 to −2.0 during the month. Mars is in the constellation of Sagittarius. It reaches its first stationary point on May 11, and then moves slowly retrograde.

JUPITER, magnitude –1.9, is now approaching the end of its evening apparition. It can only be seen in the western sky in the early evening and is unlikely to be seen after the first three weeks of the month.

SATURN passes through conjunction on May 25 and there-fore remains too close to the Sun for observation throughout the month.

Mercury and Copernicus. Mercury has been known from very ancient times, but unlike the other naked-eye planets is it never prominent because it stays close to the Sun in the sky, and is never seen against a dark background. In fact it can attain magnitude –1.9, which is brighter than any star – even Sirius.

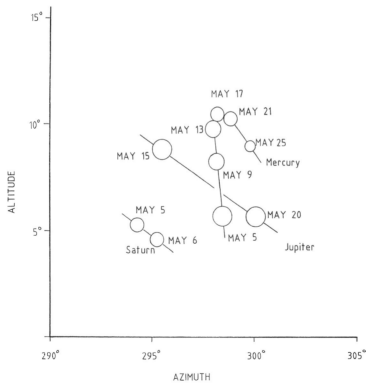

Figure 7. Evening apparition of Mercury, from latitude 52°N.

This month it is an evening object, and should not be hard to locate. On the other hand, there are many people who have never seen it at all. There is a famous story here: it is said that Copernicus, the man who showed that the planets move round the Sun rather than round the Earth, never saw Mercury in his life because of mists rising from the river Vistula, where he lived in Poland.

This seems most unlikely. Copernicus lived from 1473 to 1543, when the skies were much less light-polluted than they are now, and mists from the Vistula are not persistent, so there is no reason to believe that Mercury eluded Copernicus. When the Editor of this *Yearbook* was in Toruń (Copernicus' home town) some years ago, Mercury happened to be at elongation, and he saw it with no difficulty at all.

Eastern elongations in the near future are as follows:

2001   Sept. 18
2002   Jan. 11, May 4, Sept. 1, Dec. 26
2003   Apr. 16, Aug. 14, Dec. 9
2004   Mar. 29, July 27, Nov. 21
2005   Mar. 12, July 9, Nov. 3

Of course, not all of these are equally favourable.

The surface of Mercury. Mercury is a small world, and even large telescopes will show little surface detail. Usually, all that can be made out is the characteristic phase – first seen definitely by Giovanni Zupi in 1639. Early maps proved to be very inaccurate, which was not surprising; the best of them was drawn by E. M. Antoniadi and published in 1934. Antoniadi used the 33-inch (0.83-m) refractor at the Observatory of Meudon (Paris), and made his observations during daylight, when both Mercury and the Sun were high over the horizon.

Antoniadi believed – wrongly – that the Mercurian atmosphere was dense enough to support dust clouds. He also believed that the rotation period was synchronous – that is to say, equal to the revolution period round the Sun (88 Earth days). If this had been the case, part of Mercury would have been in permanent sunlight and another part in permanent darkness, with only a narrow 'twilight zone' in between. In fact, the true rotation period is 58.6 days, two-thirds of a Mercurian 'year'. There is a detectable magnetic field, and the iron-rich core of the planet may be larger than the entire globe of the Moon (Mercury's diameter is 4876 km).

The only spacecraft to have encountered Mercury is Mariner 10, which made three active passes: in March and September 1974, and March 1975. It showed a landscape superficially like that of the Moon, though with important differences in detail: there are craters, valleys, mountains and 'lobate scarps'. There are also broad intercrater plains, of a type not found on the Moon. The most imposing feature is the Caloris Basin, which is 1300 km in diameter and is bounded by a ring of smooth mountain blocks; unfortunately only part of it was in sunlight during the Mariner passes. The largest crater, Beethoven, is 625 km across.

Part of Mercury remains unmapped, and we must await the launch of a new space probe. However, there is no reason to suppose that the remaining regions will be markedly different from those visible to Mariner 10. Life of any kind seems to be completely out of the question.

June

New Moon: June 21   *Full Moon*: June 6

Solstice: June 21

MERCURY passes through inferior conjunction on June 16 and remains too close to the Sun for observation throughout the month, except for observers in the tropics, who should be able to detect it low above the north-eastern horizon at the beginning of morning civil twilight for the last few days of the month.

VENUS, at magnitude −4.2, continues to be visible as a morning object in the eastern sky before dawn. It attains its greatest western elongation (46°) on June 8. Observers in the British Isles will note that by the end of the month Venus can be seen for almost two hours before sunrise.

MARS reaches opposition on June 13, and therefore is available for observation throughout the hours of darkness. Closest approach to the Earth occurs on June 21, the difference of 8 days being due to the eccentricity of the oribit of Mars. It will then be 67 million kilometres from the Earth. Reference to Figure 1 (accompanying the notes for January) shows that Mars is now moving retrograde, and at the beginning of June moves back from Sagittarius into Ophiuchus. The magnitude of Mars at opposition is −2.4. For observers in the latitudes of the British Isles this is a very disappointing opposition since Mars is now at a declination of −27° and therefore only 12° above the southern horizon at transit, as seen from southern England, and only 7° as seen from southern Scotland.

JUPITER passes through conjunction on June 13 and therefore remains too close to the Sun for observation throughout the month.

SATURN, having passed through conjunction in May, remains too close to the Sun for observation throughout June for observers in the

British Isles, because of the long duration of twilight in these latitudes. Farther south, observers are more fortunate and should have the opportunity of glimpsing the planet, low above the eastern horizon before the morning twilight inhibits observation, by the middle of the month.

This month's total solar eclipse. With memories of August 1999 in mind, many people will travel to see the total eclipse of June 21. The track crosses the African continent, though over countries which are politically rather unstable – Angola, Zambia and Zimbabwe – and there will also be 'cruise ships' off the coast.

This is a very long eclipse, since totality lasts for nearly 5 minutes, and weather conditions are expected to be good along most of the track. The Sun is near the peak of its 11-year cycle of activity, and so the corona should be of 'maximum' type; there may also be spectacular prominences, though of course one can never be sure.

The next total eclipses fall on December 4, 2002 (South Africa, Indian Ocean, part of Australia) and November 23, 2003 (Antarctica). The 2003 eclipse should be fascinating, though weather conditions are unpredictable and most of the spectators are likely to be penguins.

Libra. This is a good time to look for Libra, the Scales or Balance, one of the least brilliant of the Zodiacal constellations. From Britain it is always rather low down, though from southern countries it is of course much higher in the sky.

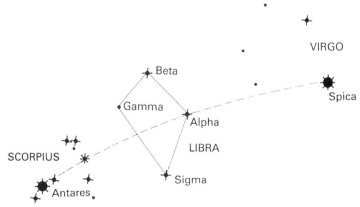

Figure 8. The constellation Libra.

Libra lies inside the large triangle formed by Arcturus, Spica and Antares (Figure 8). Its four main stars – Alpha, Beta, Gamma and Sigma – are between magnitudes 2.7 and 3.9; Sigma Librae was formerly included in Scorpius, as Gamma Scorpii. Libra itself was once known as Chelae Scorpionis, the Scorpion's Claws; some Greek legends associate it, rather loosely, with Mochis, the inventor of weights and measures.

It cannot be said that there is much of immediate interest in Libra, though Alpha is a wide optical double; the components are of magnitudes 2.8 and 5.2, and the separation is 231 seconds of arc. Beta Librae is often said to be the only single star to have a distinctly greenish hue; it is of spectral type B8, and is 105 times as luminous as the Sun. The distance is 121 light-years. The colour is at best very fugitive, and most observers will see the star as white or slighly bluish.

Probably the best way to identify the constellation is by using Antares and Spica; Alpha Librae lies about midway between these two brilliant stars.

July

EARTH is at aphelion (farthest from the Sun) on July 4 at a distance of 152 million kilometres (94.5 million miles).

MERCURY attains its greatest western elongation from the sun on July 9, but the long evening twilight means that it will not be visible to observers in the British Isles. It is a morning object for observers in the tropics for all except the last week of the month. Further south it is visible during the middle two weeks of the month, low above the east-north-east horizon, around the beginning of morning civil twilight.

VENUS is still a brilliant morning object, magnitude –4.1, visible in the eastern sky before dawn.

MARS is now just past opposition and during the month its magnitude fades from –2.2 to –1.5. At the beginning of July it is still visible for most of the hours of darkness. Mars is in the constellation of Ophiuchus and, after reaching its second stationary point on June 19, resumes its direct motion.

JUPITER, at the beginning of the month, is still too close to the Sun for observation. However, after the first few days of July it may be detected by equatorial and Southern-Hemisphere observers; a week later and it becomes visible to observers in the British Isles. Jupiter has a magnitude of –1.9 and is visible low in the eastern sky before dawn.

SATURN, already observable in the early mornings by equatorial and southern observers, gradually becomes visible to those in the British Isles after the first week of the month. Saturn is in the constellation of Taurus, magnitude +0.2, half a magnitude brighter than Aldebaran.

NEPTUNE comes to opposition on July 30, in the constellation of Capricornus. Neptune is not visible to the naked eye since its magnitude is +7.8. At opposition the planet is 4351 million kilometres from the Earth.

Ophiuchus in the Zodiac. This month Mars lies in the constellation Ophiuchus, the Serpent-bearer. This large constellation was also known as Sepentarius; it is associated with Aesculapius, the mythological 'doctor' who became so skilled in medicine that he was even able to restore the dead to life. To avoid depopulation of the Underworld, Zeus (Jupiter) reluctantly disposed of Aesculapius with a thunderbolt, but then relented sufficiently to place him in the sky.

Ophiuchus is not ranked as a Zodiacal constellation, but it does cross the ecliptic between Scorpius and Sagittarius. Of its brightest stars, the northernmost (Alpha), lies at declination +12°, and the southernmost (Theta) at −25°, so that Ophiuchus covers a wide area. Astrologers, of course, are very worried about Ophiuchus, and do not quite know how to deal with it – yet another instance of the absurdity of the whole astrological cult.

Barnard's Star. One faint star in Ophiuchus is of special interest. Its official designation is Munich 15040, and it is generally known as Barnard's Star in honour of Edward Emerson Barnard, the American astronomer who first drew attention to it. Its apparent magnitude is 9.5; it is a red dwarf, with a luminosity only 0.00045 that of the Sun. At its distance of 6 light-years, Barnard's Star is our closest stellar neighbour after the members of the Alpha Centauri group. It has the greatest proper motion known – 10.29 seconds of arc per year – so that it covers one degree in 351 years.

Early in the twentieth century, Peter van de Kamp, Director of the Sproule Observatory in the United States, made a long series of measurements of the movements of Barnard's Star and came to the conclusion that it was attended by at least one planet – probably two. This was in fact the first announcement of the detection of an extrasolar planet by what is now termed the astrometric method. It seemed very convincing, and for many years van de Kamp's results were accepted. Then, however, it was found that the apparent movements of the star were spurious, and were due to faults in the telescopic equipment. The 'Barnard planet' was discounted – and there is no evidence of any planet there.

Subsequently, many extrasolar planets have been found by the astro-metric method. Final proof came in 2000, when the star Tau Boötis, 50 light-years away, was found to have a planetary companion whose spectrum could actually be seen. There is now no reason to doubt that planetary systems are very common in the Galaxy, and in other galaxies also.

The position of Barnard's Star is RA 17h 55m.04, dec. –04° 33'. Close by lies a little group of stars, 66, 67, 68 and 70 Ophiuchi; 70 is a famous binary, with a period of 88 years. In 1777 the Polish astronomer Martin Poczobutt separated out this area into a new constellation, Taurus Poniatowski (Poniatowski's Bull), but, like many other proposed groups, it has not survived, and is no longer to be found on modern star maps.

Neptune at opposition. Neptune, now in Capricornus, is not hard to identify – binoculars show it easily – but details are hard to make out. During the pass of Voyager 2, in 1989, the main atmospheric feature was the Great Dark Spot, which was then thought to be of the same nature as the Great Red Spot on Jupiter, though lacking the latter's coloration. However, it is now possible to see surface features using the Hubble Space Telescope, and the Great Dark Spot seems to have disappeared, though other spots have been seen. Evidently Neptune's atmosphere changes much more rapidly than had been expected.

Neptune's orbit is fairly circular: the eccentricity is 0.009, less than for any other planet apart from Venus. The distance from the Sun ranges between 4456 and 4534 million kilometres; the orbital period is 164.8 years. Neptune is slightly smaller than Uranus – its equatorial diameter is 50,550 km, as against 51,130 km for Uranus – but Neptune is the more massive of the two, and unlike Uranus it has con-siderable internal heat. As a result, the surface temperatures of the two planets are almost the same, even though Neptune is so much farther from the Sun.

August

MERCURY passes through superior conjunction on August 5 and remains unobservable from the latitudes of the British Isles throughout the month. During the second half of the month observers in equatorial and southern latitudes will be able to detect the planet as it moves slowly away from the Sun and becomes visible as an evening object (Figure 9).

VENUS, magnitude –4.0, continues to be visible as a brilliant morning object. It is now visible in the eastern sky for several hours before dawn.

MARS continues to be visible as an evening object, though only low in the south-western sky for observers in northern temperate latitudes. During August its magnitude fades from –1.5 to –0.9. Mars is in the constellation of Ophiuchus.

JUPITER is a morning object in Gemini, magnitude –2.0, visible in the eastern sky until dawn. For observers at the latitudes of the British Isles the planet may be seen low above the east-north-eastern horizon shortly after midnight by the end of August. Venus, two magnitudes brighter than Jupiter, spends the early part of the month close to the larger planet, and on the night of August 5/6 the separation is only 1°.

SATURN, magnitude +0.1, continues to be visible as a morning object in Taurus.

URANUS comes to opposition on August 15 in the constellation Capricornus. It is barely visible to the naked eye since its magnitude is +5.7, but it is readily located with modest optical aid. At opposition the planet is 2837 million kilometres from the Earth.

The Perseids. August is the 'Perseids month'. This annual shower, associated with the periodic comet Swift–Tuttle, is reliable: meteors can be seen at any time between around July 27 and August 20. The maximum of the shower occurs on August 12, so that this year the Moon will not be obtrusive.

The rings of Uranus. Uranus, at opposition this month, is just visible with the naked eye, though detail is beyond the range of most telescopes. The ring system was discovered in 1977, during observations of an occultation of the star SAO 158687; both before and after the occultation the star 'winked', because it was temporarily hidden by the ring material. Since then the rings have been imaged by the Voyager 2 spacecraft (1986) and by the Hubble Space Telescope. They are dark and obscure, quite unlike the glorious icy rings of Saturn.

It is worth remembering that in 1787, six years after the discovery of the planet, William Herschel reported the existence of a ring; he described it as 'short, not like that of Saturn'. He was using his 20-foot (6-m) focal-length reflector. In fact he was being misled by optical

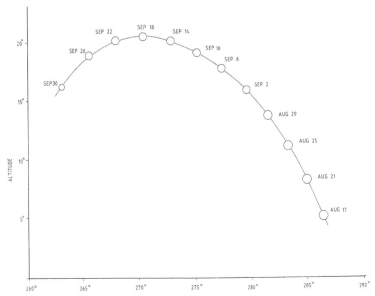

Figure 9. Evening apparition of Mercury, from latitude 35°S.

effects produced by the telescope, and by 1793 he had realized that his 'ring' did not exist. No telescope of that period could possibly have shown the true ring system.

Herschel also announced the discovery of six satellites of Uranus. Two of these were Titania and Oberon. The remaining four seem to have been non-existent; one of them may have been Umbriel, but there is considerable uncertainty. Twenty satellites are now known. Ariel and Umbriel were discovered by William Lassell in 1851, Miranda by Gerard Kuiper in 1948, and ten from Voyager 2 images; four more remote, asteroidal satellites were found in 1998–99. All the satellites move more or less in the plane of Uranus' equator, so that their movements are technically retrograde – remember that the tilt of Uranus' axis is 98°: more than a right angle.

The Summer Triangle from Australia. The brilliant stars Vega, Deneb and Altair form a large triangle, known commonly as the Summer Triangle (the result of a chance comment made by the Editor of this *Yearbook* during a television programme forty years ago!). However, the three stars are in different constellations, and the nickname is entirely unofficial. Moreover, it does not apply to the Southern Hemisphere, from where the three stars are best seen during winter.

Their declinations are as follows:

Deneb (α Cygni)   +45°
Vega (α Lyrae)   +39°
Altair (α Aquilae) +09°

Thus Deneb and Vega are just circumpolar from England, but Altair is not. Deneb, the northernmost of the three members, does not rise at all from latitudes south of –45°, so that as seen from Australia and New Zealand it is always low down, and from the southernmost part of New Zealand's South Island it is never seen. From these regions, the 'Triangle' is at its best during August evenings.

Appearances can be deceptive. Deneb appears the faintest of the three, but is in fact much the most luminous: it is the equal of about 70,000 Suns. Vega could match 52 Suns, but Altair only 10.

September

New Moon: September 17   *Full Moon*: September 2

Equinox: September 22

MERCURY remains unsuitably placed for observation for those in the British Isles throughout September. However, for observers in equatorial and southern latitudes this will be the most favourable evening apparition of the year. Figure 9 shows, for observers in latitude 35°S, the changes in azimuth (true bearing from north, through east, south and west) and altitude of Mercury on successive evenings when the Sun is 6° below the horizon. This condition is known as the end of evening civil twilight, and in this latitude and at this time of year occurs about 30 minutes after sunset. The changes in the brightness of the planet are indicated by the relative sizes of the circles marking Mercury's position at five-day intervals. It will be noticed that Mercury is at its brightest before it reaches greatest eastern elongation (27°) on September 18. During the month its magnitude fades slowly from –0.1 to +0.7.

VENUS is a brilliant morning object, magnitude –4.0. It is well placed for observation in the eastern sky for an hour or so before sunrise.

MARS, magnitude –0.6, is still visible in the south-western quadrant of the sky in the evenings. Mars is in the constellation of Sagittarius, and its path among the stars for September onwards is shown in Figure 10.

JUPITER continues to be visible as a brilliant object in the early morning skies, magnitude –2.1. Observers in the British Isles will be able to see it well before midnight, by the end of September. A daylight occultation of the planet by the gibbous Moon is visible from the British Isles on September 12, roughly between 13ʰ and 14ʰ GMT. The occultation occurs near the southern limb of the Moon, when its altitude is only 16°. Of course, a telescope is needed to witness the phenomenon.

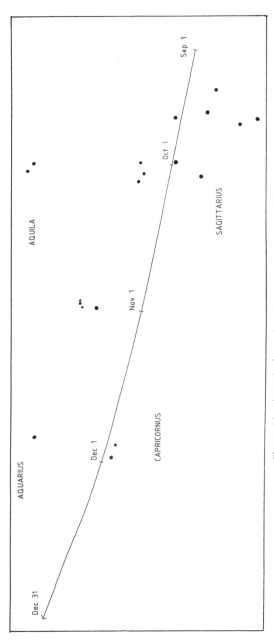

Figure 10. The path of Mars form September to December 2001.

SATURN continues to be visible as a morning object in the eastern sky, magnitude 0.0. The planet reaches its first stationary point on September 27, and then commences its retrograde motion.

Planetary occultations. Occultations of planets by the Moon are not too uncommon, but occultations of planets by other planets are very rare indeed. The last occasion when Jupiter occulted a planet (Uranus) was on August 15, 1623; of course this was not observed – Uranus was not discovered until 1781. On January 3, 1818 Jupiter was occulted by Venus, but no records have been found.

On November 22, 2065 Venus will again occult Jupiter, but Venus' elongation from the Sun will be only 8°W. Mercury will occult Jupiter on October 27, 2088 and April 7, 2094, but its elongation from the Sun will be no more than 5°, so that these events will be very difficult to observe.

The W of Cassiopeia. During September evenings Cassiopeia is not far from the zenith as seen from British latitudes, though it never rises from far-southern countries. The five main stars make up an obvious W or M pattern (Figure 11). Details are as follows:

Star	Proper name	Magnitude	Luminosity Sun = 1	Spectrum	Distance light-years
Alpha	Shedir	2.23 var?	200	K0	120
Beta	Caph	2.87	14	F2	42
Gamma	—	1.6–3.2	6000 var	B0p	780
Delta	Ruchbah	2.68	11	A5	62
Epsilon	Segin	3.38	1200	B3	520

Gamma is an unstable 'shell star'; it suffers occasional outbursts, and has risen to magnitude 1.6 (as in the late 1930s, though for the past few decades it has hovered around magnitude 2.2). The reddish Alpha (Shedir) has long been suspected of variability. Officially it is now listed as 'constant', but it may well fluctuate over a small range – perhaps from magnitude 2.1 to 2.4. It is interesting to compare it with Beta, which is a normal white star and definitely not variable.

The Milky Way passes through Cassiopeia, which is therefore a very rich area. Cassiopeia and the Great Bear (Ursa Major) lie on opposite sides of the Pole Star, and are around the same distance from it; when

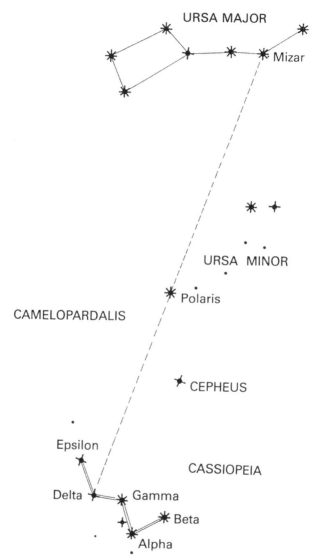

Figure 11. The constellation Cassiopeia, on the opposite side of Polaris to the Plough in Ursa Major.

the Bear is high up, Cassiopeia is low down, and vice versa. However, both are circumpolar from British latitudes.

Borrelly's Comet. This periodic comet returns to perihelion this month (September 14). It is never a bright object, but its orbit is well known; the period is 6.8 years, and the comet has been seen at most returns since its discovery by the French astronomer Nicolas Borrelly in 1904. Generally it is very obscure and badly defined, though on occasions, as in 1981, it develops a distinct tail.

October

New Moon: October 16   *Full Moon*: October 2

Summer Time in Great Britain and Northern Ireland ends on October 28.

MERCURY passes through inferior conjunction on October 14, but then moves rapidly away from the Sun. Although unsuitably placed for observation by those in southern temperate latitudes, for observers in northern temperate latitudes this will be the most favourable morning apparition of the year. Figure 12 shows, for observers in latitude 52°N, the changes in azimuth (true bearing from north, through east, south and west) and altitude of Mercury on successive mornings when the

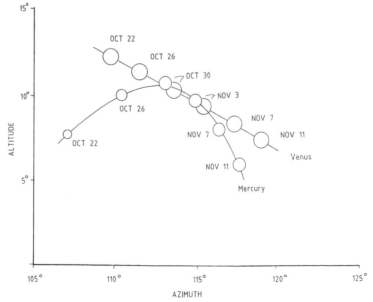

Figure 12. Morning apparition of Mercury, from latitude 52°N.

Sun is 6° below the horizon. This position of the Sun is known as the beginning of morning civil twilight, and in this latitude and at this time of year occurs about 35 minutes before sunrise. The changes in the brightness of the planet are indicated by the relative sizes of the circles marking Mercury's position at five-day intervals. It will be noticed that Mercury is at its brightest after it reaches greatest western elongation (19°) on October 29.

VENUS, magnitude –3.9, continues to be visible as a brilliant morning object in the eastern sky before dawn. It is gradually drawing closer to the Sun, being less than 20° away by the end of the month.

MARS continues to be visible in the south-western quadrant of the sky in the evenings, at magnitude –0.2. Mars is moving steadily eastwards among the stars, passing from Sagittarius into Capricornus during October.

JUPITER continues to be visible as a brilliant morning object in the south-eastern sky, at magnitude –2.3. Jupiter is in Gemini.

SATURN, magnitude –0.1, continues to be visible as a morning object in the eastern sky, though by the end of October observers in the latitudes of the British Isles should be able to locate it low above the east-north-eastern horizon by about 19^h.

The Sword Handle and the Caldwell Catalogue. In 1781 Charles Messier drew up his famous catalogue of star clusters and nebulae, containing 103 objects; later editions increased this total to 109. However, Messier was not in the least interested in nebulae. He was a comet-hunter, and drew up his catalogue so that he could avoid wasting time upon objects which merely appeared cometary. It is ironic that it is because of his catalogue that Messier is best remembered today.

Deliberately he omitted many objects which could not possibly be confused with comets, and of course he was limited to the sky as seen from France, where he spent the whole of his life. There seemed to be room for a new catalogue, listing the most important objects omitted by Messier, and the Caldwell Catalogue, also containing 109 objects, is now being widely used. For example, one object in this Catalogue, C14, is the famous Sword Handle in Perseus (Figure 13); it is composed of two separate clusters, NGC 869 and 884 (otherwise known as h and χ Persei), visible with the naked eye. Binoculars show them well, and they make a glorious sight in a wide-field telescope. Between the two clusters is an obvious red star. Both lie at around 7000 light-years from us.

The Caldwell objects are arranged in order of declination, from C1, an open cluster in Cepheus (dec. +85°) to C109, a planetary nebula in Chamaeleon (dec. −81°). All are visible with small telescopes, and almost all are easy binocular objects. Some of the Caldwell objects in the Northern Hemisphere are as follows:

C	NGC	Constellation	Type	Name
4	7023	Cepheus	Reflection nebula	—
6	6543	Draco	Planetary nebula	Cat's Eye Nebula
9	—	Cepheus	Nebula	Cave Nebula
11	7635	Cassiopeia	Nebula	Bubble Nebula
13	457	Cassiopeia	Open cluster	Phi Cassiopeiae cluster

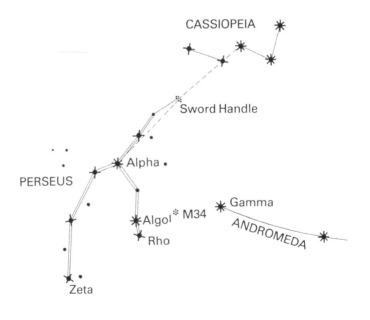

Figure 13. The Sword Handle in Perseus, near the constellation Cassiopeia.

C	NGC	Constellation	Type	Name
14	869/884	Perseus	Double cluster	Sword Handle
20	7000	Cygnus	Nebula	North America Nebula
23	891	Andromeda	Edgewise-on galaxy	—
31	IC 405	Auriga	Nebula	Flaming Star Nebula
33	6992/5	Cygnus	Supernova remnant	E. Veil Nebula
34	6960	Cygnus	Supernova remnant	W. Veil Nebula
41	—	Taurus	Open cluster	Hyades
42	7006	Delphinus	Globular cluster	—
55	7009	Aquarius	Planetary nebula	Saturn Nebula
63	7293	Aquarius	Planetary nebula	Helix Nebula
64	2362	Canis Major	Open cluster	Tau Canis Majoris cluster
65	253	Sculptor	Galaxy	Sculptor Galaxy

A full description of each object can be found in the book *Observing the Caldwell Objects* by David Ratledge (Springer-Verlag, London, 2000).

November

MERCURY, for observers in the tropics and northern temperate latitudes, continues to be visible as a morning object until nearly the middle of November. Observers in the latitudes of the British Isles should refer to the diagram given with the notes for October. Remarkably, Venus and Mercury remain within 5° of each other for almost three weeks (from October 23 to November 11), and within 2° from November 1 to 11. Minimum separation, on November 3, is only 0°.6. For observers in southern temperate latitudes Mercury remains too close to the Sun for observation.

VENUS is a brilliant morning object with a magnitude of –3.9. However, it is moving closer in towards the Sun so that the period available for observation is shortening noticeably from week to week and by the end of the month it is only visible for a short while low above the south-eastern horizon before sunrise.

MARS, magnitude +0.2, continues to be visible as an evening object in the constellation of Capricornus.

JUPITER continues to be a brilliant object in the night sky, magnitude –2.5. Jupiter, in Gemini, reaches its first stationary point on November 2, and then moves slowly retrograde.

SATURN, as it approaches opposition early next month, is now visible for the greater part of the night. Saturn, magnitude –0.3, is moving slowly retrograde in the constellation of Taurus, north of Aldebaran. An occultation of Saturn by the Moon, late on November 3, is visible from the British Isles.

Comet Tempel–Tuttle. This is the parent comet of the Leonid meteor stream, which can sometimes produce really spectacular displays – as in

1833, 1866 and 1966; there was a reasonable display on November 16, 1998 and a rather better one, of brief duration, on November 18, 1999. Some Leonids are seen every year around this time, but major 'storms' occur only when the comet is near perihelion. The last return was that of 1998; the period is 33 years.

The comet is never very bright. Historical research has shown that it was seen in 1366 when it passed Earth at around 9 million kilometres and rose to magnitude 3; since then it has never attained naked-eye visibility. For example, at the return in 1966 it never exceeded magnitude 16. Its perihelion lies just inside the orbit of the Earth; the movement is retrograde. The next perihelion passage is due in 2031, so that we may then hope for another major Leonid storm.

The 'Last in the River'. The long, sprawling constellation of Eridanus, the River, begins close to Rigel in Orion and extends down to the south polar region. Despite its large area – 1138 square degrees – it contains only four stars above the third magnitude. These are Alpha (Achernar), magnitude 0.5; Beta (Cursa), 2.8; Theta (Acamar), 2.9; and Gamma (Zaurak), also 2.9.

Achernar, declination –57°, is the nearest really brilliant star to the south celestial pole; the pole itself lies in Octans, about midway between Achernar and the Southern Cross. The name 'Achernar' is a transliteration from the Arabic *Al Ahir al Nahr*, 'the End of the River', but this leads to a curious problem. Achernar is too far south to be seen from Alexandria, where Ptolemy compiled his classic star catalogue, and the name may really apply to Theta (Acamar), which does rise from Alexandria. Moreover, some old records rank Acamar as being of the first magnitude, whereas it is now only just above the third. It is a fine binary, with components of magnitudes 3.4 and 4.5; the separation is over 8 seconds of arc, and this is one of the finest pairs in the sky. The distance from us is 55 light-years; both components are white, and are respectively 50 and 17 times as luminous as the Sun. Both components are stable stars, and all in all it is most unlikely that any fading has taken place since Ptolemy's time.

Achernar is a B5-type star, 400 times as powerful as the Sun and 85 light-years away. It is a bluish-white; some old reports describe it as red, but this is certainly because the observers were looking at it when it was low down, so that its light was reddened.

The first Mars mission. This is the 39th anniversary of the first attempt to send a probe to another planet. On November 1, 1962 the Russians launched Mars-1, hoping to obtain data from closer range. In fact the mission was unsuccessful; contact with Mars-1 was lost when the distance had increased to just over 100,000 km, and was never regained. Even today the Russians have had almost no luck with Mars, and virtually all our information has been drawn from American missions – plus the Hubble Space Telescope.

In 2000 there was considerable interest in a NASA announcement about possible surface water on Mars. Generally the atmospheric pressure there is below 10 millibars, though in a few places (such as the floors of the Hellas and Argyre basins) it is slightly greater. Surface water on any permanent scale is out of the question, but it is possible that water may exist below the crust, occasionally gushing out and remaining liquid for a brief period. We hope to discuss this in detail later in the 2002 *Yearbook*, when more information is to hand.

New missions are planned for the near future, and within a few years we ought to know whether there is, or is not, any trace of life on the Red Planet.

December

New Moon: December 14   *Full Moon*: December 30

Solstice: December 21

MERCURY passes through superior conjunction on December 4 and is too close to the Sun for observation for most of the month. However, those near the equator should be able to locate it low in the south-western sky at the end of evening civil twilight during the last week of the month, while for observers in southern temperate latitudes the opportunity occurs only during the last few days of December.

VENUS, magnitude –3.9, is a bright morning object visible low above the south-eastern horizon for a very short while before dawn. Observers at northern temperate latitudes will be able to see it only for the first fortnight of December, but for those in southern latitudes the period of observation extends for three weeks.

MARS is still visible in the south-western quadrant of the sky in the early evenings. It has a magnitude of +0.6. During December Mars continues to move eastwards and passes from Capricornus into Aquarius. As it does so it is also moving northwards in declination, and despite Mars moving closer to the Sun it means that, for observers in the British Isles, Mars is actually setting slightly later in December than it did in October.

JUPITER is now visible for the greater part of the night as it moves towards opposition early next month. Its magnitude is –2.7. The path of Jupiter among the stars is shown in the diagram given with the notes for February. For observers in the British Isles the early sunset times mean that the planet is visible low in the east-north-eastern sky as soon as it gets dark. On the last day of the month, Jupiter, one day before opposition, is 626 million kilometres from the Earth.

SATURN reaches opposition on December 3 and is therefore visible throughout the hours of darkness. The magnitude of Saturn is –0.4. It is moving slowly retrograde in Taurus, and passes 4° north of Aldebaran on December 12. At opposition Saturn is 1204 million kilometres from the Earth.

Phaethon and the Geminids. The Geminid meteor shower, which extends from December 7 to 16 (maximum on the 13th), is usually rich; the zenthal hourly rate is 75, equal to that of the Perseids. This year the Moon will not interfere, so we may expect a good view.

Most major streams have identifiable parent comets – such as the Eta Aquarids and the Orinids (P/Halley), the Perseids (P/Swift–Tuttle), the Taurids (P/Encke) and the Ursids (P/Tuttle). No comet has been identified with the Geminids, but it is probably significant that the orbit closely matches that of an Apollo-class asteroid, (3200) Phaethon, which is around 5 km in diameter.

Apollo asteroids are often regarded as ex-comets which have lost all their volatiles, and certainly the evidence is reasonably good; for instance, Comet Wilson–Harrington of 1949 had a decided tail, but has now taken on the appearance of an asteroid, and has been given an asteroid number (4015). It may well be that Phaethon was indeed a comet, and in this case it could be the parent of the Geminids, though we cannot be sure.

Saturn at its brightest. Saturn is now almost at its maximum brilliancy. It reaches perihelion in 2003, and the ring system is wide open, so that the planet is a magnificent sight in even a small telescope. Saturn is now brighter than any star apart from Sirius and Canopus; when the rings are edgewise-on, as they were in 1995, the opposition magnitude is only +0.8, comparable with Aldebaran. Moreover, the position in Taurus is well north of the celestial equator; for observers at the latitudes of Britain, conditions are not far short of ideal.

Annular eclipses. This month's annular solar eclipse ought to be widely observed, since the track crosses parts of the United States; it will not be seen from Britain. This is also true of the annular eclipse of June 10, 2002, when the track will cross the Pacific. Next comes the annular eclipse of May 31, 2003; this will be seen from parts of northern

Scotland, but the altitude will be low, and – clouds permitting! – a more favourable site will be Iceland.

An annular eclipse is interesting to watch. The corona cannot be seen, and in many cases the drop in light-level is surprisingly low – but remember that the danger of direct viewing through a telescope or binoculars is as great as it is when there is no eclipse in progress. The only really safe method is to use projection.

Eclipses in 2001

There will be four eclipses, two of the Sun and two of the Moon.

1. *A total eclipse of the Moon on January 9* is visible from the western Pacific Ocean, Australia, Indonesia, the Philippines, Asia, the Indian Ocean, Africa, Europe (including the British Isles), the Atlantic Ocean, eastern South America, Iceland, Greenland, the Arctic Ocean, N.E. and N. North America and Bermuda. The partial eclipse begins at 18^h 42^m and ends at 21^h 59^m. Totality lasts from 19^h 50^m to 20^h 52^m.

2. *A total eclipse of the Sun on June 21* is visible as a partial eclipse from most of South America, the Atlantic Ocean, Africa (except the north), the Southern Ocean, Madagascar and the western Indian Ocean. The eclipse begins at 10^h 36^m and ends at 13^h 32^m. The path of totality starts in the South Atlantic Ocean east of South America, and crosses Angola, Zambia, northern Zimbabwe, Mozambique and southern Madagascar. The maximum duration of totality is 4^m 57^s.

3. *A partial eclipse of the Moon on July 5* is visible from the Pacific Ocean, Australasia, Antarctica, the Indian Ocean, Asia (except the extreme north), eastern and southern Africa, and Asia Minor. The eclipse begins at 13^h 35^m and ends at 16^h 15^m. At maximum eclipse, 50 per cent of the Moon is obscured.

4. *An annular eclipse of the Sun on December 14* is visible as a partial eclipse from the Pacific Ocean, Hawaii, the USA and part of Canada, the north-west of South America and the western Caribbean. The partial phase begins at 18^h 03^m and ends at 23^h 41^m. The track of annularity starts in the western North Pacific Ocean, and passes south of Hawaii before crossing southern Nicaragua and northern Costa Rica. The maximum duration of annularity is 3^m 54^s.

Occultations in 2001

In the course of its journey round the sky each month, the Moon passes in front of all the stars in its path, and the timing of these occultations is useful in fixing the position and motion of the Moon. The Moon's orbit is tilted at more than 5° to the ecliptic, but it is not fixed in space. It twists steadily westwards at a rate of about 20° a year, a complete revolution taking 18.6 years, during which time all the stars that lie within about 6½° of the ecliptic will be occulted. The occultations of any one star continue month after month until the Moon's path has twisted away from the star, but only a few of these occultations will be visible from any one place in hours of darkness.

There are nineteen lunar occultations of bright planets in 2001: one of Mercury, two of Venus, one of Mars, six of Jupiter and nine of Saturn.

Only four first-magnitude stars are near enough to the ecliptic to be occulted by the Moon: Aldebaran, Regulus, Spica and Antares. However, none of these stars undergoes occultation in 2001.

Predictions of these occultations are made on a worldwide basis for all stars down to magnitude 7.5, and sometimes even fainter. The British Astronomical Association has produced a complete lunar occultation prediction package for personal computer users.

Occultations of stars by planets (including minor planets) and satellites have aroused considerable attention.

The exact timing of such events gives valuable information about positions, sizes, orbits, atmospheres and sometimes of the presence of satellites. The discovery of the rings of Uranus in 1977 was the unexpected result of the observations made of a predicted occultation of a faint star by Uranus. The duration of an occultation by a satellite or minor planet is quite small (usually of the order of a minute or less). If observations are made from a number of stations it is possible to deduce the size of the planet.

The observations need to be made either photoelectrically or visually. The high accuracy of the method can readily be appreciated when one realizes that even a stopwatch timing accurate to a tenth of a second is, on average, equivalent to an accuracy of about 1 kilometre in the chord measured across the minor planet.

Comets in 2001

The appearance of a bright comet is a rare event which can never be predicted in advance, because this class of object travels round the Sun in enormous orbits with periods which may well be many thousands of years. There are therefore no records of the previous appearances of these bodies, and we are unable to follow their wanderings through space.

Comets of short period, on the other hand, return at regular intervals, and attract a good deal of attention from astronomers. Unfortunately they are all faint objects, and are recovered and followed by photographic methods using large telescopes. Most of these short-period comets travel in orbits of small inclination which reach out to the orbit of Jupiter, and it is this planet that is mainly responsible for the severe perturbations that many of these comets undergo. Unlike the planets, comets may be seen in any part of the sky, but since their distances from the Earth are similar to those of the planets their apparent movements in the sky are also somewhat similar, and some of them may be followed for long periods of time.

The following periodic comets are expected to return to perihelion in 2001, and to be brighter than magnitude +15:

Comet	Year of discovery	Period (years)	Predicted date of perihelion
47P/Ashbrook–Jackson	1948	7.5	Jan. 6
41P/Tuttle–Giacobini–Kresák	1858	5.4	Jan. 6
73P/Schwassmann–Wachmann 3	1930	5.4	Jan. 27
44P/Reinmuth 2	1947	6.6	Feb. 19
45P/Honda–Mrkos–Pajdušáková	1948	5.3	Mar. 29
24P/Schaumasse	1911	8.2	May 2
19P/Borrelly	1905	6.8	Sep. 14
71P/Clark	1973	5.5	Dec. 2

Minor Planets in 2001

Although many thousands of minor planets (asteroids) are known to exist, only a few thousand of them have well-determined orbits and are listed in the catalogues. Most of these orbits lie entirely between the orbits of Mars and Jupiter. All these bodies are quite small, and even the largest, Ceres, is only 913 km (567 miles) in diameter. Thus, they are necessarily faint objects, and although a number of them are within the reach of a small telescope few of them ever attain any considerable brightness. The first four that were discovered are named Ceres, Pallas, Juno and Vesta. Actually the largest four minor planets are Ceres, Pallas, Vesta and Hygeia. Vesta can occasionally be seen with the naked eye, and this is most likely to happen when an opposition occurs near June, since Vesta would then be at perihelion. Below is an ephemeris for Vesta in 2001; Ceres, Pallas and Juno are not favourably placed for observation during the year.

Vesta

					Geo-centric distance	Helio-centric distance	Elonga-tion	Visual magni-tude
		RA 2000.0		Dec.				
		h	m	°	'	AU	AU	°	
Jun.	20	2	54.70	+10	52.6	3.119	2.499	44.5W	8.3
	30	3	10.41	+11	53.2	3.034	2.506	50.0W	8.3
Jul.	10	3	25.66	+12	45.8	2.941	2.512	55.7W	8.3
	20	3	40.33	+13	30.4	2.839	2.519	61.5W	8.3
	30	3	54.26	+14	6.8	2.731	2.525	67.6W	8.2
Aug.	9	4	7.27	+14	35.3	2.616	2.531	73.9W	8.2
	19	4	19.18	+14	56.0	2.497	2.536	80.6W	8.1
	29	4	29.70	+15	9.3	2.374	2.541	87.6W	8.0
Sep.	8	4	38.57	+15	16.0	2.250	2.546	95.1W	7.9
	18	4	45.48	+15	16.6	2.127	2.550	103.1W	7.7
	28	4	50.05	+15	12.0	2.007	2.554	111.7W	7.6

Vesta (*cont'd*)

		RA		Dec.		Geo-centric distance	Helio-centric distance	Elonga-tion	Visual magni-tude
			2000.0						
	h	m	°	′		AU	AU	°	
Oct. 8	4	51.99	+15	3.5		1.895	2.558	121.0W	7.4
18	4	51.00	+14	52.1		1.794	2.561	131.0W	7.2
28	4	46.98	+14	39.1		1.709	2.564	141.8W	7.0
Nov. 7	4	40.10	+14	26.2		1.643	2.566	153.1W	6.8
17	4	30.89	+14	14.8		1.602	2.568	164.5W	6.6
27	4	20.31	+14	7.1		1.588	2.570	172.7W	6.5
Dec. 7	4	9.60	+14	5.1		1.603	2.571	166.4E	6.6
17	4	0.00	+14	10.7		1.647	2.572	155.0E	6.8
27	3	52.54	+14	25.2		1.715	2.573	143.4E	7.0

A vigorous campaign for observing the occultations of stars by minor planets has produced improved values for the dimensions of some of them, as well as the suggestion that some of these planets may be accompanied by satellites. Many of these observations have been made photoelectrically. However, amateur observers have found renewed interest in the minor planets since it has been shown that their visual timings of an occultation of a star by a minor planet are accurate enough to lead to reliable determinations of diameter. As a consequence many groups of observers all over the world are now organizing themselves for expeditions should the predicted track of such an occultation cross their country.

Meteors in 2001

Meteors ('shooting stars') may be seen on any clear moonless night, but on certain nights of the year their number increases noticeably. This occurs when the Earth chances to intersect a concentration of meteoric dust moving in an orbit around the Sun. If the dust is well spread out in space, the resulting shower of meteors may last for several days. The word 'shower' must not be misinterpreted – only on very rare occasions have the meteors been so numerous as to resemble snowflakes falling.

If the meteor tracks are marked on a star map and traced backwards, a number of them will be found to intersect in a point (or a small area of the sky) which marks the radiant of the shower. This gives the direction from which the meteors have come.

The following table gives some of the more easily observed showers with their radiants; interference by moonlight is shown by the letter M.

Shower	Limiting dates	Maximum	RA		Dec.	
			h	m	°	
Quadrantids	Jan. 1–4	Jan. 3	15	28	+50	M
Lyrids	Apr. 20–22	Apr. 22	18	08	+32	
Eta Aquarids	May 1–8	May 4	22	20	−01	M
Ophiuchids	June 17–26	June 19	17	20	−20	
Delta Aquarids	July 15–Aug. 15	July 29	22	36	−17	M
Piscis Australids	July 15–Aug. 20	July 31	22	40	−30	M
Capricornids	July 15–Aug. 25	Aug. 2	20	36	−10	M
Perseids	July 27–Aug. 17	Aug. 12	3	04	+58	M
Orionids	Oct. 15–25	Oct. 21	6	24	+15	
Taurids	Oct. 26–Nov. 16	Nov. 3	3	44	+14	M
Leonids	Nov. 15–19	Nov. 17	10	08	+22	
Geminids	Dec. 9–14	Dec. 13	7	28	+32	
Ursids	Dec. 17–24	Dec. 23	14	28	+78	M

Some Events in 2002

ECLIPSES

There will be two eclipses, both of the Sun.

June 10–11:   annular eclipse of the Sun – Asia, northern Australia, North America.

December 4:   total eclipse of the Sun – Africa, Australia.

THE PLANETS

Mercury may be seen more easily from northern latitudes in the evenings about the time of greatest eastern elongation (May 4) and in the mornings around greatest western elongation (October 13). In the Southern Hemisphere the corresponding most favourable dates are around February 21 (mornings) and September 1 (evenings).

Venus is visible in the evenings from late February to October, and in the mornings from November onwards.

Mars does not come to opposition in 2002.

Jupiter is at opposition on January 1.

Saturn is at opposition on December 17.

Uranus is at opposition on August 20.

Neptune is at opposition on August 2.

Pluto is at opposition on June 7.

Part II

Article Section

Is there Life in the Universe?

PAUL MURDIN

At one time it was not possible to ask whether there was life on other worlds, or even whether it had ever started. What sense did it make to ask such a question if there was only one world, our own, and the world had always been as it is? But as soon as it occurred to philosophers that our world was perhaps one of many, then the question of whether life had evolved on any of the other worlds made sense. The questions were first posed over 2000 years ago. What is 'life'? What does life need as an environment? What, if anything, makes it special?

These questions became more pressing when Galileo used his telescope to view the planets and found that they were worlds like ours. The Moon had mountains and plains. Jupiter had its own system of moons, in orbit around it. Venus showed a succession of phases and was clearly a world in its own right. Did this mean that there might be people on the Moon, on Jupiter, on Venus? Astronomers next realized that the stars were suns, at immense distances. They might also have planetary systems, very hard to distinguish at such distances. Could there be people on these remote planets?

We now know that the number of stars is huge, and that planets are formed at the same time as their parent star (see 'The Origins of Planets' in the *1999 Yearbook of Astronomy*). This suggests that planets, and therefore perhaps other beings like ourselves, are ubiquitous in the Universe.

The question of how common life is in the Universe has attracted astronomers, even though astronomers are not specialists in the science of 'life' – their interest in the issue of whether life exists on other worlds has to do with how the stage was set for life to appear. What sort of stage should astronomers look for? Science fiction writers have been able to imagine an enormous variety of habitats and the life forms that might inhabit them. Science fiction is interesting and provocative, but it opens up such wide possibilities that, when we are faced with all of them, we cannot decide where to start. Scientists have to place some limits on what to look for.

The first observation one can make is that life on Earth is based on carbon chemistry. As far as is known, no other atom has this ability to such a great degree. Silicon is sometimes put forward as an alternative to carbon since, especially in combination with oxygen atoms, it makes complex, plate-like molecules. We call the masses of 'inorganic life' that form in this way 'rocks'. Rocks are as near to 'life' as silicon makes. But silicon does not make the large and therefore complex molecules that carbon can.

Carbon is made in stars in abundance, so this is the cosmic source of life's most basic raw material. The carbon atom has the ability to link with others to form long chains, making possible the formation of chemical compounds of great complexity. Carbon compounds of a certain degree of complexity are found in interstellar space, so this is the source of the raw material of the so-called prebiotic soup from which life is thought to have arisen.

Silicon can never make anything like the characteristic, long, double-helix molecules called DNA. DNA molecules are the basis for life, and each species has a characteristic form of DNA. The DNA molecule is made up of a sequence of smaller units which, like letters, make up a 'script' that spells out the genetic code of its living host creature. The unwinding of one strand of DNA from the other in the double helix, and the formation of new DNA as components link themselves in the right sequence onto each unwound strand, are what constitute the replication process that is one of the characteristics of life.

Living organisms also need proteins. Proteins are organic molecules that life uses as catalysts, as transportation molecules (for example, haemoglobin transports oxygen in blood) and as support structures (for example, collagen makes skin). Proteins are made on the same principle as DNA, from strings of units called amino acids. There are a very large number of amino acids, but only 20 are used in life on Earth. They form a very rich 'vocabulary' of proteins, used in the 'script' of life.

Whether extraterrestrial forms of life use exactly the same 'vocabu-lary' of biochemicals is an interesting question. Maybe there is only one vocabulary that works. But maybe, like spoken and written languages, there are several ways of implementing the scripts of life. When and if we obtain and examine life from some other planet (Mars, perhaps), we shall have the chance to see what differences there may be between it and our own terrestrial biochemistry. This will be of great scientific significance, as well as of interest to the pharmaceutical industry.

Amino acids contain a carbon atom that is not centrally situated in the molecule, and each amino acid can exist in two forms that are reflections of each other, like a left hand and a right hand. Only one of the two forms of each amino acid is used by life – the left-handed form. Sugars have a similar asymmetry – and life uses the right-handed forms of sugars. Life molecules like proteins, sugars and DNA therefore have a property called 'chirality', or 'handedness'. Nature makes some of life's molecules by ordinary, inorganic chemistry, and these do not show strong chirality. If you find chirality in a naturally occurring soup of organic molecules, it could indicate that the molecules were made by life.

This is not entirely a logical conclusion, however, because there are some other ways in which chirality can be induced. For example, if you shine strongly polarized light into a soup in which there are equal numbers of left- and right-handed molecules, some of one sort switch into the other, giving the soup an imbalance of chirality. It is not known whether the chirality of biological molecules is a consequence of the way life works, or a prerequisite for life to start. If it is the latter, then astronomers have to explain how chirality can arise in organic molecules in space. Perhaps it occurs when interstellar grains on which there are organic molecules pass a source of strongly polarized light, such as a pulsating neutron star, a pulsar. This must be a chancy process, but even if it occurs only a few times, the chiral organic molecules could move into other regions and seed more chirality through prebiotic chemistry (chemistry which is like the chemistry of life, and may be a precursor of life processes, but is not actually produced by life). The pulsar that induced chirality in the chemicals that seeded terrestrial prebiotic chemistry (if that is indeed what happened) has long since faded into an inert neutron star – an unidentifiable cold cinder from the fire that flash-cooked the prebiotic soup.

Chemical reactions that build more and more complex molecules need energy sources to drive them. For life on Earth the predominant energy source is sunlight – plants use photosynthesis as the chemical means to create cellular structures. This is not the only possible source, however, and the 'black smokers' or geothermal vents in the deep ocean have colonies of life surrounding them. These life forms use geothermal energy as their energy source.

It is possible to relate organisms to one another by examining their DNA. The closer one species is to another, the more similar their DNA will be. By looking at the sequence of DNA forms it is possible to trace the evolutionary chain that connects species to one another, right back to the presumed common ancestor of all life on Earth. Recent analysis of the molecular sequencing of the DNA of a range of life forms seems to indicate that the common ancestor of life on Earth was a thermophilic (living at high temperature) archaeon. (Archaea are a newly discovered type of organism that provides a structural link between bacteria and the higher multicellular organisms like you and me.) If this is right, then it seems that life on Earth first started under the ocean surface, not in the sunlight where we live. Astronomers have identified the processes that put the chiral chemicals on the Earth, and geologists have identified the fire that simmered them into life.

Life chemistry needs a medium in which to operate. Biochemical compounds need to get together and react in the way that life operates here on Earth. They need to be mobile – not frozen into solids – and close to one another – not dispersed like gases. The solvent that provides the required medium on Earth is water (see 'Water: A Cosmic History' in the *2000 Yearbook of Astronomy*). It is abundant, and it is made of simple elements (hydrogen and oxygen) which are found everywhere in the Universe. It has the property that, although its molecules are light in weight, they stick weakly together, so it is liquid over quite a wide range of temperatures, provided it exists under an atmospheric pressure of over 6 millibars. Water also is a key chemical in biochemical reactions, and 'likes' to react with organic molecules. Liquid water is the key environmental factor for the existence of life, as we can tell on Earth by comparing the near sterility of the dry deserts and icy poles with the fertility of the temperate humid zones.

Liquid water survives most readily and for long times in the 'Goldilocks zone' in the Solar System, the region in which the temperature on a planet is neither so cold that water freezes, nor so hot that it evaporates. This is partly a matter of the planet being the right distance from the Sun, but also a matter of how much carbon dioxide there is in its atmosphere. Too close to the Sun, and with too much carbon dioxide, Venus suffers from a runaway greenhouse effect. Too far from the Sun, and with the carbon dioxide condensed out of the atmosphere as dry ice, Mars has only a small greenhouse effect and is too cold now for liquid water (except in regions where there might be geothermal springs). But by no coincidence (we do live here, after all!), the Goldilocks zone encompasses the orbit of Earth.

Life evolved in water. A rain of organic chemicals fell from interstellar space onto the early Earth, brought in on the comets that melted on impact and formed the seas and lakes. Mixed with carbon dioxide and phosphates in rocks, the gases hydrogen cyanide, cyanoacetylene, cyanogen, formaldehyde and hydrogen sulphide from space were energized by geothermal vents, and reacted to form more complicated organic molecules such as amino acids and nucleotides. These prebiotic molecules are the building blocks of DNA and proteins.

Some complex prebiotic molecules may even have been made in space and brought directly to Earth on comets, or in micrometeorites and sand grains from space. Astrochemistry experiments in which chemists at the NASA Ames Research Center have simulated the conditions of interstellar space show that quite complicated molecules can be made on interstellar grains energized by weak ultraviolet light. Hexamethylenetetramine is one: it is a molecule with six carbon atoms, and in warm acidic water it makes amino acids. Quinone is another molecule made in the Ames Research Center's experiments. In its structure it is similar to the molecules that help chlorophyll to harness light energy to build the cells of plants.

If interstellar grains or comets carrying amino acids produced by such astrochemistry pass a neutron star emitting polarized light, the prebiotic material may develop chirality. As explained earlier, this may be how the handedness develops, and makes possible biochemistry.

The idea that comets, or their 'emanations', could lead to the spontaneous generation of life on the Earth was first expressed by Isaac Newton. It was given its modern form in 1908–11 by the father-and-son team of Thomas C. Chamberlin and Rollin T. Chamberlin in a paper called 'Early terrestrial conditions that may have favored organic synthesis'. They suggested that 'planetesimals', the small bodies that merged to form the planets, may have been a source of the organic material from which life evolved. 'The planetesimals are assumed to have contained carbon, sulphur, phosphorus and all the other elements found in organic matter,' they wrote, 'and as they impinged more or less violently upon the surface formed of previous accessions [sic] of similar matter, there should have been generated various compounds of these elements.' The basic ideas of the theory were revived by the Soviet astrobiologist Alexander Oparin in 1938, and given their modern form by J. Oró and Chris Chyba, the director of the SETI Institute and a student of Carl Sagan's.

Unfortunately, no clear evidence that might support this theory has survived from the time of the Earth's bombardment by comets and other sources of prebiotic chemistry from space. The structure of the primitive Earth was completely altered when a large asteroid collided with the proto-Earth about 500 million years after the formation of the Solar System. This collision created the Moon. Not only did this impact all but obliterate all signs of previous events, but ever since then the movements of the Earth's crust known collectively as plate tectonics have churned over the surface materials. As the Earth's climate has cycled between glaciations and interglacial periods, changes in sea level and downpours of rain have washed away any remaining traces of early living structures. Oxygen produced by the burgeoning of life has converted early organic molecules into carbon dioxide. All this activity on the Earth has made it very difficult to say what the primitive Earth was like.

There is, however, experimental evidence of this theory in the form of simulations of the conditions under which early life formed. The creation of life has yet to be achieved by some future Professor Frankenstein, but prebiotic chemistry was created in 1953 by Stanley Miller. Miller was a Ph.D. student of Harold Urey's at the University of Chicago. He put simple organic chemicals in a flask of water from which any oxygen gas had been removed, and passed an electric spark through a mixture of gases over the water that was thought to represent the composition of the primitive atmosphere. He was guided by the idea that it was electrical discharges (lightning) that created biological molecules in the atmosphere, rather than geothermal energy in the deep oceans, but hundreds of similar experiments have since been carried out with a variety of chemicals and energy sources, with much the same results. Miller found amino acids in the black sludge produced by his experiment. Nucleotides have also been produced, and indeed a similar range of organic molecules is always produced, provided there is no free oxygen.

At some point, it appears that, given the right ingredients, a source of energy and water as a solvent, the organic chemistry of the Earth crossed the boundary between inanimate chemistry and life processes. There is a gap in our knowledge of how this happened – it is always good to know that there are some things left for new generations of scientists to find out! Reproduction was enabled by the splitting apart of the DNA (or its more primitive relation, RNA), rebuilding a pair of the DNA helices by assembling nucleotides onto each half-spiral. A certain amount of randomness crept into this method of reproduction – mistakes of reproduction were made. These mutations created slightly different forms of life, which then competed with existing forms in their habitats. Survival during changes of habitat or success in reproduction provided the systematic selection of those 'mistakes' that were, in fact, more favourable. Natural selection became the driving force of evolution.

The most favourable habitats for the first, primitive life forms on Earth included water with the right temperature, acidity, salinity and nutrient sources. The life that evolved under water was protected from any harmful ultraviolet radiation. Life certainly needs the right conditions, but recent discoveries have shown just how wide a range of conditions can be 'right'. The species that exist under the most extreme conditions are called extremophiles. Extreme habitats on Earth currently under study as places where strange life forms have evolved include Lake Vostok, an ice-covered lake in Antarctica. This is a terrestrial environment which is the closest we have to the conditions on Jupiter's moon, Europa.

The Lake Vostok Initiative, led from NASA's Jet Propulsion Laboratory and other agencies, plans to take samples from the lake once an international consortium can decide how to go about it. The issues are how to do it safely (the pressure of the ice floating on the water of the lake may cause the water to gush like an oil well as soon as the ice is penetrated by drilling) and how to maintain the lake water pristine, uncontaminated with organisms from the surface. One plan is to use a hot water lance to break through, inserting a robotic probe that will sterilize itself as it descends, looking at the chemistry and the biology of the lake. Ice near the hole through which it is inserted will re-freeze and close the hole again. In many respects this mission makes the same demands as a space mission – a robotic craft sent on a one-way trip, remotely operated, working in extreme conditions and radioing data back to base. Scientists plan to practice on similar, smaller lakes nearby.

Other examples of life surviving under extreme circumstances are the Antarctic cryptoendoliths. These organisms (their name means 'hidden inside rocks') live just below the surface of rocks on cold, dry Antarctic hillsides. These hillsides are about as close to the temperature of the cold deserts of Mars as the Earth gets. When a rock is broken open, the cryptoendoliths can be seen as a layer of green inside layers of blue and yellow substances. The organisms themselves deposit the layers to protect themselves against the fierce ultraviolet light from the Sun over Antarctica. They leach water and nutrient from the rocks.

In controversial discoveries, microbiological organisms living inside rocks have been identified down to depths of kilometres below the surface of the Earth. They have no need of photosynthesis, and gain their energy from chemical processes, flourishing in the interstices of rocks. Discoveries of life below ground, in boiling geothermal cauldrons like the black smokers and in extreme environments in the Antarctic show that life is tenacious. Once it takes hold on a planet it will survive and live even in extreme habitats, provided there is water and an energy source.

The most extreme environment that tests life's survival capability is space. Of course, space is dry. Humans survive in space by taking what they need with them. The Mir space station, in orbit and almost continuously inhabited for 15 years, was regularly visited by supply spacecraft, bringing not only new science experiments, videos and books for the bored astronauts, but – most importantly – water.

It is important for life not to be exposed to too much radiation, lest it receives a fatal dose. The Apollo astronauts absorbed about as much radiation as they could stand during their flights to the Moon when they passed through the concentrations of radiation in the Van Allen Belts surrounding Earth. An astronaut on a space walk must be recalled back into the spacecraft if there is a danger of increased radiation from a solar storm.

One of the most hostile places imaginable for life to survive in is the totally dry surface of the Moon, unprotected by any atmosphere from radiation. But some life can survive, if not flourish, even there. An early lunar probe left a camera on the Moon's surface. It was retrieved 31 months later during the November 1969 Apollo 12 mission. When it was examined back on Earth, biologists found streptococci bacteria. These cold germs had been deposited on the equipment by a technician who had sneezed while getting the equipment ready for its journey to the Moon. They had survived a couple of years' exposure to space. Water in them had evaporated, they had been frozen and they had gone into suspended animation, but they had survived being irradiated by ultraviolet light and cosmic rays from the Sun.

This bears on the interesting question of whether bacteria can travel across space by natural means, moving from one planet to another.

This is called the panspermia hypothesis, and dates from the late 19th century. Louis Pasteur showed that the abundance of yeast that grows in wine in fact derives from pre-existing traces of yeast. Commenting on the failure of attempts, up to then, to produce organisms from non-living matter, Hermann von Helmholtz asked rhetorically in 1874 how life arose on Earth and whether seeds have been carried from one planet to another, germinating wherever they have fallen on fertile soil. The Swedish chemist Svante Arrhenius developed the panspermia hypothesis in a book called *Worlds in the Making*. Incidents such as the survival of the Apollo programme's cold germs, and detailed scientific experiments in space on the Mir space station and other space laboratories, suggest that bacteria can indeed survive for millions of years in space. If ejected into space, say on a rock knocked off a biologically active planet, bacteria may find their way in suspended animation to another watery planet, where they can revive and successfully reproduce.

This transport mechanism exists. The SNC meteorites (see 'Meteoritics at the Millennium', *2000 Yearbook of Astronomy*) are Martian rocks, ejected from Mars by the glancing impact of an asteroid, and eventually finding their way to Earth. If life exists on Mars, then it could have travelled here on such a meteorite. Life certainly exists on Earth, and there have been asteroid impacts here too. Somewhere on Mars there are, no doubt, terrestrial rocks. It is tantalizing to speculate that Mars has been seeded by terrestrial life.

So life is tenacious, and appropriate life forms can survive in extreme habitats – the cold watery depths of a polar lake, or the even colder vacuum of space. Of course, there are limits to the environments in which life will continue. Life can cope with changes in its environment, but not if the changes are too large. Since evolution takes a long time, life needs stability on a long time scale. To what degree is this stability provided by Earth, and other planets in the Universe?

When I took my children to the Disneyland at Anaheim in California, the two boys (aged seven and eleven) sought out the adrenalin rush of the Matterhorn Bobsleigh, but my daughter (aged three) enjoyed the sedate rotations of the Teacup Roundabout. She sat primly in the large pink teacups, as small as a shrinking Alice at a Victorian tea party. The teacups circled in a sedate and orderly way. There were certainly no collisions, as there are between dodgem cars at fairgrounds. The fairground attendants may set out to instil an orderliness in the progression of the dodgems, and point to notices that demand 'No Bumping'. But the notices are ignored, and teenage lads with shrieking girls at their side race, foot down, against the traffic flow, bumping into the other cars. Collisions are inevitable.

We think of our Solar System as an orderly rotating collection of planets, like the Teacup Roundabout, and this image is fostered by elementary treatments of Newton's theory of gravitation and the motion of planets. If the Sun and a planet are both perfectly spherical, well separated, with the Sun very massive and the planet very small, and there are no other planets in the system, and gravity is the only force that affects the Solar System – then the planet's orbit will be perfectly repetitive. If there are more planets than this one, but they are all so small that the pull of one planet on another is completely negligible – then, again, the motions of the planets will be perfectly repetitive.

As soon as the Solar System departs from this ideal, as of course it does, an element of chaos creeps into the motions of the planets, which approach a little closer to the turbulence of the dodgem cars. The interactions between the planets, as they pull close and then separate, add a tug to each planet that is additional to the pull of the Sun. The planets and the Sun all rotate, and each body raises a tide on all the others, so none of the planets nor the Sun are perfectly spherical. The Sun emits radiation and a solar wind of particles, so its influence on the planets includes non-gravitational forces, like puffs of air in the sails of a yacht.

All these factors make the motions of the planets in our own Solar System a little erratic. They twist and turn, they oscillate in their spin, and they approach the Sun and recede. These effects have caused the climate of our own planet to change, in the Milankovitch cycles. The spin axis of the Earth itself spins (or precesses), and the eccentricity of the Earth's orbit changes. The combination of these effects means that the amount of solar radiation received by the Earth changes cyclically, and the way it varies through a year also changes, producing different modes of the Earth's seasons. These differences are illustrated by taking two extreme examples.

If the Earth's axis were perpendicular to the plane of its orbit, sunlight would never fall exactly on the two poles, but would fall in full strength at noon on the equator. By contrast, if the spin axis lay in the plane of the orbit, at a certain time the north pole would be pointing at the Sun and the southern hemisphere would all be dark, and six months later vice versa. Obviously the seasonal changes, the behaviour of the polar caps, the shift of water between north and south as one cap melted and the other froze – all these effects would be very different in the two extremes.

The reality does not encompass as wide a variation as the two extremes of the example above. At present the Earth's axis is tilted at an angle of 23.5° degrees to the plane of its orbit. Over long periods of time the angle varies between 22° and 24.5°. The eccentricity of the Earth's orbit varies, producing changes in its distance from the Sun throughout its year. This enhances seasonal (summer/winter) differences. The change is relatively small, between 0 and 0.05, so the variation in the Sun's flux is only a few per cent.

The general cyclic development of the Earth's axial tilt and of its eccentricity is relatively easy to calculate, as these things go, but impossible to calculate and forecast accurately and specifically. What happens in the future is very sensitive to the mathematical statement of where the orbit lies now. This kind of difficulty is a feature of chaos theory. It is, however, possible to make general statements about the range and period of variation.

As I have mentioned, the Earth's climate follows what are called Milankovitch cycles. The predominant cycles have periods of 23,000–100,000 years, corresponding to the ebb and flow of ice ages. This affects the climate, particularly, of the polar caps. Although these climate changes are measurable and significant, they are not overly large. Moreover, the Earth has some internal adjustment mechanisms that keep its climate changes within certain limits, if the changes are not too large. If, for example, the Earth receives more solar radiation, it warms. More water is evaporated from its oceans. This makes the atmosphere cloudier. The whiteness of the clouds reflects solar radiation. This reduces the solar radiation that the Earth takes in, and the Earth cools.

Formulated under the name of the Gaia hypothesis, this concept of the Earth almost as a living organism is due to James Lovelock. It means that, once life takes hold on a planet, it will maintain the planet in a state that is suitable for life's continuance. This gives life on a planet like Earth the time to develop. The Gaia hypothesis is valid only if the changes in the circumstances of the Earth are small – say up to a change in solar radiation of a factor of two. Why have I chosen this figure as a limit? The reason is that it encompasses the amount by which astronomers have calculated the Sun to have increased its output since it was born some 5 billion years ago (this is a normal part of the ageing process for a star like the Sun). In spite of this increase in brightness of the Sun, the Earth has sustained life since the collision that formed the Moon over 4 billion years ago.

The Gaia mechanism is not infallible and will not work in extreme circumstances. It did not work for Venus. Venus was hot, being so near to the Sun. When Venus received water from cometary impacts, this water evaporated into its atmosphere under the Sun's heat, and perhaps was never liquid on Venus. Life (it appears) did not, therefore, develop on Venus, and could not create an oxygen atmosphere to counter the effect of the volcanic eruptions that pumped sulphur dioxide into the atmosphere, creating unusually cloudy conditions. All this created a major greenhouse effect in its atmosphere, and Venus got even hotter. Further cometary impacts and the heat evaporated more water. The greenhouse effect ran away, rather than regulating itself in a Venusian equivalent of the Gaia mechanism.

The Earth has shown a remarkable stability in its history. Of course, there have been large changes. Continents formed, broke up and drifted apart, altering the flow of oceanic currents and changing the climate. Some 100 million years ago, for example, the disposition of the continents deflected warm water from the equator towards Antarctica, making it verdant during its summer, although it froze in winter. As the continents separated, this warming stream was no longer deflected into the south polar regions and the Antarctic became a snowbound waste. Such dramatic changes perhaps caused wholesale extinctions of some of the species that had been dominant under the conditions that prevailed previously. But other species would have replaced them and thrived in the new conditions. Life went on, developing.

This might have happened on Mars. Even though Mars has evidently changed a great deal during the history of the Solar System, the changes may not have been absolutely catastrophic to the continued existence and evolution of life there – if it had started and got established before the change occurred. This contributes to scientists' optimism about the possibility of life on Mars.

In general, the evolution of life needs a relatively stable platform, a planet whose temperature and climate remain stable – or change not too quickly – or, if there are sudden changes, they are not too large. Our own Earth seems to have stood up favourably when judged by these criteria. Unlike Venus, it is at a distance from the Sun that permits liquid water to exist on the surface – much closer to the Sun, and Earth would have had a steamy climate, perhaps a dry one. Farther from the Sun than the asteroids, Earth would have been frozen like Europa, perhaps with extremophile life in isolated niches, but evidently without life that can take a hold across the surface of and regulate the climate of the whole of its planet.

The favoured inner part of the Solar System is not without risks, however. Inside the asteroid zone, collisions are possible between the asteroids and the planets. As I have mentioned, only a few hundred million years after its formation the proto-Earth collided with an asteroid the size of Mars. This created the Moon. The iron cores of the merged proto-Earth and asteroid combined to produce the rather large iron core of the Earth.

Later collisions between the Earth and asteroids were not so catastrophic, but were certainly large. Such wholesale effects are also not self-regulated in the way that the Gaia hypothesis maintains. After the colossal impact in which the Moon was created, the Earth's surface suffered further impacts by asteroids, but luckily not another big one. The largest known crater on Earth is the Chicxulub crater in Mexico, some 200 km in diameter. There is no crater on Earth like Hellas on Mars, that affected half the planet, nor even one the size of the Aitken Basin at the Moon's south pole.

It is the existence of the Moon near the Earth that has stabilized the Earth's tilt. The Moon is quite large compared with the Earth, certainly by comparison with other planets and their moons. Sometimes, in fact, the Earth and Moon are regarded as a twin planet, rather than a planet and satellite. Because it is relatively so large, the Moon's gravity limits the wobble of the Earth. Although it wobbles a little, the Earth wobbles much less than Mars, which has just two tiny satellites, Phobos and Deimos. The Earth's chaotic seasonal cycles are therefore small, and the Milankovitch cycles are relatively minor, on a planetary scale (although climate-transforming on a regional scale). The formation of the Moon early on the Earth's life was the price the Earth paid for later stability. The formation of the Moon, as well as creating the Earth's large iron core, contributed to the tectonic mobility that causes the continents to slide over the Earth's surface, and to its geothermal activity.

The eccentricity of the Earth's orbit is small, and the massive planet Jupiter is far enough away that its perturbing effect on Earth's orbit is small, compared with its effect on the nearer Mars. Earth can think of itself as the 'lucky planet' because its climate and geology are benign, and its prevailing conditions maintain water as liquid.

This is not true of the two dozen or more extrasolar planetary systems found so far, in orbit around some nearby stars (see 'The Discovery of Other Planetary Systems', *1997 Yearbook of Astronomy*). For a start, several of the planets are in orbit around binary stars. Our Sun is a single star, but most stars are members of multiple star systems – pairs, triples or more. The Lone Star state is the peculiar one. Three of the planets are in a binary star system, each orbiting one of the stars, with the other star orbiting at a larger distance. There is one case in which a planet orbits both stars (sunrise and sunset on this planet will be as was imagined for Luke Skywalker's desert home in the film *Star Wars*).

The orbit of a planet in a binary system is pulled by the cyclic tugs of the pair of stars. In a more extreme case, where the stars and the planet were closer together, the planet could well be ejected from the system into interstellar space. If not, the planet's orbit will be perturbed and it will move alternately closer to and farther from its parent star or stars, with episodic drying-out periods. It was no surprise to me that Luke Skywalker lived in a desert, given the double star sunset that was shown on screen. It did surprise me to find that his planet had an atmosphere, since I would expect it to have suffered extreme climate changes.

Most known planetary systems have 'hot jupiters', massive Jupiter-sized planets close to their sun. On current thinking, massive jupiters do not form close to their suns: they form in cold regions distant from their parent stars. If that is the case, then the jupiters migrated to their present positions, coursing across their solar systems. Even if this were not so, a surprising number of these jupiters have very eccentric orbits and move back and forth, closer to and farther from their stars. We do not have the technology to be able to tell whether any planetary systems contain small Earth-sized planets. But if the 'hot jupiter' planetary systems do have such 'earths', the earths will have suffered. An earth in such a system will have been pulled by the migrating or eccentric jupiter, and tugged into outrageous, unstable orbits, sometimes hot, sometimes cold. The climate changes would be severe. The sub-zero epochs would plunge the earth into frozen stasis. Perhaps some life forms could survive in such conditions, in special niches – near geo-thermal vents, under ice or in caves under the permafrost. But the superheated epochs, with the temperature over 100°C, would set off greenhouse episodes, and the earth's water would begin to escape as steam into its upper atmosphere, and then as water vapour into the surrounding space.

Some earths in such an unstable planetary system, reacting to a rampaging jupiter, will have been accreted and assimilated by the jupiter if they came into their feeding zones. Like Comet Shoemaker–Levy 9, the earth will drop into the jupiter's atmosphere. Instead of mushroom clouds the size of continents, as were seen rising above Jupiter's horizons in 1994 from the cometary impact (see 'The Impact of Comet Shoemaker–Levy 9 on Jupiter and on the World of Astronomy', *1997 Yearbook of Astronomy*), in a collision with an earth the whole of the jupiter's atmosphere would oscillate. The planet would vibrate slowly, like a falling drop of water filmed in slow motion, with small droplets splashing into the space around. Needless to say, in such a collision the earth would be roasted, and its water would evaporate, and be dissipated, or merged into the water in the jupiter.

Some earths in systems like the ones recently discovered might have found themselves, not in eccentric, looping orbits, but ejected from the planetary system altogether. Its occupants, if any, would look back to their receding sun, as over a few years it diminished in brightness and warmth to the same chill gleam as any other star. Its climate would chill, its oceans freeze, its habitats become more and more extreme. Its life would retreat into niches which, however, would themselves contract and disappear. The planet would be doomed to a dark and cold journey through interstellar space, a lonely existence, illuminated for brief periods by a distant encounter with another star. It would pass such a star unseen, except for an echo of its presence in the disturbance it might cause to the star's Oort cloud of comets, some of which it would perturb from their orbits and send plunging in towards their star (see 'The Planets of Interstellar Space', *1992 Yearbook of Astronomy*).

Like comets, some earths in other solar systems that also contain disturbing, eccentric jupiters might also be sent plunging towards their star rather than outwards into space. Their water would evaporate from the earth's sunlit side, trailing in a wake behind, like a comet's tail. The plunge into the star's atmosphere and surface would cause a splash, small on a stellar scale, a puff of material from the star's corona like a spontaneous coronal mass ejection from our own Sun. The earth material would be assimilated into the star's atmosphere. There is actually some evidence for this possible consequence of an in-spiralling earth in known planetary systems with close hot jupiters. Their stars are unusual in that their atmospheres have spectra with rather stronger spectral lines than average. Spectral lines are caused by the absorption of starlight from the star's surface by metallic atoms in its atmosphere. Stronger lines than average imply that there is more metal material than average. This is what you could expect if the star's atmosphere had ingested an earth.

What does all this mean for the existence of life in other planetary systems? I think that the ubiquity of organic molecules in space means that organic chemistry has a chance to be everywhere in the Universe. If the organic molecules need to be chiral and must be irradiated by a pulsar, then this might reduce the chance that organic molecules seed life, but this idea is more speculative even than most of the other ideas in this article, and I set it aside.

Water certainly is ubiquitous, and even though it may be dried out from terrestrial-type planets when they are formed near their suns, the leftover fragments of icy material (comets) are likely to resupply water to the rocky surfaces of the terrestrial planets. There is a range of watery habitats that can result on individual planets, asteroids and satellites. For example, its 'Goldilocks' position in a planetary system ('just right', like the Earth) might lead a whole planet to be covered in water. Or there may be a localized watery zone near a geothermal vent or under an icy sea. This may well mean that liquid water is also universal, at least in niche environments. The fact that life burst so soon onto the surface of the Earth seems to indicate that if watery conditions exist, and the organic chemistry is deposited (as in a comet impact), and there is a source of energy (like geothermal energy), then life is likely to develop. Alternatively, if it is very difficult to form life and (against my expectations) it has only happened once (here on Earth), even so, it is possible that terrestrial life has been distributed at least in the near zone of the Galaxy by being propagated on meteorites from the Earth like the SNC meteorites in reverse.

But we have to remember that the first signs of life on Earth were relatively simple creatures, like archaea. There were single-celled organisms, which assembled in colonies, and developed into complex creatures like ourselves. This evolution took a long time to get under way. Once it was under way, a wonderful variety of life forms appeared, but there must have been many failed developments. This indicates that a stable platform is necessary for complex creatures to evolve – it literally takes billions of years of the right conditions.

By contrast, most of the extrasolar planetary orbits that we know of are not stable. Even within our own Solar System, apparently, the planet Mars has not been lucky and stable for the 4.5 billion years of the life of the Solar System. To pass on your genes into complex life, you have to be a bacterium born in the right planetary system; perhaps you even have to be born on a planet with a stabilizing moon. While one massive collision may be useful to make a large, stabilizing moon, your planet has to avoid a significant number of massive collisions which would cause a severe climate change, stop it from developing an atmosphere or otherwise put back evolution too much.

While life may be common in the Universe, complex and therefore intelligent life may be rather rare. The Universe is so large, and the number of stars so big, that I would hesitate to say that we, the most complex life that we know of, are unique in the Universe. But I think we may be at least unusual.

SUMMARY

Tending to make life common	Tending to make life rare
Stars are numerous.	
Planets are associated with many stars.	
Carbon is made abundantly.	
Organic chemicals form in interstellar space.	Chirality is necessary in prebiotic chemicals (?) and is induced by polarized light from a pulsar (?).
Water is abundant.	Water dries out in too much heat or too low a pressure.
Comets and asteroids distribute water to planets that have dried.	Planets may suffer large bombardments at the 'wrong' times.
There is a 'Goldilocks zone' in planetary systems which is neither too hot nor too cold for water to be liquid.	Many planetary systems have large planets that are in eccentric orbits or migrate and disturb planets in the 'Goldilocks zone'.

Cont'd

Tending to make life common

Life evolves near geothermal sources and moves on to a planet's surface to be sustained by its sun.

Once life takes hold on a planet, it will tend to adapt the planet to sustain life, even if the planet changes.

Life may be propagated through space.

Tending to make life rare

In the real Universe, planetary systems create oscillations in their planets that cause destabilizing climate changes.

Twin planets like the Earth–Moon system do not oscillate much; but such twin systems are made by freak cases.

Astronomy of the Plains Indians

COLIN TAYLOR

In my early travels across the Great Plains of North America in pursuit of my ethnological studies, I often camped out under the starry sky and, not surprisingly, began to muse on how the original inhabitants of the region, the Plains Indians, rationalized the astronomical phenomena which nightly unfolded in the clear heavens above them.[1]

Later, I discussed the subject with Paul Murdin, who told me of a topic which was increasingly capturing the interest of astronomers, namely *archaeoastronomy* – the study of the astronomies of indigenous peoples – and we agreed to collect and exchange information on the subject. He later published an article based on an examination of Plains Indian historical records in which he described their use of astronomical phenomena, particularly spectacular meteor showers, as points in their calendar (Murdin 1984). These records were commonly referred to as Winter Counts, and the meteor showers were called by the Teton Sioux (Lakota) *Wicáhpi-Linh'pàya*, 'the-falling-of-stars'.

Since those early days, it has been my good fortune not only to amass extensive published and other data on Plains Indian astronomy, and study artefacts produced by Plains Indians which have astronomical associations, but also to discuss the topic with knowledgeable individuals, both red and white. The topic is vast and still unfolding, and what follows is but the tip of the iceberg.

HISTORICAL BACKGROUND

The Great Plains form the very heartland of North America. This is a land of sun, wind and vast grasslands, stretching from north to south more than 3000 km, from the Saskatchewan River in Canada almost to the Rio Grande in Mexico. The western and eastern boundaries are approximately those of the foothills of the Rocky Mountains and the Mississippi–Missouri valleys. In all, the region encompasses an area of some 2.5 million km[2].

During the 18th and 19th centuries, when contact was first made with the white man, the Great Plains were largely dominated by Siouan and Algonquian linguistic groups although others, such as Uto-Aztecan and Athapaskan, were also represented. In the northern part of the region (now present-day Alberta, Saskatchewan and Montana) lived such tribes as the Blackfeet, Cree, Plains Ojibwa and Gros Ventre; to their south (present-day Wyoming, southern Montana and the Dakotas) were the Sioux, Cheyenne, Crow, Mandan, Hidatsa and Arikara; the Southern Plains (present-day Texas, Nebraska and Oklahoma) were occupied by the Comanche, Kiowa, Wichita and Pawnee. Most of these tribes had migrated into the region after the introduction of the horse by the Spaniards in the south-west, and of the gun by the English and French in the north-east – a gradual process which started in about 1650. It brought together peoples of great diversity of background and history, although their populations were relatively small. For example, one of the largest tribes – the Algonquian-speaking Blackfeet – numbered no more than 15,000 in the 1780s, while the Lakota (the most nomadic of the Sioux group) numbered about 10,000.[2]

Of all the five hundred or so tribes in North America, it was perhaps the thirty or so Plains Indian tribes whose environment afforded them a largely unobstructed view of the dark night sky, and they routinely observed the celestial panorama above them. As with many other ancient cultures, what they saw there had a significant impact on their art, mythology, religion, ceremonies and architecture.[3] Reconstruction and documentation of this knowledge and how it suffused the culture of the people has recently been of considerable interest to archaeo-astronomy researchers, and the cosmological concepts and lore of the Plains tribes in particular have caught researchers' attention. This field clearly has considerable potential for further research. It provides us with insights into the basic urge of human nature to explain the natural phenomena that continuously unfold before them, not least the panorama of the heavens which, although seen, can never be touched.

EARLY REFERENCES

From the earliest times, it has been recorded that the Plains tribes viewed the heavens with interest, generally tempered with great reverence. The explorer David Thompson, who travelled across the Northern Plains in the 1750s, reported that the Cree had names for a number of the brightest stars and constellations, such as Sirius and Orion, and that the changing seasons were marked by observing the rising of Orion for winter and the setting of the Pleiades for summer. The Sun and the Moon were described as 'divinities' and, though not worshipped, were always spoken of with great reverence.

Nearly a century later, in response to a US Government Survey document drawn up in 1847, the fur trader Edwin Denig reported from Fort Union on the Upper Missouri (on the present-day North Dakota border) details of Cree astronomical concepts, a number of which were remarkably insightful. The Sun was considered to be the Great Master of Life which gave heat and light to all things, while the Moon was conceived of as another world, receiving light from the Sun and stars. The Milky Way was referred to as the Chief's Road, and was regarded as a division which separated the sky into two parts. Polaris was referred to as the Stationary Star, and Ursa Major as the Trail of Stars, while the aurora borealis was called the Dance of the Dead – spirits who were enjoying themselves in the upper regions of the night sky. Mythology aside, the Cree, as well as the Assiniboin, Denig reported, had deduced that the stars of Ursa Major revolved around Polaris, and used its orientation as a clock when they were travelling at night.

In addition to subdividing time by the different phases of the Moon, such as 'moon on the increase', 'half moon', 'decreasing moon', 'small moon', 'dead moon', and so on, the Cree – in common with other Northern Plains tribes – had names for the 13 moons of the year. Subdivisions were particularly important to a tribe closely related to the Cree – the Blackfeet – who, in association with one of their most important ceremonials, the Beaver Bundle[4] complex, counted 26 days for the Moon and recognized four days during which it was invisible – reasonable even for today's astronomers who still debate this issue.

A SIOUX SHAMAN EXPLAINS GRAVITY

The white man's concept of gravitational force was, however, challenged. When Denig (a highly educated man) attempted to explain the laws of motion and gravitation to the Assiniboin, a highly intelligent tribal member observed that if at midnight the people were all on the underside of the Earth, what was there to stop the Missouri from spilling out and all the people from falling off? Flies, spiders, birds and the like, he said, had small claws by which they could adhere to the ceiling and other places, but man and water had no such support!

Half a century later, almost by an accident of circumstance, Dr J. R. Walker, a distinguished physician to the Lakota, gained insight into the Sioux cosmos. After he and Finger, a noted shaman, had together witnessed a meteor, or 'falling star', Finger agreed to explain the Sioux concept of energy and the place of the stars, Moon and Sun in the Sioux cosmos. 'When the meteor fell you cried in a loud voice, "*Wohpa*! *Wohpe-e-e-e*!" Why did you do this?' asked Walker. Finger replied, 'Because it is *Wakan*' (holy). Walker: 'What is *wohpa*?' Finger: 'It is one of the stars falling.' Walker: 'What causes the stars to fall?' Finger: '*Taku Skan Skan*' (abbreviated in the sacred language of the shaman to *Skan*). This fascinating dialogue continued for some time – the fall of a stone, the flow of a river, the falling of a star, the movement of everything was due to *Skan*. 'He causes everything that falls to fall and he causes everything to move that moves.' The place of the Sun, Moon, stars, meteorites and the sky in the Sioux cosmos, was then explained. *Skan*, Finger said, was superior to the Sun and the Moon, for *Skan* was 'there for all the time', whereas the Sun and Moon were there only half the time. The stars were *waniya*, or spirits. When a child is born, *Skan* takes one of these spirits and gives it to the child; on death, the spirit returns to the stars. One particular 'falling star' – obviously a meteor – was identified as a beautiful holy woman, who in Sioux mythology brought many good things to the tribe. Finally, Finger explained that *Skan*, the source of energy that gave movement to all things observed in the Sioux world, 'was everywhere' and that 'all that mankind can see of Him is the blue of the sky'.

Very similar concepts were expressed by the Caddoan-speaking Pawnee, who lived to the south-east of the Sioux. Their equivalent of *Skan* was *Tirawahat*, whose dwelling-place was the blue sky dome.

Clearly, as was commented on by more than one white observer, the immensity of the heavens filled the Sioux and other Plains tribes with awe. In attempting to rationalize what they observed, in their unique way they pondered on what still remains a mystery to modern science – gravity.

Astronomical knowledge was thus woven into the fabric of the Plains Indian culture in a multitude of ways. Not only did it make a marked impression on ceremony and material culture, but it also became a rich source of mythology and legend.

PAWNEE AND BLACKFEET STAR-LORE

Nowhere is the power of the skies so forcibly expressed in the culture of a Plains tribe than with the Pawnee – more specifically, one branch of that tribe, the Skidi, who in historical times (c. 1500–1870) occupied the region of present-day central Nebraska. In Pawnee mythology, the Morning Star, *Opirikuts* – almost certainly Mars[5] – is a leader of men, helping with the creation of the Universe and travelling with his brother, the Sun, to the land of the western stars in an attempt to overcome the power of the Moon, who has killed all previous, approaching man-stars. This hero figure uses the power of a sacred bundle – a collection of objects which included a piece of meteorite – to overcome the obstacles Moon puts in his way and thus enter the woman-star village.

Such mythological descriptions were obviously based on accurate and detailed observations of the sky (Figure 1). Mars first appears in the morning sky, remains there for some time, then moves westwards with the Sun. Each day it rises earlier, taking about 14 months to cross the night sky. As it moves it becomes brighter, appearing to gain strength, but after a while the brightness fades. About every six or seven years, when Mars reaches the western evening sky, it has a close conjunction with Venus – the Evening Star. This knowledge was woven into Pawnee mythology as male Morning Star being rewarded for his battles with the stars in his journey westwards, the Evening Star being described as a beautiful woman much desired by male stars.

Little wonder that, because of this deep interest in the stars and the planets, much of the Pawnee world – their gods and their calendar – was based on the panorama of the changing sky. Such elements as the Sun, Moon, stars, meteorites and lightning appeared on artefacts used

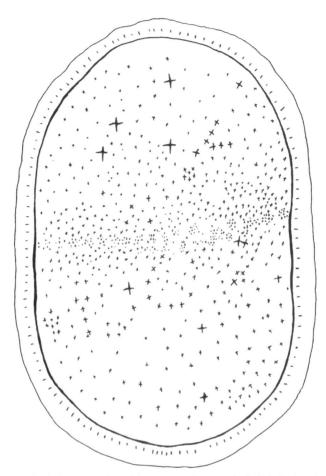

Figure 1. The Skidi Pawnee Chart of the Heavens. The original, of which this is a sketch, is painted on finely tanned buckskin and measures 56 by 38 cm. This is a schematic rather than a representational depiction of the heavens. Although certain groups of stars can be identified (e.g. the Pleiades, upper right of centre, and the Milky Way across the middle), the chart was intended not for use as a star map, but rather to capture the powers of the stars and bring them to the Skidi whenever the chart was opened out. The Chart of the Heavens embodies the complex Pawnee star mythology, and reflects their extensive knowledge of naked-eye astronomical phenomena, which were incorporated in their ceremonial and religious rites. [Taylor, 1994, p. 70]

in rituals and ceremonies of the Pawnee and of several other Plains tribes, as well as on the so-called Winter Counts (Figures 2 and 3).[6]

Evidence is emerging that complex ceremonies and thought associated with astronomical phenomena were certainly not confined to the

Figure 2. An 18th-century Crow pictograph of a foot-warrior carrying a large shield. Among the many Crow shields which carried similar designs was that of Arapoosh, who was killed in battle in 1834. Crow informants have said that designs such as this represented the Moon, and recent research (Cowdrey 1995) suggests that this is an ancient Crow motif that represents one of the most prominent of lunar features, Mare Serenitatis – the Sea of Serenity. [From the Pictograph Cave near Billings, Montana]

Figure 3. Ratutsakntesa, 'Sun Chief', a Grand Pawnee, photographed probably in about 1870. His robe is embellished with star symbols. Much Pawnee ceremonial, ritual and mythology was constructed around the heavenly bodies. [Photograph from the author's collection]

Pawnee. The Algonquian-speaking Blackfeet, for example, integrated their astronomical knowledge in the decoration of their tipis, the portable buffalo-hide dwellings. Most painted tipis had a darkened area at the top to represent the night sky, with white disks for star-groups (the Great Bear and the Pleiades). The smoke flaps were painted with six black dots on one ear, to represent the bunched stars (possibly a reference to the Milky Way), while seven starlike images were on the other ear to represent the Plough. At the back of the tipi was a figure in the form of a Maltese cross representing the Morning Star, while a border at the bottom of the tipi had rows of figures representing 'fallen stars' (meteors). A ceremonial altar within the tipi was decorated with

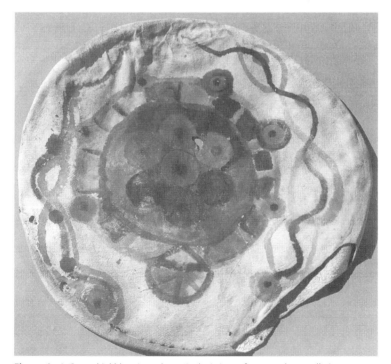

Figure 4. A Crow shield bearing schematic depictions of stars and constellations, among them Aldebaran and Betelgeux and Rigel. The wavy lines may represent the diurnal motion of the stars across the sky. Aldebaran, and Sirius are shown at their heliacal risings; such stars have been 'perceived as infallible markers of seasonality, and of Time' (Cowdrey 1995, p. 14). [Photograph by John Painter]

coloured earths displaying images of the Moon, Morning Star, Mistaken Morning Star (see below) and marks representing sunbeams. Unusual solar activity, 'when the Sun paints his face', was also represented on the altar, in bands of black, red and green earth. Such tipis with their associated rituals were believed to have originally been a gift of the Sun, and when sold they commanded a high price – up to ten horses!

Likewise, ceremonial regalia of the Blackfeet were embellished with symbols representing Sky as well as Underwater powers, some of which – in the case of the Beaver Bundle ceremonials – seem to have been used in documenting the lengthy and complex rituals associated with the Bundle.[7] Tribal history records that the first Beaver Bundle contained representations of aquatic animals; then, at the request of the beavers, the Sun, Moon and Morning Star enhanced the ceremonial, hence the sky symbols. The ceremony was of immense complexity, and it became an intellectual challenge to master it. Thus, the Bundle was to be opened only at each full moon, and it was also said that if particular attention was paid to the Moon by the Beaver Bundle's owner, he could use it for weather forecasting. Another of the owner's duties was to act as a timekeeper: the various phases of the Moon – recorded by using notched sticks – enabled an important event such as a birth, battle, treaty or the age of a person to be dated, a suitable fee being charged for such a consultation.

Interwoven with the symbolism evident in such artefacts were mythological tales which underline the deep interest that the Blackfeet had in the night sky. An example is the story of Mistaken Morning Star, who was said to be the son of Morning Star. As with Dr Walker, who was with a Lakota shaman when a meteor fell, leading to a discourse by the shaman on the Sioux concept of gravitational force, so too the ethnologist Walter McClintock, quite by chance, gained insights into the depth of Blackfeet astronomical awareness. McClintock was in the company of Brings-Down-The-Sun, a distinguished Blackfeet medicine man, who related how his father had taught him to 'read the signs in the sky'. Thus, if the Sun paints his face (sunspots), a big storm was said to be coming; when the fires of the north men (aurorae) show in the sky, a heavy wind is coming; a 'feeding star' (a comet), is a sign of famine and sickness; and if the Sun hides his face (an eclipse), a great chief is about to die. The rainbow is the lariat – it is the Thunder roping the rain, and the storm will slow up.

It was July 1905 when, by chance, the two men observed a conjunction of the planets Venus and Jupiter just before daybreak. The phenomenon evoked a display of deeper astronomical knowledge than the previous conversation had indicated, and that knowledge was obviously ancient since it had been woven into the fabric of Blackfeet mythology. Viewing the conjunction, Brings-Down-The-Sun explained to McClintock that the Blackfeet were certainly aware that at times these two stars 'travelled together in the sky'. Described as father and son, who had many adventures as they moved through the stars, the son, he said, was then often mistaken for his father because Mistaken Morning Star appeared first above the horizon, while his father – the true Morning Star – rose soon after. McClintock was obviously impressed with this display of astronomical knowledge, and carefully footnoted his field notes.

Later, other anthropologists, such as Clark Wissler of the American Museum of Natural History, recorded further details of Blackfeet star myths, many, if not all, based on accurate observations of cyclic astronomical changes. References were made to the Seven and Bunched Stars, the North Star, the Plough (Great Dipper), other parts of Ursa Major and the Pleiades. Wissler found that the myths explained the origin of tipi designs, buffalo-calling rituals and the Sun Dance ceremonials, and particularly the role of Elk Woman, who was principal leader in the Sun Dance and who, it was related, dug a forbidden turnip out of the sky, leaving a hole there. Is this a reference to one of the dark rifts in the Milky Way, picked out by some keen-eyed shaman in the distant past?

THE MEDICINE WHEEL IN THE LAND OF THE CROW

A fascinating structure, one of more than a hundred scattered across the Central and Northern Plains, but notable for its great size, is the so-called Medicine Wheel (Figure 5), located in the Bighorn Mountains of modern-day Wyoming. It is a circular outline of piled limestone rock, approximately 26 m in diameter, flattened on one side, with a central cairn from which radiate 28 spokes that connect to the outer stone rim. Known to Anglo-Americans since at least the 1880s, the most recent archaeological investigations suggest that the initial construction began during the late prehistoric period – certainly prior to 1700. Regardless

Figure 5. The Medicine Wheel in the Big Horn Mountains of Wyoming. The site is about 3000 m above sea level and dates back at least to AD 1700. The wheel, some 24 m in diameter, is constructed from hundreds of limestone boulders and has 28 spokes. Archaeological evidence suggests that the Medicine Wheel was a religious site and also a Native American astronomical observatory. [Photograph by the author]

of who the original builders were, every indigenous society that encountered it contributed to the structural and ideological complexity of the site, and both prehistoric and more recent Native American peoples who lived in, or passed through, the region incorporated the Medicine Wheel into their world-view as a sacred entity. Of particular interest is the emphasis given to astronomical associations and how, by its very existence, it has elicited from various tribal intellectuals – such as those from the Sioux, Crow, Arapaho, Shoshone, Cheyenne, Cree and Blackfeet – references to the importance of the heavenly bodies in their cultures.

Thus, the Cheyenne link the Medicine Wheel to the sacred Medicine Lodge used in the Cheyenne *Massaum*, or Earth renewal ceremonial. The commencement of the ceremonial round was signalled by celestial events, such as the heliacal rising of the red star Aldebaran on about June 22, closely coinciding with the summer solstice. Aldebaran flashes briefly in the early dawn; approximately 56 days later comes the heliacal rising of Sirius in the south-east. The *Massaum* itself was traditionally held at about the middle of this period, and one particularly important day was linked with the heliacal rising of Rigel, which flashed across the horizon from the south-east. Significant too is that Rigel appears exactly 28 days after Aldebaran's first rising, and is then followed by the rising of Sirius, 28 days later: note that there are 28 spokes in the Bighorn Medicine Wheel.

There is not the space here to describe the astronomical associations of the Medicine Wheel in more detail. It should be recorded that on visiting the Medicine Wheel, various Native American scholars have emphasized the importance of astral knowledge in their cultures – the products of four with four (16) and with seven (28), the lunar cycles, and their many religious deities which were manifested in the various planets and constellations. All of these could be connected with the Medicine Wheel. Recent, independent archaeoastronomical investigations by Anglo-Americans have confirmed that the Medicine Wheel was used to observe culturally significant astronomical movements connecting the risings of Aldebaran, Sirius and Rigel with the summer solstice.

Thus, perhaps more than anything, Medicine Wheels[8] such as that in the Bighorn Mountains document the Plains Indians' sources of renewal and power, much of which pivoted on cyclic, dramatic and often spectacular astronomical phenomena which have fascinated all mankind from time immemorial – *Wohpe-e-e-e*!

NOTES

1. The vista of the night heavens on the Great Plains was again recently brought home to me by Don Moccasin, during the course of an evening sweat-lodge ceremonial at Mission in South Dakota (the Brulé Sioux Reservation) in October 1999. The amazingly clear night sky and a panorama of stars was stunning to us all – as similar views must have been to the old-time Plains tribes.
2. The history of the Plains tribes is discussed in considerable detail by Taylor (1994).
3. The architectural symbolism of the Skidi Pawnee is discussed in some detail by Nabokov and Easton (1989, pp. 136–9).
4. The Plains tribes possessed a large number of so-called medicine

bundles – collections of objects and materials which were considered to hold spiritual power, and were used in various ceremonies. The Beaver Bundle was one of the oldest and most complex.

5. Chamberlain (1982, pp. 89–91) pointed out that the identification of the Skidi Pawnee Morning Star as Mars (as opposed to Venus) is nicely consistent with their mythologies and ceremonies.

6. A Winter Count was a tanned buffalo or elk hide upon which the tribal historian – the 'keeper of the count' – would, each year, paint a pictograph representing the most important or unusual event of the year just passed. This was usually done after consulting other recognized tribal historians.

7. The costume which seems to relate to the Blackfeet Beaver Bundle – and the influence of the Sun, Moon and comets on Blackfeet ceremonial – is now in the Department of Ethnography, British Museum, London. This is discussed in some detail by Taylor (1993). For the Cheyenne, see Nagy (1994), who has discussed not only the use of astronomical symbolism on costume but also on shields; much relates to protective-type symbolism. Cowdrey (1995) has related features of the lunar surface (e.g. Mare Serenitatis, the Sea of Serenity), as well as the brightest geometric asterism in the Northern Hemisphere – that is, Sirius, Betelgeux, Rigel, Aldebaran and the Pleiades, to symbols on Crow shields.

8. An Arikara saying is, 'Eventually one gets to the Medicine Wheel to fulfil one's life.'

BIBLIOGRAPHY

Campbell, Gregory R., and Thomas A. Foor (1999), The Big Horn Medicine Wheel: A Sacred Landscape and the Struggle for Religious Freedom. *ERNAS (European Review of Native American Studies)*, Vol. 13, No. 2, pp. 21–35.

Chamberlain, Von Del (1982), *When Stars Came Down to Earth: Cosmology of the Skidi Pawnee Indians of North America*. Maryland, MD: Ballena Press, Center for Archaeoastronomy Cooperative Publication, University of Maryland.

Cowdrey, Mike (1995), *Spring Boy Rides the Moon: Celestial Patterns in Crow Shield Design*. Obispo, CA: Privately published by the author.

Denig, Edwin Thompson (1930), Indian Tribes of the Upper Missouri.

Extract from the *Forty-Sixth Annual Report of the Bureau of American Ethnology*, edited by J. N. B. Hewitt. Washington: Smithsonian Institution, pp. 375–628.

McCleary, Timothy P. (1997), *The Stars We Know: Crow Indian Astronomy and Lifeways*. Illinois: Waveland Press, Inc.

McClintock, Walter (1937), *Painted Tipis and Picture-Writing of the Blackfoot Indians*. Southwest Museum Leaflets, No. 6. Los Angeles.

McClintock, Walter (1937), *The Blackfoot Beaver Bundle*. Southwest Museum Leaflets, Nos 2 and 3. Los Angeles.

Murdin, Paul and Lesley (1984), *Supernovae*. Cambridge: Cambridge University Press.

Nabokov, Peter, and Robert Easton (1989), *Native American Architecture*. New York and Oxford: Oxford University Press.

Nagy, Imre (1994), Cheyenne Shields and their Cosmological Background. *American Indian Art*, Vol. 19, No. 3, pp. 38–47.

Taylor, Colin F. (1993), *Saam: The Symbolic Content of Early Northern Plains Ceremonial Regalia*. Wyk auf Föhr, Germany: Bilingual Americanistic Books, Dietmar Kuegler.

Taylor, Colin F. (1994), *The Plains Indians*. London: Salamander.

Taylor, Colin F. (1995), *Myths of the North American Indians*. London: Calmann & King.

Walker, J. R. (1917), *The Sun Dance and other Ceremonies of the Oglala Division of the Teton Dakota*. Anthropological Papers of the American Museum of Natural History, Vol. XVI, Part II. New York.

Wissler, Clark, and D. C. Duvall (1908), *Mythology of the Blackfoot Indians*, Part I. New York: American Museum of Natural History.

The Dawn of Binocular Astronomy

FRED WATSON

At any given moment, how many optical instruments are directed skywards from the dark side of our planet? Thousands? Tens of thousands? Perhaps even hundreds of thousands? The answer clearly depends on many things, such as the amount of cloud cover, the time of year and which hemisphere is in darkness at the time. It is impossible to give a definite answer.

There is, however, a little that can be said about the sorts of instrument they are likely to be. For example, a handful will be telescopes with household names. These are the giants of the species: the Geminis, William Herschels and Anglo-Australians of this world, whose mirrors range between about 4 and 10 m in diameter. The 2.4-m Hubble Space Telescope will join them for the dark segment of each of its 96-minute orbits. Further down the aperture spectrum will be a much larger group of instruments, bigger than, say, 0.3 m, which fall into the category of professional equipment. Today, this group overlaps with the still larger number of telescopes used by serious amateur astronomers, with mirrors up to about 1 m in diameter.

At the very bottom of the pecking order are the humblest tools of astronomy, the hosts of instruments whose apertures are measured not in metres but in millimetres. These are nearly always refracting telescopes (ones that use lenses rather than mirrors to form the images), and they include that special category designed for terrestrial use with both eyes – ordinary binoculars. Such is the ubiquity of binoculars, and so popular is their use in both casual and serious stargazing, that it is quite possible they will outnumber *every* other class of telescope scanning the sky at any given time. And that is something to reflect on – or, if you prefer, to refract on.

BINOCULAR ASTRONOMY

Notwithstanding the sensitivity and convenience of today's high-tech CCD cameras, binoculars offer the most natural way of all to observe the night sky. Whether it be with a common-or-garden 7 × 50 night glass (in which the 7 represents the magnification and 50 mm is the diameter of each of the front, or objective, lenses) or with one of those big, stand-mounted binoculars championed by comet-hunters, the use of two eyes stimulates an intimacy with the heavens that is quite special. Of course, this is entirely understandable. We have evolved as two-eyed beings, and to use them both in direct astronomical observation is to bring to bear our most highly developed perceptive faculty on the sky in a manner with which we are immediately at ease. And for anyone trying to do serious visual observing of, say, variable stars, the use of both eyes brings real advantages.

Today, astronomy with binoculars enjoys a level of popularity greater than ever before. Paradoxically so, perhaps, because when today's amateur astronomers go shopping for new observing equipment, they are confronted with a dazzling array of high-performing telescopes. But binoculars, too, have reached a level of development that places them well above the ordinary and into the serious league of astronomical instruments. Even a modern, compact 8 × 24 model can be a useful tool in the hands of an accomplished observer. And stand-mounted binoculars with objectives up to 150 mm in diameter represent the ultimate for sky-watchers who prefer to do their astronomy with both eyes open. Between these two extremes lies a broad spectrum of binoculars of differing type, size, magnification and quality, all suitable in one way or another for astronomical observation.

Because binoculars are such versatile instruments, they are used for sky-watching by people who would never admit to an interest in astronomy. There can't be many binocular owners who haven't tried out their prized possession on the Moon, for example. And you might be surprised to know that, at the other end of the scale, professional astronomers are prone to relieving the stress of large-telescope observing by spending a few minutes outside in contemplation of the binocular sky. The instruments they use are often quite small, perhaps no bigger than 8 × 30, so as to fit conveniently into the briefcase or backpack they carry on their observing trips. But these astronomers enjoy a special privilege denied to most people. The odds are that they will be conducting their research at an observatory on a remote site, far from city lights and pollution. At such locations the sky is truly dark, and binocular sky-watching benefits enormously as a result – on moonless nights, stars and nebulae become spectacular when viewed even with modest binoculars.

HOW LONG HAS THIS BEEN GOING ON?

Some people imagine that observing the sky with binoculars is a relatively new pursuit, an offshoot of amateur astronomy that has blossomed only recently. Many might attribute its success to contemporary popularizers of astronomy – luminaries such as the Editor of the *Yearbook* you now hold in your hands. Patrick Moore's *Exploring the Night Sky with Binoculars* made its début in 1986, prompting several other authors to try out similar explorations of their own. These books have become very popular, and without doubt they have contributed to the outstanding level of interest in binocular observing today. Remarkably, though, a strikingly similar situation prevailed a hundred years ago. The turn of the century found binocular astronomy enjoying a wide following, surprisingly so in an era when science tended to be the province of the educated and well-to-do.

There seem to be several reasons for this. First, there was an upsurge of popular interest in astronomy as a whole towards the end of the 19th century. This is reflected in the number of astronomical societies that appeared around that time. Two good examples are the British Astronomical Association (1890) and the Astronomical Society of South Australia (1892), but there were many others. Secondly, binocular astronomy had a champion then, too, in the shape of a man who was as illustrious in his own sphere as Patrick Moore is on the world scene today. This man lived and worked in Brooklyn, New York, and we shall make his acquaintance in due course. Finally, and most importantly, turn-of-the-century binoculars had just undergone a technological revolution that had dramatically improved their performance. The new prismatic glasses then becoming popular seemed to offer much more to astronomers than the old-fashioned Galilean type.

As we shall see, that was only partly true, but the point remains that binoculars for astronomy became popular after their technology had been improved. Astronomy did not of itself drive the development of binoculars; their evolution was spurred on by far more earthly pressures. That has been true throughout the entire history of binocular astronomy. Even today, those large binoculars in the 100- to 150-mm class that are manufactured especially for astronomy owe their origin to Japanese ship-mounted binoculars of the Second World War. To trace the history of binoculars in astronomy, we must trace the history of binoculars themselves. The long awakening of binocular astronomy is intimately connected with technological development.

THE EARLIEST BINOCULARS

There is still debate and uncertainty over the early history of the refracting telescope. The focus of recorded events is The Hague in the Netherlands, where, in October 1608, the government of the States General was asked to consider a number of patent applications for what we now call the telescope. First among them was that of Hans Lipperhey, a Middelburg spectacle-maker, and the response he elicited was that he should develop a version for both eyes, and then try his luck again. Apparently, this he did, and when he fronted up to the States General two months later, he brought with him the world's first binocular. Whether or not it actually worked terribly well is another matter, but to Lipperhey goes the credit for the first two-eyed optical instrument – even though his patent for the telescope was denied him on the grounds that several others already knew of the invention.

Lipperhey's patent application (and his binocular) used the simple lens system shown in Figure 1. This combination of convex (thickest in the middle) and concave (thickest at the edge) lenses is now known as the Galilean telescope. Of course, it was Galileo who, in 1609, seized the opportunity missed by the simple spectacle-maker and used the new telescope to begin dismantling contemporary astronomy, thereby rocketing to infamy in the courts of the cardinals. But Lipperhey and his countrymen received a recognition of sorts – the instrument is still sometimes known as the 'Dutch telescope'.

While the design of the telescope itself advanced steadily during the 17th century, little attention was paid to the construction of binoculars. No doubt this was because the successful manufacture of a binocular demands the construction of two identical telescopes fixed with their

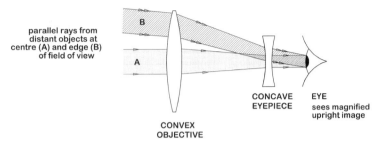

parallel rays from
distant objects at
centre (A) and edge (B)
of field of view

B

A

CONCAVE
EYEPIECE

EYE
sees magnified
upright image

CONVEX
OBJECTIVE

Figure 1. The light path through a Galilean telescope. The field of view is limited by the diameter of the objective, a drawback unique to the Galilean configuration. However, the simple two-lens construction offers low light-loss, resulting in a bright image.

axes parallel. These requirements stretched the technology of the time to its very limits, and few opticians made the attempt.

One who did was a Capuchin monk by the name of Chérubin d'Orléans, and it may have been one of his extraordinary Galilean binoculars that was first used for astronomy. Published works by Chérubin dating from the 1670s and 1680s describe his instruments as having cardboard tubes of rectangular cross-section up to 4 m long, and a much later engraving depicts three bewigged gentlemen apparently using one of these monsters for astronomy. All this would be rather hard to believe were it not for the existence of just such a binocular, about 1 m long, in the Museum of the History of Science in Florence (Figure 2). This instrument is almost certainly the earliest binocular preserved today. It is most fitting that it was probably used for astronomy by its first owner, the Grand Duke Cosimo III de' Medici.

Although binoculars themselves were few and far between, the foundations of the modern instrument were laid in a series of developments in optics during the 17th and 18th centuries. Briefly, they were:

1. The invention, in 1611, of the inverting telescope by Johann Kepler. This has a wider and more uniformly illuminated field of view than the Galilean, but presents an upside-down image to the observer (Figure 3).
2. The improvement of Kepler's design in about 1645 by the use of additional lenses to re-invert the image (Figure 4). Usually known as the terrestrial telescope, this arrangement was due to Anton Maria Schyrle de Rheita, who was also an early binocular-maker.

Figure 2. A large Galilean binocular made by Chérubin d'Orléans in the 1670s for the Grand Duke Cosimo III de' Medici. It was probably used for astronomy. [© Museum of the History of Science, Florence]

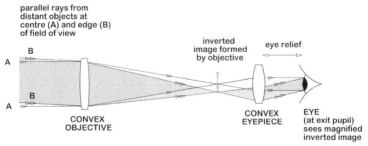

Figure 3. The basic optical system of the Keplerian, or inverting telescope. The objective forms an inverted image, which is magnified by the convex eyepiece. Light from the full area of the objective passes through the exit pupil at the location of the eye. The so-called eye relief is the distance of the exit pupil from the back of the eyepiece. The field of view depends not on the objective diameter, but on the characteristics of the eyepiece, which in practice is made with multiple components for better imaging.

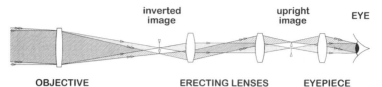

Figure 4. The terrestrial telescope devised by Schyrle in 1645 is simply a Keplerian telescope with additional lenses to render the image upright. The extra lenses give the instrument its characteristic length. The ordinary draw-tube telescope works on this principle.

3. The use of compound eyepieces in Keplerian and terrestrial telescopes from about the middle of the 17th century. The single convex lens was replaced by two spaced components (in the most common design, due to Christiaan Huygens) to improve definition and field of view.
4. The solution, in 1729, of the problem of chromatic aberration (coloured fringing) in telescope objectives by combining component lenses of different materials. The discovery was made by a London barrister, Chester Moor Hall, but the achromatic (colour-free) lens was eventually perfected and patented by the optician John Dollond.
5. The use of a simple hinge arrangement to allow the two halves of a binocular to be adjusted to match the separation of the user's eyes (the inter-pupillary distance). The Venetian optician Lorenzo Selva described such an instrument in 1787.

BINOCULARS COME OF AGE

Despite these various advances, it was a reversion to the simplest optical system of all that brought the first commercially successful binocular. The instrument was a rudimentary opera glass consisting of two small Galilean spyglasses mounted side by side, their extending eye-tubes moving independently for focusing. It was introduced in 1823 by the Viennese optician Johann Friedrich Voigtländer, founder of an optical dynasty that shortly afterwards moved to Brunswick in Germany, where it became famous for the manufacture of cameras. Voigtländer's basic design was quickly adopted by enterprising Parisian opticians, who added a bridge to the eye-tubes and a central focusing wheel to produce the instrument everyone recognizes today as an opera glass (Figure 5).

By the middle of the 19th century, outdoor versions of the little opera glasses were also being manufactured throughout Europe. Although they used the same Galilean optical system, they tended to be larger, more robust and less ornate than their theatre-going counterparts. Their magnification was usually greater, too; up to ×5 or ×6 in the best glasses, compared with ×2 or ×3 in an opera glass. Properly termed 'binocular field glasses' (but commonly known simply as 'binoculars'), they appeared in different guises as manufacturers coined fanciful names for them: race glasses, marine glasses, hunting glasses, pilot glasses.

As time went on, various improvements appeared – usually in response to military demands. Refinements in higher-quality instruments included extending ray-shades to keep out direct sunlight and rain, adjustable bridges to suit a range of inter-pupillary distances, and sling-loops for the attachment of neck-straps – once the message had got through that a binocular dropped on the floor was frequently rendered useless by its two halves going out of parallel.

Figure 5. An ivory-and-gilt opera glass dating from the 1870s. Instruments like this used the simple Galilean optical system, and were produced in very large numbers during the second half of the 19th century. Towards the end of this period, astronomy with opera glasses became a popular pastime.

Optically, the most significant refinement was the incorporation of achromatic objectives and eyepieces. The individual components of each lens were cemented together, so that to all intents and purposes the instrument retained the simplicity of having only two lenses in each half. This was a very important aspect of the Galilean binocular, particularly when used at the faint levels of illumination encountered in astronomy.

Why was this so? The principal light-loss in a lens is caused by partial reflection as the light enters and leaves it, crossing its two polished air/glass surfaces. In a typical Galilean instrument, the total wastage of light resulting from its passage through the two lenses is about 17% – a modest amount compared with the light-loss in the instruments that were to follow. Complex optical systems with many elements are costly in terms of light-loss, a defect that was not properly remedied until the development of anti-reflection coatings in the 1930s. Until then, a well-designed Galilean offered the brightest image of any binocular type available. It also boasted the greatest freedom from ghosting and flaring – effects produced when the unwanted reflected light finds its way into the eye. Today, optical instruments have sophisticated anti-reflection coatings on all their optical surfaces, reducing light-loss almost to zero. Poor transmission in binoculars is simply no longer an issue.

THE DAWN OF BINOCULAR ASTRONOMY

The mass production of Galilean opera and field glasses in huge quantities during the second half of the 19th century led to an awakening to their possibilities for astronomy. Their use for observing stars and star clusters in particular rated a mention in some popular astronomy books of the time, though a telescope was always regarded as the more desirable instrument. But then, onto the scene (in the USA, at least) strode binocular astronomy's first great advocate. This man was not a scientist, but a journalist with a burning enthusiasm for the night sky and, by virtue of his profession, a particular eloquence in communicating its beauties. His name was Garrett P. Serviss, and he lived from 1851 until 1929, spending virtually his whole life in the state of New York. By his writing and lecturing he did more to popularize astronomy than any American before him; truly, he was the Carl Sagan of his age.

Astronomy with an Opera-Glass is but one of Serviss's books. It was, in fact, his first, appearing in 1888 as a digest of articles he had written for a popular science magazine the previous year. It is a book of great charm, and its clear exposition and sound practical advice made it a best-seller that ran to at least eight editions. Serviss's title was well chosen, for he believed that the relatively wide field of view of opera glasses made them more suitable for astronomy than their higher-magnification outdoor counterparts – though he did include advice for users of field glasses with magnifications of up to ×7.

The flavour of the book can be gleaned from a few excerpts. Here, for example, is Serviss waxing lyrical as an apologist for the ancient legends of the constellations:

> While we may smile at these stories, we cannot entirely disregard them, for they are intermingled with some of the richest literary treasures of the world, and they come to us, like some old keepsake, perfumed with the memory of a past age.

And again, exhibiting a dry humour as he discusses certain deficiencies of the constellation Taurus:

> The constellation-makers did not trouble themselves to make a complete Bull, and only the head and fore-quarters of the animal are represented. If Taurus had been completed on the scale on which he was begun, there would have been no room in the sky for Aries; one of the Fishes would have had to abandon his celestial swimming-place, and even the fair Andromeda would have found herself uncomfortably situated. But, as if to make amends for neglecting to furnish their heavenly Bull with hind-quarters, the ancients gave him a most prodigious and beautiful pair of horns, which make the beholder feel alarm for the safety of Orion.

Finally, he had a real flair for understatement:

> In attempting to view the planets with an opera-glass, too much must not be expected . . .

That did not, however, prevent Serviss from detailing just what might be expected from opera-glass views of the planets – with as much enthusiasm and insight as in his descriptions of other celestial vistas better suited to the instrument.

Astronomy with an Opera-Glass certainly advanced the cause of binocular sky-watching on Serviss's side of the Atlantic. Its influence outside the USA is more difficult to judge, but at the very least it reflected the spirit of the time in Britain and Europe, and probably made some contribution to it. The message was clear: binoculars were worthwhile instruments both for casual star-gazing and for more serious astronomical work such as variable-star observing and comet-hunting.

SIGNOR PORRO AND PROFESSOR ABBE

Meanwhile, the technology of binoculars was moving on. At the time *Astronomy with an Opera-Glass* was being written, it was possible to go out and buy new types of binocular that overcame the main defect of the Galilean: namely, its very restricted field of view at magnifications greater than about ×6.

Both Kepler's inverting telescope (Figure 3) and Schyrle's terrestrial telescope (Figure 4) had by then appeared in binocular form. Inverting binoculars were much the rarer of the two, being produced mainly for astronomical use at observatories. The Munich firm of Steinheil, for example, manufactured an instrument that closely resembled a Galilean binocular in appearance but was actually fitted with convex eyepieces. Having few optical components, it did not suffer unduly from light-loss, but of course the upside-down images rendered its application very limited. Comet-seeking was its main purpose. (Some thirty years later, the exigencies of war resulted in an inverting binocular being manufactured by the London firm of Dollond to allow naval signals to be read in poor conditions. No doubt a few of these unusual instruments eventually found their way into the hands of astronomers.)

More practical than the inverting binocular was the so-called binocular telescope. Such instruments were often known in Britain as 'deer-stalker's binoculars', but Serviss would no doubt have been more familiar with the American 'long-John' – an eloquently descriptive name. Although they were much more expensive than Galilean binoculars, they appeared in quite large numbers. Ordinary draw-tube telescopes based on Schyrle's arrangement of lenses had been common-place for well over a century. To make a binocular version, you simply took two of these, mounted them side by side, and – *violà!* – you had your deer-stalker – or long-John (Figure 6). Certainly, the models produced during the late 19th century offered magnifications of up to ×15 or ×20 with an apparent field of view (the angular diameter of the illuminated image presented to the eye) of around 35°. While that is pitifully small by today's standards, it was two or three times that of a large Galilean.

Of course, the drawback with these instruments was their inordinate length. This made them unwieldy (especially for astronomy) and prone to accidental misalignment. What was needed was a way of re-inverting the image in a Keplerian telescope that did not require all those additional lenses. In fact, though very few opticians were aware of it, the solution had already been provided as long ago as 1854 by an obscure Italian artillery officer named Ignazio Porro. This inventive soldier was familiar with optics through his experience of using surveying instruments, and he had devised and patented two different combinations of right-angled glass prisms that would neatly turn an image upside down. Introduced into the light-path of an inverting telescope, they turned it into a terrestrial one; moreover, they had the effect of folding up the

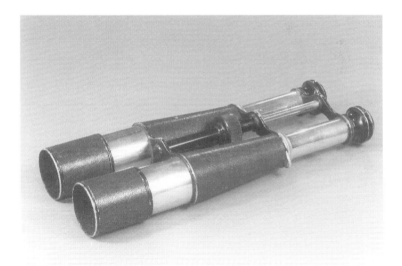

Figure 6. A late-19th-century binocular telescope, or 'deer-stalker's binocular'. Instruments of this type consisted simply of two terrestrial telescopes mounted side by side, offering much higher magnification than the Galilean type. However, they were more expensive. They were also rather unwieldy (particularly for astronomy), and prone to misalignment.

light-path to shorten the instrument. Porro's invention was successfully incorporated into hand-held telescopes manufactured in small numbers in France in the 1850s. Today we would call them prismatic monoculars.

The obvious next step of making a binocular version was attempted by a number of optical firms. Success, however, eluded them. The problem was reminiscent of the tribulations of 17th-century binocular-makers: manufacturing methods were simply not up to the fine tolerances required. Even the one design that got as far as the optical instrument trade (a product of the Parisian firm of Luquin et L'Hermite) quickly faded into obscurity because, basically, it didn't work.

The spark of genius that eventually turned prismatic binoculars into everyday objects belonged to one of the greatest scientists of his day, the German physicist Ernst Abbe (Figure 7). Abbe taught at the University of Jena, and he was also a partner in the optical instrument manufacturing firm of Carl Zeiss. In 1873 he independently re-invented Porro's prisms, and subsequently designed a binocular that incorporated them. Faced with the problem of obtaining the right optical glasses for his project, he simply enlisted the help of a chemist, Otto Schott, and with him founded a glass factory to overcome the difficulties. He had a similar 'can-do' approach in his collaboration with Zeiss for the manufacture of fine components.

Abbe tried to patent his prismatic binocular in 1893, but was astonished to discover that a patent already existed. He had been completely unaware of Porro's work and the subsequent attempts to manufacture binoculars. Undismayed, he resorted to a clever aspect of his own design that was entirely original. He had placed the prisms in such a way as to make the objectives more widely separated than the observer's eyes, thereby enhancing the observer's stereoscopic perception (Figure 8). By basing his application on this striking three-dimensional effect, Abbe won his patent, and the new binoculars began to emerge from Zeiss's factory the following year.

Produced in ×4, ×6 and ×8 versions, the new prismatic glasses were a vast improvement on most of what had gone before. Of course, they were more expensive than Galilean binoculars, but not outrageously so. To our eyes they look remarkably modern – their inventor had chosen the optimum arrangement of the optical components, and it had no need of improvement. Abbe's persistence in the development of prismatic binoculars was soon rewarded. With their compact, finely

Figure 7. Ernst Abbe, the German optical physicist who designed the first successful prismatic binocular. He also made significant contributions to microscopy and optical theory. Although he was a professor at the University of Jena, his partnership with the optical instrument maker Carl Zeiss gave his work an immediate practical application. This photograph dates from 1893, the year Abbe applied for his binocular patent. [© Optical Museum, Jena]

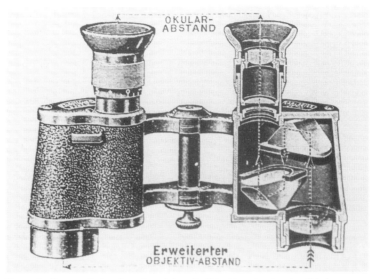

Figure 8. The manufacturer's sectioned view of a Zeiss binocular, showing Abbe's arrangement of the Porro prisms to increase the separation of the objectives relative to that of the eyes and enhance the stereoscopic effect. The engraving depicts one of Zeiss's 1907 models, which incorporated improvements on the original 1894 series. It established the pattern of binocular design for decades to come, and countless thousands of people have had their first telescopic views of the night sky through an instrument like this.

engineered construction and pleasing stereoscopic enhancement, the new Zeiss glasses were an immediate success.

ASTRONOMY AND THE NEW PRISMATIC BINOCULARS

Because Abbe's patent was awarded on the grounds of increased objective separation, other manufacturers found themselves free to develop prismatic binoculars – as long as the objective separation was the same as (or less than) the eyepiece separation. It did not require any great genius to work out that the way to do this was to arrange the prisms so that they stepped the optical axis vertically, rather than horizontally. Thus were the floodgates of prismatic binocular manufacture opened during the closing years of the 19th century. First to compete with Zeiss were Continental firms. Voigtländer launched the assault, describing themselves in their advertising as the 'original makers of . . . binocular field glasses'. They did not trouble to add that this was their opera glass of 1823 rather than a modern prismatic instrument – no doubt they hoped no one would notice. The Berlin firm of Goerz followed with their Trieder binocular (Figure 9), of which more in a moment. Well-known British manufacturers such as Ross, Watson, Dallmeyer and Aitchison soon joined them.

The scientific world took great interest in these developments. After all, binoculars were regarded as novel scientific instruments rather than merely accessories for tourism, sport, and so on, as they are today. Thus, astronomers were made aware of the benefits of the new glasses at an early stage. Most astute in this respect was the firm of C. P. Goerz of Friedenau in Berlin. They were quick to realize that astronomers were the only users of binoculars who would gain no benefit from enhanced stereoscopic perception. While the Zeiss glasses extended the range of three-dimensional vision very significantly (to more than 10 km in the ×8 model, for example), the horizons of astronomers are infinitely more distant, and stereoscopic enhancement is irrelevant. Convinced that they could therefore compete with Zeiss on an equal footing in astronomy, Goerz launched a major advertising campaign in April 1899.

A lengthy supplement in the scientific journal *Nature* on the 6th of that month tells the story:

> Goerz's Trieder-Binocular [is] particularly suitable for observations of Variable Stars on account of its extraordinarily wide field of view (= 40 degrees apparent) and the perfectly uniform distribution of light over the whole field.

An account of the advantages of the Trieder over Galilean binoculars follows, after which the supplement continues:

> The Trieder-Binocular is made with either of these 4 magnifications [×3, ×6, ×9 or ×12], but we beg to point out that 12 fold magnifying power is rather high for portable glasses, for hand use, so that it is not easy to keep the stars in steady position in the field of view. We, therefore, recommend 3 to 9 fold magnifying powers.

Figure 9. The Goerz binocular of 1899 with an original instruction booklet. This instrument was typical of its day, being based on an optical arrangement that avoided infringing Abbe's patent. It also had an unusual sliding adjustment for the eyepiece separation. Goerz promoted these binoculars for astronomical use, especially for observing variable stars.

On clear, moonless nights, the Trieder-Binoculars will show stars of the following magnitudes with sufficient distinctness to enable the observer to make determinations of the intensity of their light on Argelander's method, viz.:

Trieder-Binocular [×3]: Stars up to the 7.5th magnitude
  ,,   ,, [×6]: ,, ,, ,, ,, 8 ,, ,,
  ,,   ,, [×9]: ,, ,, ,, ,, 8.5,, ,,
  ,,   ,, [×12]: ,, ,, ,, ,, 9 ,, ,,

We also make the Trieder-Glasses in the form of Monoculars, that is to say for one eye . . .

The Trieder-Binoculars are also excellently suitable for use as Terrestrial Telescopes for theatre, hunting, field, travelling, races, the army, navy, &c.

While the prose hardly compares in elegance with Serviss's, some interesting issues are raised. The point about the uniformity of illumination of the field of view, for example, is well made. And the warning about the use of the ×12 model will strike a chord with anyone who has ever attempted to observe the sky with hand-held high-powered binoculars. But when it comes to the measurement of star magnitudes by Argelander's method, Goerz's advertising copy is rather optimistic, to say the least.

It does get the technique right. F. W. A. Argelander was a most capable astronomer and former director of the Bonn Observatory, who had died only 24 years earlier. His *Stufenschätzungsmethode*, or step-estimation method, was still seen as state-of-the-art in the visual measurement of star magnitudes. Indeed, it is used today by many observers of variable stars. It requires the careful estimation of star brightnesses against a sequence of comparison stars, and it assumes that the field of view of the telescope is completely uniform. However, it is not the uniformity of illumination that is at issue here, so much as the capabilities of the glasses in revealing faint stars. It is questionable whether stars of the quoted magnitudes would even be visible in the binoculars, let alone measurable.

If the effects of night-sky background glow are ignored, the limiting magnitude of a telescope depends only on the diameter of its objective and the efficiency with which its optical system transmits light. The same is true of binoculars. Nowhere in Goerz's supplement is the diameter of the binoculars' objectives specified, but that is not surprising, since it was considered of little importance at the time. The '7 × 50' type of specification we use today was not adopted for another 20 years. In fact, the objective diameters were 15 mm for the ×3 and ×6 models and 20 mm for the ×9 and ×12 versions, sizes typical of their day. Taking into account the 37% light-loss caused by the ten air/glass surfaces in the optical path, we can roughly estimate the limiting magnitudes for these glasses as about 7.1 for the ×3 and ×6 models, and 7.8 for the ×9 and ×12.

These figures are based on a naked-eye limit of 6.0, which is attainable by most observers. They are very different from those given by Goerz, which step upwards neatly with magnification. In fact, magnification does influence detectability considerably, because at higher magnifications the sky-background glow is diluted and the contrast of faint objects is enhanced. It is therefore possible that the real limits for these binoculars are closer to the figures quoted by Goerz, even though they do look a bit too neat and tidy to be true. It would be interesting to discover the identity of the astronomer who provided these figures, and whether they were arrived at by observation or educated guess. Unfortunately, the chances of doing that are virtually non-existent. The Goerz company ceased to exist in 1926, when it was subsumed into a new venture called Zeiss-Ikon.

The astronomical advertising seems to have had no ill effect on the company's turn-of-the-century fortunes. The final sentence of the supplement seems to be the most pertinent one. The Trieder binoculars were produced in large numbers and became well regarded for terrestrial use – perhaps nowhere more potently than in South Africa, where Boer farmers used them to great effect in taking on the might of the British Army.

A PREMATURE TWILIGHT

With the turn of the century came a boom in the optical instrument trade as people sought to replace their outmoded binoculars with the new prismatic instruments. That included astronomers, influenced no doubt by the seductive advertising of the manufacturers. The new binoculars were produced in a wide variety of designs as makers jostled to find particular selling points within the restrictions imposed by Abbe's patent for the Zeiss product. Although no one said so (except Zeiss), it was tacitly assumed that Abbe's design was the best.

While the new binoculars certainly brought higher magnification than the Galilean type, together with a wider and more uniform field of view, they were not necessarily everything that an astronomer's heart could desire. As we have seen, the ten air/glass surfaces in most binoculars produced severe light-loss, with increased ghosting and flaring. There were other drawbacks. Having more optical components, the new glasses were more easily damaged than the Galilean type. They were also peculiarly susceptible to fungus-growth on their internal optics, especially in moist climates. But most unsatisfactory of all for astronomers was the small size of their objectives, which severely limited their light-grasp.

As the 20th century began, only one manufacturer was producing binoculars with objectives more than 20 mm in diameter, and that was Zeiss, who had introduced a range of 'large' instruments with 25-mm objectives in 1896. Even these were confined in their astronomical usefulness to little more than the Moon and the brighter planets – they were effectively only one-inch telescopes. A British firm instigated the move to larger apertures. In August 1903, Aitchison introduced a range of binoculars with 35-mm objectives. So revolutionary was this considered that the binoculars were fitted with variable iris diaphragms to allow the light input to be reduced during the day! Nevertheless, for observing star clusters and nebulae they were still eclipsed by a large, light-efficient Galilean. Finally, it was Zeiss who, in 1910, introduced a binocular that matched the diameter of the light beam emerging from the eyepiece to the 7 mm of a fully dilated pupil, thereby producing optimum illumination. Its effectiveness at low light levels – even with 30–40% light-loss – was quickly demonstrated, and its 7 × 50 specification soon became the standard for night glasses. These instruments were very expensive when they were first introduced, but no doubt a few became the pride and joy of some well-heeled astronomers.

The end of the Edwardian period brought to a close the intense competition between binocular manufacturers that had spawned such a rich variety of designs. Abbe's patent expired in 1908, and manufacturers quickly adopted the Zeiss 'stereo-prism' pattern for their own instruments. Binoculars took on a general uniformity of appearance that lasted for almost half a century.

In the same year, German military authorities approved the design of the 'Fernglas 08' ('1908-model binocular'), a highly specified ×6 Galilean instrument which, by the standards of the day, was very suitable for astronomical use. It was robustly engineered, and had a high degree of optical correction. But when it eventually emerged from the production lines of German optical manufacturers, astronomy was the last thing of the minds of its potential owners. Tensions had been growing throughout Europe, and armaments had grown alongside them. Just twenty years after the appearance of the first Zeiss binoculars, political brinkmanship cascaded into the slaughter of the Great War. Binoculars – prismatic and Galilean alike – suddenly became optical munitions, and in great demand. It was not long before they faced one another in their scores across the muddy wastes of no man's land. For the moment at least, binocular astronomy was but a distant memory.

ACKNOWLEDGEMENT

Some years before Serviss wrote *Astronomy with an Opera-Glass* in America, a young woman in England was given a high-quality opera glass of unusual and delicate proportions. It is not known whether she ever turned the instrument on the night sky, but there must have been some predisposition towards astronomy in her family. That predisposition eventually manifested itself in the capable and energetic form of her great-nephew – a fellow by the name of Patrick Moore. When Patrick kindly offered to donate his Great-Aunt Alice's opera glass to my collection of early binoculars, I wondered if there was something I could do in return. The only thing I could think of was this article. So thank you, Patrick!

FURTHER READING

Ashbrook, Joseph, 'Garrett P. Serviss and Some Brooklyn Amateurs', *Sky & Telescope*, **49**(1), 17–18, 1975.
Hearnshaw, J. B., *The Measurement of Starlight: Two centuries of Astronomical Photometry*, Cambridge University Press, 1996.
Moore, Patrick, *Exploring the Night Sky with Binoculars*, Cambridge University Press, 1986 (6th edn, 2000).

Serviss, Garrett P., *Astronomy with an Opera-Glass*, D. Appleton & Co., New York, 1888 (and later editions).

Watson, Fred, *Binoculars, Opera Glasses and Field Glasses*, Shire Publications, Princes Risborough, 1995.

Photographing the Elusive Eclipse

BOB TURNER

Never mind the people, the eclipse of August 11, 1999 must have been attended by millions of cameras taking pictures of virtually nothing. Never before have so many willing photographers crowded into a narrow strip of land to record images of the underside of darkening cloud. Watching the television, you could see thousands of camera flashes – but the photographs showed what? The underside of cloud is far too far away to illuminate with a flash, and even if the eclipse had been visible, you can't take flash pictures of the Moon (unless, that is, the flash is pretty big and the shutter is opened about 2½ seconds after the flash!).

The eclipse of 1927 was quite widely seen but little photographed, as very few people owned a camera in those days. The 1999 eclipse was seen by very few from Britain, but photographed by virtually everybody. It's strange how these things work out. We all have our eclipse memories which we carry around with us. 'Yes, I remember going out into the playground with a piece of smoked glass.' 'It was wonderful!' But as you talk to people, you realize that many are confusing having seen a partial eclipse with having experienced a total. Most people remember an eclipse. At most partial eclipses there is a perceptible darkening of the sky, so the question 'Did it get dark?' is not very helpful in establishing what people actually experienced. Only the sight of totality makes people talk about the Sun as a spectacle. But this was the one we were all waiting for – a total eclipse visible from the Britain. There have been three total eclipses this century that have touched our shores: in April 1921 in northern Scotland, in June 1927 from Wales through to Yorkshire, and now the big one – August 11, 1999, in Cornwall.

Although it seemed that the weather conspired against most eclipse-watchers, even those under a leaden sky marvelled at this act of nature.

We had all waited a long time for this date, and for many the experience of daytime darkness, plus the views on the television, made this event memorable even though totality was not seen. The European part of the track, from Cornwall through France and Germany, seems to have been generally overcast. But there were some holes in the cloud base, one of which was over the English Channel at a position of 0°6'.8 W, and 49° 51'.2 N, just off the French coast north of Le Havre, where the author was waiting, but I must admit, not very patiently. The morning had been quite clear, but we could see cloud coming in from the west, and were steaming at about 10 knots to keep ahead of the weather front.

My own photographic plan was based on the solar activity seen about an hour before first contact by viewing the Sun in hydrogen alpha. I had kept a daily record of prominences since the start of August. A major northern sunspot group had rotated off the disk on the 8th, which, although looking very active in white light, produced virtually no hydrogen alpha activity at all. The disk was fairly in active on the morning of the eclipse (Figure 1), with sunspot groups on the east and west limbs, and three very nice spots in a line almost centred on the disc. The limb was a mass of prominences, with eight eruptions evident. Photographs in hydrogen alpha taken at the same time showed the disk features (Figure 2), but the moving boat made a longer exposure for the limb features impossible.

From knowing where the second and third contact points would occur, I was able to predict that the main group of prominences would be on the emerging limb, and tailored the photographic programme to suit. I took pictures of the partial phase in hydrogen alpha, and managed to get the Moon's limb crossing one of the centralized spots – which was fun if nothing else (Figure 3). The main plan was to photograph in white light the mid-eclipse (Figure 4) to give a general view and then try to get a series of pictures of the emerging photosphere, also in white light (Figure 5). As it is possible to get an almost instant image with the digital camera I was using (see below), mid-eclipse was used to set the light exposure. The digital images were then converted to JPEG format on the computer and image-processed to obtain the final results.

The telescopes used were a 60-mm Solaris refractor fitted with a hydrogen alpha 0.07-nm filter operating at 656 nm, and for the total phase an 85-mm $f/18$ refractor. The shutter speed was 1/125 of a second.

To photograph the eclipse I used a Kodak professional DCS 660 digital camera. With a 3040 × 2008 pixel CCD, I had over 6,000,000

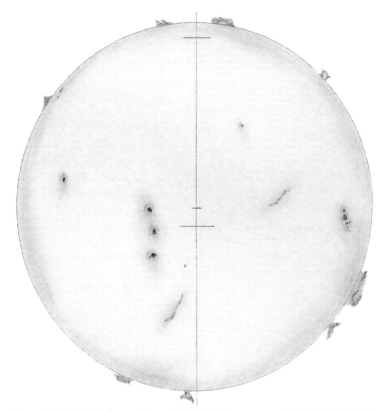

Figure 1. The Sun in hydrogen alpha at 07:00 UT, Wednesday August 11, 1999. Bandwidth 0.07 nm at a wavelength of 656.28 nm. North is at the top, but east–west is reversed by the configuration of the telescope. Eight groups of prominences are visible, with several filaments (prominences seen in silhouette against the solar disk) and three major sunspot groups. Sunspot penumbras are not so prominent in hydrogen alpha as when viewed in white light: they tend to blur into the granulation at the top of the photosphere. [Drawing by R. F. Turner]

pixels to play with. It's robust, it's big and it's heavy – but what a camera! It has a burst of 1 frame per second, which is to say it can record several images at 1 per second, before those images are written to its internal store, and it has an ISO range of 80 to 200. This, combined with the most amazing range of shutter settings, gives everything the astronomer needs to get 'that picture'.

The camera performed beyond expectation during totality and produced marvellous images, but the real test was to see whether it could operate at a specific frequency with a bandwidth of only 0.07 nm. Previous attempts to capture digital pictures with a black and white CCD have been successful. With that kind of imaging you record only shades of grey, but colour – well, that's something else. With the camera operating at the red end of the spectrum only about 20 to 25% of the pixels were expected to function, and the images were somewhat degraded, but they still showed disk details quite well at about 1/500 to 1/300 of a second. The prominences on the solar limb are much fainter and required about 1/30 of a second to ½ second, but although they photographed beautifully the overexposed disk bled into the area of the image occupied by the prominences. An occulting disk would have preventing this from happening.

The solar corona was of uniform structure, as was expected from a Sun approaching sunspot maximum, and had a lovely pearly green tinge. The diamond ring had a tiny spark of light in its centre for about 1½ seconds – an effect I have not seen before. The tiny amount of high

Figure 2. The full solar disk photographed in hydrogen alpha about 30 minutes before first contact. The exposure was set midway between the limb and the centre of the disk timings, at 1/150 of a second, to try to get all features on one picture. On the original image all the filaments and spots seen in white light are visible, as are six of the eight prominence groups. The disk details are somewhat overexposed and the limb features underexposed when viewed on a computer screen, and transforming the image to the printed page has resulted in further loss of clarity.

Figure 3. A hydrogen alpha image taken during the partial phase, showing the lunar limb crossing the uppermost of the group of three sunspots lying north–south on the solar disk (see Figure 1). As with Figure 2, the translation from a hydrogen alpha computer image to the printed page has resulted in a certain amount of image degradation.

Figure 4. Mid-eclipse in white light, with the exposure set for the inner corona, f/8 at 1/125 of a second. All the prominences seen at 07:00 UT were still visible, and one group showed separation from the solar disk. Since the photograph was instantly accessible as an electronic image, this exposure was used to check that the exposures for the run of pictures during the emergence of the photosphere were set correctly.

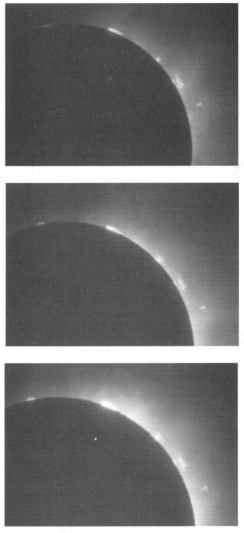

Figure 5. With the exposure set at f/8 and 1/125 of a second, a series of pictures was taken of the emerging limb. From the hydrogen alpha images obtained earlier, the major grouping of prominences was predicted to be showing at third contact. The exposures were made at 1ᵐ 35ˢ (top), 1ᵐ 50ˢ (middle) and 2ᵐ 5ˢ (bottom) into the eclipse. The images show the prominences emerging from the lunar limb; the exposure was changed slightly as the groups brightened. Several seconds after the last image was taken, the photosphere was fully exposed.

cloud had no detrimental effect on imaging the eclipse, but shrouded out Mercury, although Venus remained an easy object. Since the Moon's apparent diameter was 1.03 times that of the Sun, the darkness was not intense, and the light from around the edge of the shadow was sufficient to read by. Totality was a glorious spectacle, and one of the prettiest eclipses I have ever seen – a truly marvellous sight.

When will the next viewable total solar eclipse be? The year 2001 is exciting. On July 21 there is a total eclipse that starts in the Atlantic, crosses Africa and ends in the Indian Ocean. Its track crosses Angola, Zambia, Zimbabwe and Mozambique, and should provide many sites where good weather is assured. The greatest duration of totality is 4^m $56^s.6$, in the Atlantic just off Angola. December 14 sees an annular eclipse visible mainly from the Pacific, passing over Costa Rica and ending in the Caribbean. This should prove interesting, as annular eclipses are very odd sights, especially in their final stages when you can see a 75 to 80% partial phase. In 2002 there is an annular eclipse in June over the Pacific, with no landfall, but on December 4 a total eclipse of maximum duration 2^m $3^s.7$ starts in Angola, Botswana and South Africa and travels across the South Pacific, ending in Western Australia. An annular eclipse on May 31, 2003 will be seen from Northern Scotland, Greenland and Iceland, and in November that year a total eclipse of 1^m 57^s maximum duration will be visible only from Antarctica.

So what about the UK? As noted, 2003 brings an annular in Scotland. After this there are lots of near misses, especially in September 2081, but for the next total eclipses visible from Britain observers will have to wait until September 23, 2090, and July 23, 2093.

Volcanic Io

DAVID HAWKSETT

When the Italian astronomer Galileo Galilei first pointed his new telescope at Jupiter, one of the critical discoveries of his age was made. Four tiny dots of light accompanied this prominent planet, changing position from night to night. Galileo realized that these faint objects behaved just like the Moon circling the Earth. The implications were profound: if Jupiter had four moons of its own, then not everything revolved around the Earth. This discovery, above all others, was to put to rest the notion that Earth was the absolute centre of the Universe. These four new worlds became known as the Galilean satellites, after their discoverer, and they have been scrutinized by astronomers ever since. Many more moons have since been discovered orbiting Jupiter, but they are all tiny and are almost certainly asteroids captured by Jupiter's gravity.

Io is the closest of the Galileans to Jupiter, only 350,000 km from the cloud tops, closer than our Moon is to the Earth. But while the Moon leisurely orbits our world in 27 days, Jupiter's immense gravitational embrace forces Io to hurtle around in only 42 hours. Next comes Europa, 250,000 km farther out, followed by Ganymede, at 1 million km from the cloud tops, and then Callisto at 1.8 million km. All four Galilean satellites are large worlds. Io and Europa are similar in size to our Moon; Ganymede is actually larger than the planet Mercury, while distant Callisto is slightly smaller. Watching this dynamic miniature Solar System through a telescope is very popular with star-gazers. In the course of their orbital dance the Galileans pass in front of Jupiter, trailed or preceded by their own shadows. They also disappear into and emerge from behind Jupiter or its shadow. It was by precisely timing these events in 1676 that the Danish astronomer Ole Römer calculated the first reasonably accurate value for the speed of light.

Telescopic observations had shown Io to be the reddest object in the Solar System, but because of its size and distance from the Earth, very little else was known about it. Astronomers had to wait until the space age to begin to unlock the secrets of this intriguing world. In the early 1970s the American space agency NASA sent its first missions to the outer Solar System. Pioneers 10 and 11 performed an initial reconnaissance of the Jovian system in 1973 and 1974, but their observations of Io were long-range and yielded very little detail. Their mission was to prove that it was possible to reach the outer Solar System, and so to pave the way for a much more thorough survey.

The Voyager mission was dubbed the 'Grand Tour' of the Solar System. Launched in 1977, the two craft would take two years to reach Jupiter. There they would undergo a gravitational slingshot, using the momentum of Jupiter to propel them towards Saturn. Voyager 2 would continue all the way to Uranus and Neptune, making it one of the most successful long-duration probes in the history of spaceflight. The team of scientists for the Voyager missions consisted almost entirely of experts on the giant planets themselves. The Galilean satellites were expected to be ancient relics like our Moon: all the mission scientists expected to find were craters, preserving a record of impacts from the early history of the Solar System. Because of this there was only one geologist initially assigned to the Voyager team!

During the period of heavy bombardment at the birth of the Solar System, when débris of all sizes was swept up by the planets, the immense gravitational field of Jupiter would have drawn in many comets and asteroids. Being so close to Jupiter, Io would have been struck many times and should have preserved the scars of this intense battering. But as Voyager 1 approached Io, not one impact crater was visible in any of the images returned to Earth – instead, the surface of Io was revealed to be a jumble of striking colours (Figure 1). Its fiery mixture of yellows, oranges and white have often caused this world to be described as a 'giant pizza', but it was not these colours that caused the most excitement. Several hundred black features were visible, many of which were associated with what looked like flows and haloes. These were clearly volcanoes. The lack of impact craters implied a very young geological age for the surface of Io. This small world had obviously undergone intense activity, long after the heavy bombardment had ceased, which had resurfaced it, completely obliterating all traces of early impacts.

A breakthrough came after the encounter was over. Four days after Voyager 1 had sped through the Jovian system, Linda Morabito was performing rather mundane work on the images at the Jet Propulsion

Figure 1. Taken by Voyager 1, this image shows the Loki plume erupting 200 km above the limb of Io. The heart-shaped feature to the lower left marks the fallout from the Pele plume, the first volcanic eruption ever seen off the Earth.

Laboratory in Pasadena, California – mission control for the spacecraft. As a member of the navigation team her job was to constrain precisely the spacecraft's trajectory as it headed onwards to Saturn. She enhanced an image of a crescent Io to make sure that the dim background stars were where they were expected to be if Voyager 1 was on course. It was at this point that she noticed something unusual. With the contrast increased, a large arc-like feature appeared off the limb of Io (Figure 2). Her first thought was that it was one of the other Galilean satellites partially hidden behind Io, but this was easy to check, and turned out not to be the case. The large size of this feature ruled out its being a newly discovered satellite, as anything this large would already have been observed from Earth. No camera defect could have produced the feature, so the only conclusion was that it was something to do with Io

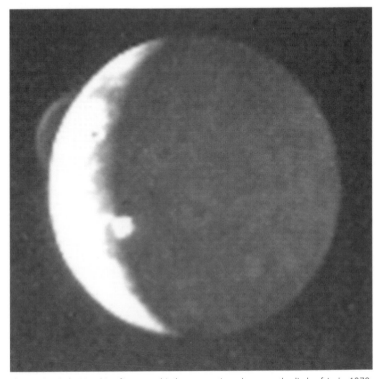

Figure 2. Linda Morabito first saw this huge eruption plume on the limb of Io in 1979. Rising 280 km into space, it was named Pele after the Hawaiian goddess of fire.

itself. Its umbrella shape was directly above one of the most prominent of the volcanic calderas. What Linda Morabito had discovered was the first active volcanic eruption ever seen on another world. The dimensions were staggering – the volcanic plume reached a height of 280 km, and the extensive halo around the caldera marked the fallout from this enormous eruption. This discovery was the highlight of the whole Voyager mission, and it made headline news around the world.

Immediately, other images were analysed and eight more volcanic plumes were identified. Few people had expected any kind of geological activity on Io. On Earth, volcanism is caused by heat produced deep in its interior from the decay of radioactive elements such as uranium and thorium. The same is true for other rocky worlds such as Mars. Being smaller than Earth, with fewer radioactive elements in its core, Mars has dissipated most of its internal heat and most of its volcanic activity seems to have stopped a few billion years ago. Io is smaller still, and should never have had enough internal heat to fuel its current activity, so what bizarre process was responsible for the plumes?

Just one week before the Voyager 1 encounter, planetary scientists Ray Reynolds, Pat Cassen and Stan Peale had published a paper in which they had calculated the gravitational effects that Jupiter and the Galilean satellites have upon one another. Any object in a body's gravitational field will experience some distortion because one side of the object is closer to the body's centre of gravity than its other side is. But if the gravitational field changes, there will be a change in the distortion which will produce friction and heat inside the object. The orbits of Io and Europa, the next moon out, are resonant, and the two satellites pull on each other when they are close together. While Io's orbit is on average circular, the effect of Europa means that it is slightly eccentric at any instant. But at the same time, being so close to Jupiter, this 'forced eccentricity' causes very powerful tides inside Io. The heat from this interior friction is just like the heat produced when you bend a spoon back and forth. Reynolds, Cassen and Peale predicted that this 'tidal heating' could be powerful enough to allow volcanic activity on Io. One week later it was realized that they had achieved a spectacular scientific coup.

In fact, the squeezing of Io's interior makes it the most volcanically active world in the whole Solar System. If you average out the heat flow over the whole surface, you find that Io emits at least 2.5 watts per square metre, giving a total of almost 100 trillion watts. This is 40 times greater than for the Earth, and more than 100 times greater than for the Moon.

The tortured interior of Io has given it a remarkable landscape with a riot of bright colours. Voyagers 1 and 2 imaged around one-third of the surface at a resolution of about 5 km per pixel, but the best images, of a region near the equator, show details as small as 0.5 km across. The terrain can be easily categorized into three types: volcanic vents, plains and mountains (Figure 3). The volcanoes themselves are the most striking features of all – hundreds of large calderas scattered across Io in a seemingly random pattern. The largest of these calderas is over 250 km across, and most are surrounded by very extensive lava flows and plume deposits. The most prominent is Pele, named after the Hawaiian goddess of fire. The fallout from this plume, the first to be discovered, can be traced for over 1000 km around the vent, forming a distinctive heart-shaped feature. The gravity on Io is only one-sixth of that on Earth and this, coupled with the almost complete lack of an atmosphere, allows the particles of the plumes to rise several hundred kilometres into space. In addition, the material leaving the vents is moving between 5 and 10 times faster than in any eruption on Earth. Pele is typical of one of the two main types of plume on Io. Pele-type eruptions reach the highest altitude (several hundred kilometres), but last only a matter of days or weeks. In contrast, the type of plume produced by Prometheus can last for years, but only reaches heights of around 50 km. By the time Voyager 2 arrived in the Jovian system in July 1979, four months after its twin, Pele had shut down but Prometheus was still going strong. Prometheus seems to have been erupting constantly for at least twenty years, and is still erupting today.

The sheer level of activity on Io is constantly altering the surface. In the four months between the two Voyager encounters there were obvious changes, even on a global scale: for example, the heart-shaped Pele deposit had become more symmetrical. It was clear that any detailed maps would quickly become inaccurate! If one were to take the total material produced in the flows and the plumes and average it out over the whole surface, it would bury the satellite under a layer perhaps a centimetre deep every year.

But what exactly was the material being erupted? Theoretical models combined with spectroscopic observations from Voyager have identified sulphur dioxide as a major component of the plumes. This highly volatile compound is thought to interact with magma under the surface, where it becomes superheated and then rises through fissures in the crust. As it approaches the surface, the sulphur dioxide boils under the decreasing pressure, and expands dramatically with enough energy to create the plumes seen in the Voyager images. These active features seem to be much more reminiscent of geysers on Earth, rather than conventional volcanoes. The many lava flows imaged by Voyager also invited an exotic explanation. The first clue came from the surface

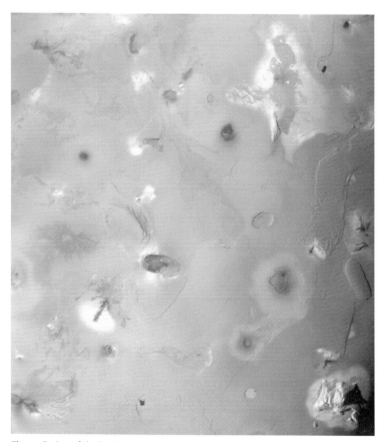

Figure 3. One of the best images acquired by Voyager 1, showing an area 1700 km across. Several large volcanic calderas can be seen along with two major mountain complexes: Euboea Montes, left of centre, and the 13 km high Haemus Mons at the lower right. The bright patches are sulphur dioxide frost.

colours: the trend from black in the calderas, through oranges and yellows to almost white, is reminiscent of the different allotropes (different forms of the same element) of sulphur. Heating elemental sulphur causes its colour to change as it forms different allotropes with increasing temperature, eventually becoming very dark brown to black. This was a tempting explanation. The changing viscosity of liquid sulphur at different temperatures could account for the variety of lava flows around many of the vents. Some of these flows are over 700 km long, and runny liquid sulphur pumped from a vent at a high rate was an ideal candidate.

Unlike most of the moons in the outer Solar System, Io is a rocky world with a density of around 3.5 g/cm^3, rather than being composed mostly of ice. There is no doubt that it possesses a large iron–nickel core surrounded by a rocky mantle. However, it was thought possible that the entire crust was sulphurous material, in much the same way that the Earth is mostly covered in water. With a melting point of only 115°C, this sulphur could easily be melted and mobilized by heat from below.

Many scientists agreed with the idea of a 'sulphur shell', and some claimed that silicate rock did not exist anywhere on the surface of Io. However, this idea soon ran into problems. Mike Carr from the US Geological Survey pointed out that volcanoes are not the only features on Io. Although mountainous regions cover only a few per cent of Io, some are around 10 km in height. Carr calculated that solid sulphur alone is not strong enough to form such high structures. This is also true for the calderas themselves – some are as deep as a couple of kilometres, with walls too steep to be supported by a material as weak as solid sulphur. Clearly, the simple model of a rocky world enveloped by a sulphur shell was wishful thinking. It turns out that to produce the vivid sulphurous colours on the surface, a composition of only a few per cent of sulphur is required. This amount of sulphur is also sufficient to produce long flows, like the distinctive radial flows from the Ra Patera volcano.

The terrain between the volcanoes and mountains has been loosely termed 'plains', but these areas also show signs of dynamic activity and alteration. Most are smooth and flat, but cliffs and escarpments surround some of them. These cliffs show plenty of evidence of erosion from a more gentle type of activity than the plumes. The clue to understanding this process comes from the composition of the surface of Io. Rather than being composed entirely of sulphur, the surface is likely to be built up as a series of layers of pyroclastic ash, sulphur and silicate lava flows, and sulphur dioxide frost. Once buried by resurfacing, the combination of pressure and geothermal (internal) heat melts the sulphur dioxide, which can then migrate through the other porous layers. When this liquid meets a cliff face it erupts explosively, evaporating in the near-vacuum at Io's surface. This action erodes the cliff faces, which gradually retreat, often forming complex scalloped patterns. The sulphur dioxide from these lateral blasts quickly condenses back into a kind of frost, leaving bright patches around their eruption point – clear indicators of recent or ongoing activity. The frost will soon be buried again by the constant resurfacing of Io but, being so volatile, the sulphur dioxide will eventually force its way back to the surface in an Ionian version of a hydrological cycle. This process adds another dimension to the complex recycling of materials at and beneath the surface.

It is not just the surface of Io that makes the moon unusual. Ground-based telescopes had watched as Io passed in front of faint stars. The sharp cut-off in starlight during these occultations suggested there was no atmosphere on Io, but results from Pioneer 10 in 1973 suggested the possibility of an ionosphere. This high-altitude layer of ionized gas did imply the existence of an atmosphere. When Voyager 1 encountered Io six years later, its infrared spectrometer detected sulphur dioxide gas above the Loki caldera. This gas does provide Io with a very tenuous atmosphere, but it is highly localized, concentrated around the sources of activity that generate it. As if its violent activity were not enough, the orbit of Io resides inside Jupiter's radiation belts, zones of deadly radiation sustained by energetic charged particles from the Sun that become trapped in Jupiter's stupendous magnetic field. This magnetic field interacts strongly with Io. It strips material from the surface and the plumes, creating a cloud of sodium atoms in Io's orbit and a plasma torus of ionized sulphur atoms in the Jovian magnetosphere. Additionally, Io is connected to the ionosphere of Jupiter by a closed electrical circuit. Inside this magnetic flux tube flows a current of several million amperes, which generates powerful aurorae near the poles of Jupiter itself.

The results from the twin Voyager fly-bys of the Jovian system had dazzled planetary scientists, and it was clear that these worlds deserved a much more detailed survey. NASA planned to return to Jupiter with the first mission actually to orbit a giant planet. Weighing in at 3 tonnes and costing $1.5 billion, Galileo was designed to be the most complex and ambitious planetary mission yet attempted. It would spend two years in Jupiter orbit, scrutinizing the giant planet and its rich variety of moons, just as its Earth-bound namesake had nearly four hundred years before. There were a dozen scientific experiments on board, including a state-of-the-art CCD camera, an infrared spectrometer, and equipment for measuring the magnetic fields and charged particles in the Jovian environment. One of the most exciting components of the mission was a small detachable probe, which would plunge into the atmosphere of Jupiter at 170,000 km/h, and relay data back to the main craft.

Galileo was the first planetary mission scheduled to be launched from the space shuttle, and it was with the shuttle that its problems began. The tragic loss of *Challenger* in 1986, with all hands, grounded NASA's shuttle fleet just months before Galileo was due to be deployed into low Earth orbit on the first leg of its trip to Jupiter. After NASA had solved its problems with the shuttle, Galileo, with its arsenal of equipment, was finally launched on October 18, 1989. It would take six years to reach Jupiter, employing a gravitational slingshot past Venus and two past Earth. During this roundabout trip the spacecraft was able to image not only these planets, but also two asteroids, Ida and Gaspra, as well as providing key observations of the impact of Comet Shoemaker–Levy 9 on Jupiter in July 1994.

One of the innovations on board Galileo was a new type of transmitter for relaying data back to Earth. Instead of the solid high-gain antenna used by the Voyager probes, Galileo employed a lightweight mesh dish which was to open like an umbrella en route to Jupiter. It was problems with this antenna that caused the mission's biggest headache. During the early part of the flight the command was sent for the motors to open the antenna, but nothing happened. It seemed that the years of being stored in a hangar, coupled with the rigours of interplanetary travel, had caused the mechanism to seize up. In space, moving parts can quickly become non-moving parts, and it seemed the whole mission was in jeopardy. The engineers tried everything they could to free up the antenna, but finally admitted defeat in 1994 after having sent the 'unfurl' command to the spacecraft over 15,000 times. The science team would have to rely on the much smaller low-gain antenna to transmit data back to Earth. This would severely limit Galileo's planned observations, as images and other data would have to be stored on the onboard tape recorder, with its limited capacity, for later relay to Earth at a trickle.

On December 7, 1995 the spacecraft closed in on Io, using the moon's gravity to reduce its velocity and begin its series of long loops around Jupiter. This was the only opportunity to see Io from up close during the whole mission. The deadly radiation belts around Jupiter, in which Io orbits, presented a distinct hazard to the spacecraft. To ensure its survival, Galileo would have to keep its distance after this daring manoeuvre. In the original mission plan, the probe would take high-resolution images of features on Io only metres across during this fly-by, but, because of the problems with the main antenna, Io scientists were dealt a double blow. Not only did the whole mission have to be scaled down, but also the atmospheric probe was descending through Jupiter's cloud tops during the Io fly-by, and this was a top mission priority. All Io volcanologists remember where they were while the crippled orbiter was concentrating its limited resources on the signals from Jupiter's atmosphere, oblivious to the tantalizing volcanic land-scape racing below only a few hundred kilometres away.

The prime Galileo mission was to last two years, and the observations of the Jovian system have been staggering. New details of fine structure in the atmosphere of Jupiter have been revealed and, during many close fly-bys, surface features as small as 6 m have been resolved on the surfaces of the other Galilean satellites which orbit outside the deadly radiation belts. During this time the spacecraft was able to image Io from afar. Only some of these observations matched those of Voyager for resolution, but the science team was eager to see how the surface had changed in the 17 years since Voyager.

One of the most striking differences was in the Prometheus plume. The dimensions were still roughly the same, between 50 and 100 km high, but the source of the plume seemed to have moved 80 km across the surface! It was possible that the sulphur dioxide that fed the erup-tion had migrated under the surface, but this was a question which would not be resolved until much later in the mission. The ring-shaped deposit from the Pele plume was still the most prominent feature on the surface, but its shape had become distorted as the geometry of the vent changed over time (Figure 4).

One of the major questions posed by the Voyager encounters was whether or not molten rock was erupting onto the surface, as well as plumes and sulphur flows. Observations from ground-based infrared

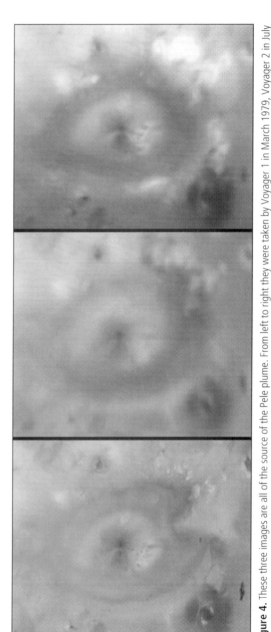

Figure 4. These three images are all of the source of the Pele plume. From left to right they were taken by Voyager 1 in March 1979, Voyager 2 in July 1979 and Galileo in June 1996; the changes over time are immediately apparent. The area shown is around 1500 km across.

telescopes had suggested temperatures of 900 K at the surface, much more typical of molten lava than of sulphur. Images from the Near Infrared Mapping Spectrometer on board Galileo have provided many charts of thermal emission from the hotspots on the surface. These results also show temperatures far hotter than can reasonably be expected for molten sulphur. And when images of Io in the darkness provided by the shadow of Jupiter were taken, they showed glowing lava on the surface. It now seems that volcanic centres can have temperatures ranging from 700 K all the way up to 2000 K! Not only is this far too hot for sulphur, but it is also significantly hotter than most terrestrial eruptions. Galileo had proved that, in addition to sulphur flows and sulphur dioxide plumes, hot molten silicate rock did indeed erupt on to the surface of Io, contrary to many of the ideas put forward after Voyager in 1979.

By far the most dramatic alteration of the surface occurred during the Galileo mission itself. The spacecraft imaged the region around Pele in April and September 1997, and it was obvious that something major had happened. Pillan Patera, to the east of Pele, had produced an enormous dark deposit of ash 400 km across, partially covering the red sulphurous deposit from the Pele plume (Figure 5). Nearly two years later, Pele, active once again, had begun to cover up the effects of the Pillan eruption with its own fallout, but the dark deposit was still visible. It seems that the two plumes are fighting for supremacy as they contest each other's boundaries.

The long-range observations of Io by Galileo yielded much from a frustrating distance, but there would soon be a chance that we would see the surface in unprecedented detail. Despite the problems with the antenna, Galileo was providing spectacular results, and funding was granted for a two-year extension to the mission, culminating in two near-suicidally close fly-bys of Io. Io volcanologists were tentatively delighted – the spacecraft had taken a battering from its years in space and two years at Jupiter. There was no guarantee that it would still be functioning at the end of 1999 for the Io encounters.

On October 10, 1999 Galileo was still alive and hurtling towards the deadly region of radiation around Io. Many people expected the electronics to be finally fried during the first encounter, but the ageing spacecraft was made of stronger stuff. The long-awaited images were soon released, causing a stir in the planetary community. By far the most exciting was the high-resolution image of Pillan Patera (Figure 6).

Figure 5. These three Galileo images of the region around Pele show dramatic changes over a three-year period. From left to right they were taken in April and September 1997, and July 1999. The black patch near the centre of the middle view shows the dramatic effect of the eruption of Pillan Patera. By July 1999 the fallout from Pele has begun to obscure the Pillan deposit.

From an altitude of only 617 km, Galileo had imaged a tiny region near the vent of Pillan with a staggering resolution of just 9 m per pixel. The black-and-white image is, at first, difficult to interpret. The Sun illuminates the scene from the right, and is very close to the horizon, throwing the landscape into sharp relief. After some perseverance it is possible to see a chaos of volcanic features: clusters of pits and domes, some with lava flows, alongside smoother areas. The smallest features visible here are around the size of a house, and the small cliff on the left of the image is up to 10 m high. While these features can be seen on other terrestrial worlds, such a variety has never been seen before in so small a region: the area covered by Figure 6 is just 7 km wide.

As the spacecraft plunged towards its encounter with Pillan Patera, it passed over the Pele vent, which was over on the night side of Io. Peering into the caldera, its camera could easily make out a thin curving line of lava, over 10 km long and up to 50 m wide, glowing in the darkness (Figure 7). This effect is often seen in the lava lakes on Hawaii, thousands of times smaller than Pele, as a thin crust of rock breaks up as it meets the edge of the caldera, exposing the molten lava beneath.

Galileo was also able to answer the question of how Prometheus had moved 80 km across the surface. During the close fly-by, the spacecraft discovered an enormous caldera 28 km across, to the east of the plume itself (Figure 8). It now seems likely that molten lava from this volcano spills out onto the surface, from where it runs through lava tubes, extending to the west, eventually coming into contact with layers rich in sulphur dioxide. The resultant interaction causes the volatiles in the ground to explode violently, forming the Prometheus plume itself. Depending on the length and orientation of these tubes, the plume could erupt from anywhere near the caldera, giving the impression of a moving volcano, and demonstrating a spectacular example of 'two-tier' volcanism.

On November 25, 1999 Galileo was once again heading towards Io. Only four hours before the closest approach of 300 km, radiation caused the onboard computer to reset and enter standby mode. Veto commands were hurriedly transmitted from Earth, and the spacecraft's instruments were reactivated in time for half the observations of the surface and the seething plasma torus to be salvaged. One of the best images from this second encounter shows molten lava spraying 1.5 km above the surface (Figure 9). Many planetologists had postulated that such 'fire fountains' would exist on Io, but they had never been seen

Figure 6. Galileo took this black and white image on October 10, 1999. It shows a region 7 km wide near to the vent of Pillan Patera, source of the Pillan plume. Illumination is from the right, and the scene shows cliffs 10 m high and features as small as houses. This is the most detailed image of Io yet taken, with a resolution of 9 m per pixel.

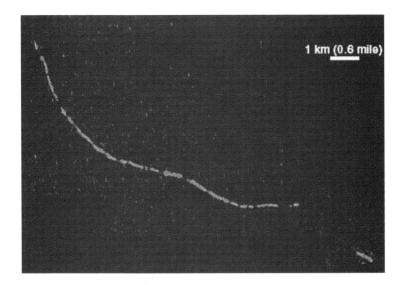

1 km (0.6 mile)

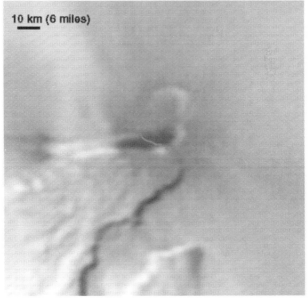

10 km (6 miles)

Figure 7. The thin curving line is molten lava in the Pele caldera, glowing in the Ionian night. The bottom part of the picture superimposes this ribbon over a daytime image of the caldera.

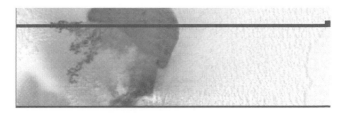

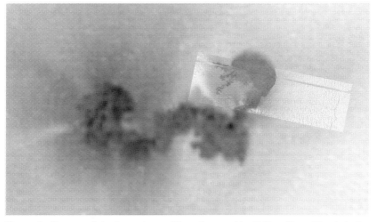

Figure 8. Close-up of the Prometheus caldera discovered by Galileo. The caldera is to the right, and lava has run through lava tubes to the west, interacting with volatiles in the crust and causing the plume.

from this close. The glowing lava was so bright that it actually over-loaded the CCD camera on the spacecraft, causing the centre of the image to 'white out' and pixels to bleed into one another as electrons spilled over the detector. This oblique view also shows some of the eroded cliffs first seen by Voyager. With details as small as 185 m across, it is possible to see the complex patterns in the cliffs, formed as buried sulphur dioxide liquefies and bursts through the cliff walls.

As I write this, Galileo is, amazingly, still functioning normally, hav-ing survived two close encounters with Io. By the time this *Yearbook* reaches the bookshelves, this highly successful, robust spacecraft will have encountered Io once more, if all goes well. At present none of the world's space agencies have any plans to revisit Io. Its location in Jupiter's radiation belts makes it a difficult target for close scrutiny. If NASA proceeds with its plans to launch a Europa orbiter in the next

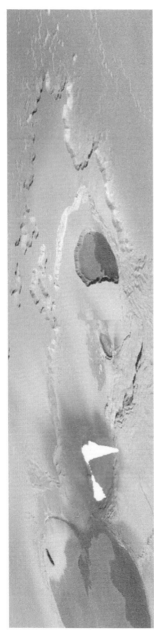

Figure 9. One of the best images acquired by Galileo during its second close fly-by of Io in November 1999. It is an oblique view covering an area 300 km across. A fire fountain of molten lava is spraying 1.5 km into the sky. This material is so bright that it has overloaded the camera, causing the bright smudge. Also visible are scalloped cliffs, eroded by the release of sulphur dioxide gas.

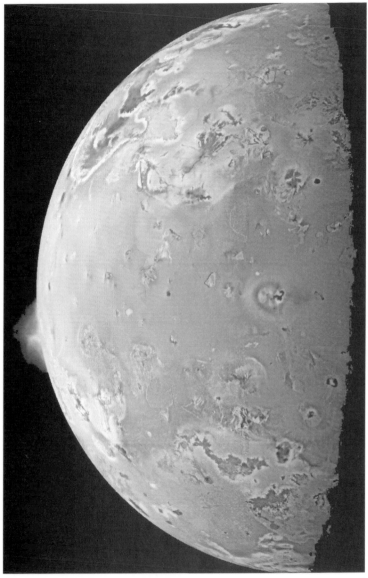

Figure 10. The eruption plume of Pillan Patera is clearly visible against the blackness of space in this Galileo image. Near the terminator is a reddish smudge, which is actually a shadow on the surface cast by the Prometheus plume.

few years, it is hoped that it will be able to make some observations of Io from this relatively safe distance. Io is a unique showpiece of the Solar System (Figure 10), and the robotic surveys of this world have taught us to expect the unexpected whenever we visit new worlds. The violence written across its surface, as if by Dante himself, provides a wonderful natural laboratory for the study of volcanic activity. The lessons learned by Voyager and Galileo will be crucial in preparing for the next great planetary survey, when the joint ESA/NASA Cassini–Huygens mission arrives at Saturn in July 2004.

The Moon's Origin: Constraints on the Giant Impact Theory

JOE McCALL

I have recently been inspired by a somewhat iconoclastic article by Don L. Anderson of Caltech, Pasadena (Anderson 1999) in which he looked at the implications of certain present-day shibboleths in Earth-mantle dynamics, especially concerning mantle plumes; and I was stung into writing this essay by a small item in the *Geoscientist* on the subject of the so-called giant impact theory for the origin of the Moon. This hypothesis – for this is what it is, no more – has been widely favoured, in America at least, because it is compatible with rotational characteristics of the Earth–Moon system. According to this hypothesis, the Moon is believed to have originated by coalescence from a zone of debris produced by a collision between two Earth-forming protoplanets.

As a geologist, long involved with planetology, I find this scenario extremely unlikely. The idea of the Earth accreting from small planetesimals is readily acceptable, but the Solar System appears to show a systematic pattern of planets rapidly accreting in orbits within the plane of the ecliptic, thus keeping them from colliding with one another. Advocates of the giant impact hypothesis (e.g. Halliday and Drake 1999) invoke a Mars-sized body colliding with the proto-Earth, but bodies of such dimensions seem to have been accreted with parsimony, and surely there is no evidence that spare bodies of this size were ever projected into eccentric orbits, such that they could by remote chance collide with the Earth, like asteroids. The asteroids' parent bodies were, apparently, quite small, and if an eccentric orbit outside the plane of the ecliptic is being invoked, surely there would need to be a host of Mars-sized bodies in such orbits for there to be such an against-the-odds chance of an Earth-collision? Where have the others gone? The alternative of one body chasing another in the same orbit, within the plane of the ecliptic, seems very unlikely. I shall leave these questions for the astronomers to answer – they may be the product of too simple a mind, for, despite a lifetime in science with a grounding in chemistry and geology, I am naive enough to worry about how you can have a 'Big Bang' explosion (Murdin 1999) before the elements of the Universe were put together – a recent popular booklet entitled *From the Beginning* (Edwards and Rosen 2000) states that 'all matter and time itself, began with a void'. How can a void explode? But I am straying from my subject.

In my lifetime, which now spans nearly 80 years, we have seen put forward ideas of the simultaneous condensation of the Earth and the Moon from a cloud of gas and dust, lunar capture, and even the Moon coming out of the Pacific Ocean – and many others besides. My contention is that the giant impact hypothesis should rank with these as an interesting, way-out hypothesis, and not be taken as gospel. The results of modern computer modelling are frequently aired in the literature and gradually come to become taken as fact – 'may be' rapidly becomes 'is' – and all models derived from the computer depend on what is fed in – 'Gigo's law'.

My friend Ted Nield, who wrote the article that triggered this brief sceptical essay, noted another problem facing this hypothesis. The colliding bodies have to be solidly accreted prior to the collision, and the event has to be fitted into a very narrow window of time, between the onset of accretion, which most scientists now believe took place quite rapidly not more than 4.57 billion years ago (this is constrained by the well-established age of the Solar System, inferred from the refractory-rich inclusions in undifferentiated meteorites: Podosek 1999), and the onset of geological processes on the Earth and Moon. He ended with the plea, 'a few finds of older rocks on Earth would not come amiss'.

The study of the Earth's oldest (Archaean) rocks was rather neglected when the present writer, in 1970, initiated the first Archaean symposium on the topic in Perth, Australia (Glover 1971) and prepared a volume containing a set of readings on the topic (McCall 1977). Unlike the situation in the 1970s, as we approach the fourth such symposium – scheduled for 2001 in Perth, Western Australia – virtually all known tracts of Archaean rocks, radiometrically dated to between 2.5 and 4 billion years, have been studied in some detail. The further back one goes in the geological timescale, the smaller the areas left exposed by geological processes, and in the end one is looking at quite small

Figure 1. The extraordinary similarity of cratered terrains on Mercury and the Moon. Top: a Mariner 10 image of the area of Mercury containing the craters Melville and Rodin (about 500 km across). Bottom: another Mariner 10 image, taken on the way to Venus and Mercury, showing the Mare Humboldtianum area of the Moon (about 300 km across).

extents of rocks, quite likely gneissose metamorphic rocks, and search-
ing within them for relict minerals or parts of minerals preserved from
an earlier geological cycle. Rocks with radiometrically determined ages
of around 3.8 billion years are well documented from Isua, Greenland
(Harland *et al.* 1989) and the Mount Narryer region of Western
Australia (Williams and Myers 1987), and the oldest rock formation
known is within the Acasta gneiss from Slave Province in Canada, a
dark basic component in the gneiss yielding a radiometric age of about
4.0 billion years (Bowring 1995). It is sobering to look at this gneiss,
of which I possess a small specimen, for it is remarkably similar in
appearance to gneiss rocks of Cenozoic age in the Alpine or Himalayan
mountain ranges, but vastly separated in time of formation.

We can, however, look back even further and see evidence of
familiar geological processes working even earlier, for recycled zircons
within the Mount Narryer rocks have yielded ages of 4.1–4.2 billion
years, older than any other known terrestrial rocks. The window for the
supposed giant impact is thus no more than 0.37 billion years, from
further terrestrial evidence. I doubt if we can do much to resolve this
problem from terrestrial geological studies, as Ted Nield hopes.

However, we can go back further in time by looking at evidence
from the Moon, which is even more constraining – radiometric dates
have been obtained for lunar rocks, almost back to the well established
time of the formation of the Solar System. 'Early events are recorded in
fragments within highland soils and evidence from relict plagioclase
cores suggest ages approaching 4.5 billion years. A dunite sample with
a radiometric age of 4.6 billion years has been interpreted as a relict of
a primordial frozen crust, the highland anorthosites. Relict lunar ages
approach meteoritic ages.' (Harland *et al.* 1999, p. 23). In 1975 Ross
Taylor commented that this suggests 'extensive melting, fractionation
and formation of the highland crust at a time close to the condensation
of the solar system at 4.6 aeons'. If we believe these radiometric dating
results, there is surely no window of time at all for the post-accretion/
solidification collision between 'Earth-forming planets' required by
the giant impact hypothesis, for the hypothetical giant impactor could
not virtually instantaneously chance to hit our orbiting planet. Besides
the astronomical questions raised above, radiometric age dating results
seem to show that there is no window of time for such an event
to occur.

There I rest my case. Podosek (1999) has discussed the unanswered questions and problems facing the giant impact hypothesis in a much more sophisticated manner than I can, but if my simple objections stir up something more than blind acceptance of the hypothesis, this brief essay will have achieved its object. Halliday and Drake (1999) note that a recent computer model based on the giant impact hypothesis has suggested a proto-Earth half its present size and a body three times the size of Mars, but that in no way detracts from my argument. Indeed, perhaps the existence of such a randomly moving inner terrestrial planetary body of this size is even more unlikely than the Mars-sized impactor originally proposed. Podosek appears, if I read him rightly, to believe that some way will be found to reconcile the giant impact hypothesis with the constraints and objections – perhaps I am naive, but I am less optimistic that he is. I believe that the key to a full understanding of the Earth–Moon system may be found in unmanned missions to recover samples from the planet Mercury. Mercury is so like the Moon in its surface features (Figure 1) that this must surely be telling us something. But what exactly is it telling us? It is a planet and not a satellite, so we do not have to indulge in complicated and way-out hypothesizing to explain its existence, but like the Moon it seems to have been arrested after its early development – dare I say that we shall find more about the origins of the Solar System by such study than by studying rocks from Mars, a complexly developed planet?

REFERENCES

Anderson, D. L. (1999) A theory of the Earth: Hutton and Humpty Dumpty and Holmes. In: Craig, G. Y., and Hull, J. H. (eds) *James Hutton – Present and Future*, Geological Society of London, Special Publication No. 150, pp. 13–35.

Bowring, S. A., Coleman, D. S., and Bunch, T. E. (1995) The 4.0 Ga Acasta gneisses: Constraints on the growth and recycling of continental crust. In 'Precambrian '95: program and abstracts', International Conference on Tectonics and Metallogeny of Early/mid-Precambrian Orogenic Belts, Montreal, p. 275.

Edwards, K., and Rosen, B. R. (2000) *From the Beginning*. Natural History Museum, London.

Glover, J. (ed.) (1971) *Symposium on Archaean Rocks*, Perth, 23–26 May 1970. Geological Society of Australia, Special Publication No. 3.

Halliday, A. N. and Drake, M. J. (1999) Colliding theories. *Science*, Vol. 283, pp. 1861–3.

Harland, W. B., Armstrong, R. L., Cox, A. V., Craig, L. E., Smith, A. G., and Smith, D. G. (1989) *A Geologic Time Scale 1989*. Cambridge University Press.

McCall, G. J. H. (1977) *The Archaean*. Dowden, Hutchinson & Ross, Stroudsburg, PA.

Murdin, P. (1999) Water: A cosmic history. In: Moore, P. (ed.), *2000 Yearbook of Astronomy*. Macmillan, London, pp. 129–52.

Nield, E. (1999) Earth and Moon. *Geoscientist*, Vol. 9, No. 8, p. 9.

Podosek, F. A. (1999) A couple of uncertain age. *Science*, Vol. 283, pp. 1863–4.

Taylor, S. R. (1975) '*Lunar Science: A Post-Apollo View*. Pergamon Press, Oxford.

Williams, I. R., and Myers, J. S. (1987) Archaean geology of the Mount Narryer region, Western Australia. Geological Survey of Western Australia, Report No. 22.

The Lives of the Stars

CHRIS LINTOTT

As I sit at my desk to write this article, outside the night is drawing in and the first stars are beginning to emerge from the twilight. Among the brightest are the two leaders of the constellation Orion, Betelgeux and Rigel, visible in the south-east during early evenings during the first few months of the year. In between these two is a row of three slightly fainter stars, Mintaka, Alnilam and Alnitak, and below these three is an object that is familiar to all observers – the Orion Nebula (M42). Glowing faintly, this small, diffuse patch of light is clearly not just another star. Examination with binoculars or, better, a telescope will reveal a glowing, green (at least to my eye) mass of gas, illuminated by the light of the four-star system Theta Orionis that is embedded in the visible part of the nebula. The key word in that last sentence was 'visible', for in fact the structure extends far beyond what we can see in the visible region of the spectrum, to cover much of Orion. M42 owes its prominence and brightness only to the shining young stars within it. For an explanation of why they are there at all, and exactly what the nebula is, we need to go right back to the beginning of a star's lifetime.

First, though, we need to go back to the beginning of our understanding of a star's lifetime. The first attempt to arrange stars into a chronological sequence was born out of the effort, in the second half of the 19th century, to classify stars by their spectral types. Building on earlier work by Carl Vogel and Angelo Secchi, Williamina Fleming of Harvard classified stars into groups, assigning A to what she believed to be the youngest group, B to the next youngest, and so on, neatly ending with P for planetary nebulae, which were assumed to represent the end of a star's life.[1] As more information was collected, defects of the classification became apparent, and the sequence was restructured by Annie Cannon to give the familiar 'O, B, A, . . .', from hottest (O) to coolest (M). It was still supposed, however, that this was an evolutionary sequence: that stars formed hot, and cooled throughout their lifetime.

All that remained to be explained was how the stars were born hot in the first place.

In the 1920s and 1930s, astrophysicists realized that the power source driving the Sun, and all stars, was nuclear fusion. Hydrogen nuclei, composed of just one positively charged proton, are converted into helium nuclei, composed of two positively charged protons and two uncharged neutrons, with an extremely small loss of mass. However, by Einstein's famous equation, $E = mc^2$, the energy released is equal to this loss of mass times the speed of light squared, and since the speed of light is a large number, we end up with a great release of energy. Once this was realized, the simple picture of a star cooling had to be let go and an alternative devised – which brings us back to the Orion Nebula.

Everything in the Universe which has mass exerts a gravitational attraction on the objects around it. The attraction between the gas and dust particles that make up the Orion Nebula and others like it is extremely slight, but there is no force to oppose it, and we have an astronomical timescale to play with: millions of years may pass before anything noticeable occurs, but slowly and imperceptibly the material begins to clump together. The larger the clump, the greater its mass, and thus the stronger the gravitational field that surrounds it, so the clumps pull in more and more material. As the process accelerates, a clump may become large enough to be visible to telescopes as a small black patch in front of the illuminated nebula. Such objects are known as Bok globules, after Bart Bok, one of the pioneers of the study of star formation, who first catalogued them. The collapse continues, and the material at the centre of what we may now term a protostar is being placed under ever increasing pressure.

This picture is a simplified one, and misses out a few elements, in particular the effect of magnetic fields. For example, free electrons moving through space set up a magnetic field which then acts on these charged particles to produce a force acting in a direction away from the forming star, in the opposite direction to the gravitational collapse. This effect is, however, never enough to stop the gravitational collapse which, for now at least, continues unabated. One other effect of the turbulent magnetic field during the early stages of collapse is to reduce the angular momentum of infalling material, allowing it to fall onto the star.[2] Later on, when infall velocities are greater, because of the higher gravitational attraction of the increasing central mass, this 'magnetic brake' has less effect, and the material goes into orbit around the protostar, forming disks of the kind that have been detected around newly formed stars in recent images. The shape of the magnetic field also influences the environment around the star. Two paraboloidal regions of the field are formed, centred on the star and together forming an hourglass shape, and the material falling in follows these field lines as the path of least resistance.

At some point the pressure at the centre of the star becomes sufficient to ignite nuclear fusion, and so switch the star on. Our protostar shines for the first time. Inflow does not stop immediately, but eventually the stellar wind[3] of the young star will begin to clear material away from its vicinity. This material also follows the magnetic field lines, which control the movement of everything around the newly forming star, and the hourglass is thus 'hollowed out' – the inside of each bulb is emptied first, then the sides. Intermediate stages with hourglass-shaped shells are seen in the infrared radiation from the cool dust.

The star is still collapsing, and now shines somewhat unsteadily in a phase known as the T Tauri stage.[4] By the end of this stage, which lasts around 30 million years for a star the size and mass of the Sun, all that remains of the nebula is the disk of 'leftover' material which will go on to form, perhaps, a planetary system such as our own, or the other 50 or so discovered over the last few years. Once the temperature at the core, which is increasing steadily all the while, reaches 10 million degrees K, hydrogen burning[5] proper can begin, and the star is ready to join the main sequence.

The main sequence is the most striking feature on any plot of the Hertzsprung–Russell diagram. The HR diagram, as it is usually called, plots temperature against stellar size. If this is done for enough stars, a band emerges running from top left (high temperature, high mass) to bottom right (low temperature, low mass) on which the majority of stars lie. This does not represent the evolutionary series that the early theoreticians looked for, but instead indicates the relationship between the mass of a star and the rate of the nuclear reactions taking place inside it: the larger a star, the higher its internal pressure, and hence the faster the reactions proceed. For the same reasons, stellar giants are the stars that shine for the least time – a true reflection of the 'live fast, die young' philosophy. The detail of these reactions is surprisingly complicated; it is not just a case of four hydrogen nuclei being squashed together and forming a helium nucleus. Instead, they form a deuterium[6] nucleus – so-called heavy hydrogen, with two protons instead of one.

This process also creates two new, bizarre particles. The first is a neutrino, a particle which interacts with everything else so weakly that most escape from the Sun without any further mishap. Many of these neutrinos are intercepted by the Earth, but most pass straight through (inspiring the poet John Updike to write the poem 'Cosmic Gall', which begins, 'Neutrinos, they are very small/And hardly interact at all . . .' – a summary I cannot hope to improve upon). It is worth pausing here to note that neutrinos pose one of the major problems of solar physics. Quite simply, we are not detecting enough of them! A neutrino telescope is very far removed from the instruments that you, I or most professional observers might use, and simply consists of a huge tank of chlorine in the form of cleaning fluid, situated deep underground. The cleaning fluid very occasionally reacts with a neutrino passing through, converting an atom of chlorine to an atom of argon, which can then be detected. The tank is underground to prevent cosmic rays (which constantly bombard the Earth's surface) from causing the same effect and swamping the neutrino signal. Such instruments are fantastically sensitive, and have easily detected bursts of individual neutrinos from events as distant as Supernova SN 1987A in the Large Magellanic Cloud, but they do not detect enough neutrinos from the Sun to agree with theory. One possible answer that has emerged over recent years is that the mass of these strange elemental particles, long thought to be zero, may in fact merely be extremely small. If these particles had mass, then more energy would be required to produce them (remember that $E = mc^2$, so producing mass uses up energy). If our calculations about the amount of energy available are correct, we should expect fewer neutrinos. If this is true, then they may well make some contribution to the thorny 'missing mass' problem, but the jury is still out. (If the new theory turns out to be correct, the next line of 'Cosmic Gall' may need some alteration. It reads, 'They have no charge, and have no mass.')

The other exotic particle created is a positron, which is like the everyday electron in every sense except that its charge is positive instead of negative. It is, in fact, the electron's antiparticle – a real-life example of the antimatter beloved of science fiction writers. When a positron collides with an electron, the two particles annihilate each other, and their masses are converted into energy (again, determined by $E = mc^2$).

The next stage is for our newly formed deuterium nucleus to collide with yet another hydrogen atom. This time helium is formed, and more importantly (at least from our perspective) radiation in the form of gamma-rays is released. It is this release of energy that heats the interior of the star, and through the mechanisms of radiation and convection it is eventually emitted into space. The exact details of how this process of heat transfer occurs are still to be agreed upon. Anomalies include the decidedly bizarre fact that the very outer layer of the Sun's atmosphere, the corona (visible during cloud-free total solar eclipses), is far hotter than the bright surface, the photosphere. There is no doubt, however, that the conversion of hydrogen into helium, by what is called the proton–proton reaction, is the major force driving the Sun. The helium that is created is not quite what we would class as normal helium. This variety, or isotope, of helium has the correct number of protons (two), but only one neutron where we would expect two. Two nuclei of this 'light helium' isotope combine in turn to form a nucleus of normal helium and a deuterium nucleus that can then react once more.

I mentioned above that the gravitational collapse of a protostar continues during the T Tauri phase. Once the main sequence and stability is reached, however, this process is halted. The outflow of radiation from the core, where the reactions are taking place, produces a radiation pressure which acts on the outer layers of the star and supports them against gravitational collapse. This equilibrium explains why stars are stable over their extremely long lifetimes, and will be important when we come to look at the changes that take place at the end of a star's life.

We are now faced with a problem. The cosmologists tell us that the Big Bang created only hydrogen and helium, and perhaps small amounts of lithium. We have seen that the major nuclear reaction in the Sun only converts hydrogen to helium, and produces nothing new, yet we know from our own world that elements heavier than lithium do exist – nearly a hundred of them, in fact. There must be some process, therefore, by which these other elements are created. The answer lies in what happens in a star's core once all the hydrogen has been used up. This does not happen until late on in the lifetime of a typical star, for example after about 10 million years for the Sun. As we have seen, although the largest and most massive stars burn brightest, the higher rate of the nuclear reactions in their core (higher because the pressure, and hence the temperature, is higher) mean that they burn their supply of hydrogen fuel much more quickly. Thus, contrary perhaps to expectation, the longest-lived stars in the Universe are not the giants, which live for just a few hundred million years, but the dwarfs, which are able to burn, albeit feebly, for many billions of years. Eventually, even a dwarf star will begin to use up all the hydrogen available to it in the core, and the nuclear reactions described above will slow down and ultimately cease. However, the star is not yet ready to cool into obscurity. As the rate at which helium is produced drops, so does the amount of energy released, and the radiation pressure that holds up the outer layers. The fragile equilibrium has collapsed – and so does the core of the star. As the core collapses, its temperature increases, heating the region around the core where hydrogen is still burning and causing an increase in the rate of reaction there. This actually has the effect of increasing the radiation pressure on the outer layers of the star, causing them to expand; the star has become a red giant like Betelgeux in Orion (where this story began). When this happens to the Sun, it will expand so much that it will swallow the inferior planets Mercury and Venus; Earth and Mars, while they may not be destroyed, will certainly be made uninhabitable. Those with a taste for long-term planning may want to start thinking now, for we have only a few billion years left!

Meanwhile, as the core temperature rises it may reach the temperature needed to ignite a different kind of reaction. This point, known as the 'helium flash', occurs when the temperature is sufficient for helium nuclei, until now inert, to begin to combine. Two helium nuclei combine to form an unstable form of beryllium, but if a third helium nucleus collides with the beryllium nucleus before it splits apart, then carbon is formed; a fourth collision produces oxygen. Each of these reactions liberates energy, providing enough energy – and hence enough radiation pressure – to stem the collapse. A whole multitude of reactions are now possible, depending on the star's temperature (which depends on its mass). The temperature decreases as we move away from the core, and we may find regions in which different reactions are occurring at the same time in some large-scale balancing act. Eventually, however, the helium at the core will run out, and the collapse will begin again, until the temperature reaches sufficient levels to start the burning of a different nuclear fuel.

This cannot continue for ever, since eventually the star will run out of straws to grasp at, and no last-minute rescue of re-ignition will halt the collapse. Only one of three paths is now open to the star. First, if its mass is less than 1.4 solar masses, the core temperature never gets high enough to clear all the hurdles and ignite all possible reactions. At some point, maybe even as early as after hydrogen burning, the core temperature never reaches the necessary level to start the next series of reactions. The star's core collapses and it sheds its outer layers, which expand to form a planetary nebula.[7] This is very much a transient stage, lasting only a few hundred thousand years, after which the expelled material diffuses away. Attuned as we are to our everyday timescale of hours, that seems like an unimaginably long time, but astronomically speaking it is a mere blink of an eye. The core collapse, in the meantime, cannot be stopped by radiation pressure and continues until the star-matter attains a huge density. Once electrons become extremely close together, they exert a pressure on one another which keeps them an 'allowed' distance apart, in the same way that if you press two marbles together a force prevents them from passing through each other. A force is thus produced which prevents the star-matter from being compressed any further. The collapse is halted, and we are left with a white dwarf star which slowly radiates its remaining energy into space as it cools. This will be the eventual fate of our own Sun. It is difficult to imagine just how dense these objects are. The usual analogies don't really enable us to comprehend the sheer scale of these objects: a teaspoonful of white dwarf material would weigh the same as a steamroller; a white dwarf with the same mass as the Earth would be just a few kilometres across. Yet even these Leviathans are not the densest objects in the Universe.

For stars with a mass greater than 1.4 solar masses, the temperature of the core is high enough to allow a sequence of further nuclear reactions, eventually leading to the production of iron. Up until this point, the various reactions have all released energy, which has provided the radiation pressure that has supported the outer layers of the star and prevented gravitational collapse. However, iron is the most stable nucleus, so to convert it to any heavier element would mean using up energy. Once iron has been produced, therefore, nuclear reactions in the core simply cease, and the star collapses at a prodigious rate. This collapse, as before, has the effect of heating the core, but this time there are no new nuclear reactions to stop the collapse, no matter how high the temperature is. As the core compresses, the protons contained within it are forced to combine with electrons to form neutrons. Once this occurs, in stars of less than 3 solar masses, neutron degeneracy pressure (like the electron pressure described above, but stronger) halts the collapse. At this point the core cannot be compressed further, and the entire collapse stops dead. This stellar emergency stop causes a celestial pile-up. A vast rebound occurs, and the infalling material explodes outwards in an incredibly powerful outburst – a supernova. All of this happens in a period of just a few seconds, and the energy involved is immense. It is in these extreme conditions that reactions take place which form elements heavier than iron, which are immediately shot out into the surrounding environment, leaving the core behind as a neutron star. If it is difficult to wrap one's mind around the weight and density of a white dwarf, then it is impossible to grasp that of a neutron star. As with many of the numbers and scales encountered in astronomy, there is simply no equivalent in our everyday world. Suffice it to say that an eggcup of neutron star material would weigh several thousand million tonnes! Just one last possible ending remains. If the star has more than 3 solar masses, then nothing can stop the collapse of the core and a black hole is produced.

The fantastic energies released in a supernova bring us almost full circle. As the energy and the material released spread out into the surrounding interstellar medium, shock waves travel outwards. Where these shock waves encounter interstellar clouds of dust and gas, they may cause the dust and gas to compress, which may spark a whole new wave of star formation. More importantly, elements heavier than helium have been created and added to the mix from which future stars will form. Our Sun is believed to be a third-generation star: all the elements within it, apart from the two lightest, hydrogen and helium, have been manufactured in previous generations of stars which have ended their lives as supernovae. All the heavier elements in the rest of the Solar System, including the Earth, and everything on it, had the same origin. In the words of the late Carl Sagan, 'We are stardust.'

ACKNOWLEDGEMENTS

Thanks to Dr Stuart Clark of University of Hertfordshire, Catherine and Ged Burgess and Ali Braden.

NOTES

1. The neatness of this system was somewhat spoiled by the omission of J, simply to make the sequence terminate at the correct letter.

2. Angular momentum is a measure of how difficult it is to stop something rotating: a system with high angular momentum would take a lot of force to stop it rotating, while a system with low angular momentum would require less force. It is determined by the mass and rotational speed of the rotating object, and its distance from the centre of rotation. An elephant on a roundabout would have a greater angular momentum than a mouse at the same distance from the centre.

3. A star's stellar wind is the outflow of material from its surface which, in the case of the Sun, is responsible for the aurorae or northern lights, and the Van Allen radiation belts surrounding the Earth.

4. The T Tauri stage takes it name from the class of variable stars whose prototype is T Tauri.

5. Hydrogen burning is the name given to the conversion of hydrogen to helium by nuclear fusion; the name 'burning' reflects the fact that hydrogen is the 'fuel' for the process.

6. Deuterium occurs on Earth as one in every thousand or so hydrogen molecules, and is utilized in our own, rather more small-scale nuclear reactors.

7. Planetary nebulae get their name from their appearance in a telescope at low power, which is similar to that of a planetary disk; this is somewhat unfortunate as they have nothing to do with planets!

FG Sagittae: A Star Evolving While We Watch

HELEN J. WALKER

When astronomers talk about stellar evolution (how stars change with time), they are normally talking about a slow process, about changes that take place over millions of years. Very occasionally we are fortunate enough to see drastic changes in a star that cause variations in temperature or brightness so sudden that the star moves significantly across the Hertzsprung–Russell (HR) diagram. The HR diagram (Figure 1) is the basic tool for graphically representing stellar evolution, using brightness (or, equivalently, magnitude or luminosity) and temperature (or, equivalently, colour or spectral type) to locate stars in such a way that different regions of the diagram contain stars at distinct stages of their lifetimes. Most stars spend most of their life on the main sequence, a swathe stretching diagonally across the HR diagram from top left to bottom right. Normally, as a star grows old it moves into the red giant/supergiant region and then into the blue supergiant region, having shed material to form around itself a planetary nebula (named for its roughly circular appearance, but nothing to do with planets). The star then gradually becomes less bright, dimming to a white dwarf. FG Sagittae (FG Sge: RA 20^h 11^m 55^s.8, dec. +20° 20′ 05″, 2000.0 co-ordinates) is a very rare example of the radical shift that occurs when a star evolves back from a blue supergiant into a red supergiant. Amazingly, in FG Sagittae we can watch this happening – at one point the star's temperature was decreasing by 250 K per year! Its behaviour has given rise to statements such as 'the star entered the instability strip in 1962' and 'the star became an R CrB variable in 1992'. In the time between me writing this article and you reading it, some new phenomenon may have occurred, the star is changing so fast.

Before 1900, FG Sagittae was assumed to be a normal old blue star; we would now say that it was in the process of becoming a white dwarf, the usual fate for a small (1 solar mass) star. A star becomes a white dwarf

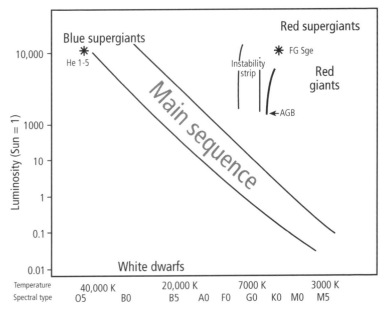

Figure 1. The Hertzsprung–Russell (HR) diagram, showing the main regions in which stars are located, including the asymptotic giant branch (AGB), to the right of the instability strip. Most stars spend most of their life on the main sequence, moving into the red giant/super-giant region as they grow old. They then move from right to left towards the blue supergiant region, having lost material to form a planetary nebula, after which they gradually dim to become a white dwarf. The initial position of FG Sagittae (labelled He 1-5) and the reddest position (labelled FG Sge, reached in about 1996) are shown.

because it is unable to burn the nuclear fuel (hydrogen or helium) it needs to create the energy it emits. The star gradually becomes less bright and shrinks in size. FG Sagittae was obviously an old star since it was surrounded by a planetary nebula, which it created 6000 to 10,000 years ago. The nebula has a completely normal composition, showing that up to then the star had been following a completely normal evolutionary track, similar to the Sun's. At the start of the 20th century, the star was referred to as the central star of the planetary nebula He 1-5, since it was *not* known to be variable; the designation FG Sagittae was applied to it only after it had been established that the star was variable, but I shall call it FG Sagittae throughout, to avoid confusion.

HOW IT STARTED

'Suddenly', in 1901, FG Sagittae started to get brighter, and throughout most of the 20th century the magnitude of the star increased. Great care is needed when measuring its magnitude, since not only does the light from the planetary nebula influence the measurement, but there is also another star, by chance, only 8″ away from FG Sagittae itself. A. van Genderen and A. Gautschy investigated the early behaviour of the star, using archival photographic plates of the region of Sagitta where FG Sagittae is located. The magnitude of the star on these plates, the photographic magnitude (m_{pg}), is very similar to the modern blue magnitude (B or m_B). They determined that FG Sagittae had a photographic magnitude of 13.96 in 1900, 13.47 in 1910, and had reached 10.73 in 1950. The maximum blue magnitude was 9.45, achieved in September 1967 (Figure 2(a)), and the star started to decrease in brightness after that. The maximum magnitude in the visual band (V or m_V) was 8.89, reached in 1971 (Figure 2(b)).

The B and V magnitudes peaked at different times because the star was changing colour, from blue to red, as well as changing brightness. The spectral type of the star was changing because the temperature changed (Figure 3). In October 1955 FG Sagittae was classified as B4 I (the 'I' signifying a supergiant), then in mid-1960 it was classified as B9 Ia, in mid-1965 it was judged to be A3 Ia, in mid-1967 it was A5 Ia, and F5 Ib in 1972. Karl Henize took the first spectrum of FG Sagittae in 1955, and in 1960 George Herbig started a series of spectral observations with the new 3-metre Shane Telescope at Lick Observatory. These observations show a star moving across the HR diagram, changing from a blue supergiant into a red supergiant. Between 1955 and 1967 FG Sagittae cooled from around 12,300 K to 8300 K, and at one time in 1965 FG Sagittae was cooling by 250 K per year (shown by the very steep change in $B - V$ in Figure 3). The cooling appears to have stopped now, and the minimum temperature was around 4500–5500 K. However, there are suggestions that the temperature may recently have increased a little. The sharp drop at the end of Figure 3 shows that the star became much redder when it emitted a cloud of dust.

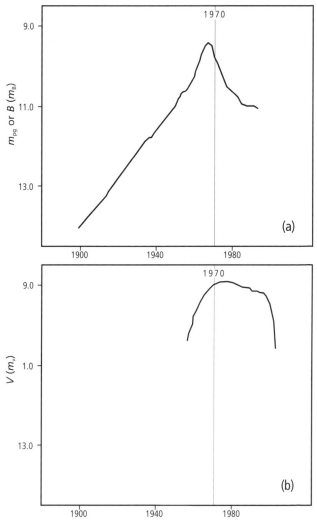

Figure 2. Changes in the magnitude of FG Sagittae during the 20th century: (a) photographic (m_{pg}) and blue (*B* or m_B) magnitudes, which are for practical purposes identical for this star; and (b) visual (*V* or m_V) magnitude. The vertical lines show where the year 1970 starts, to emphasize the different dates of the *B* and *V* peak magnitudes. The steep drop at the end of the curve in (b) comes from measurements made after 1992, when fading episodes commenced, and suggest that the dust clouds emitted by the star never completely cleared away.

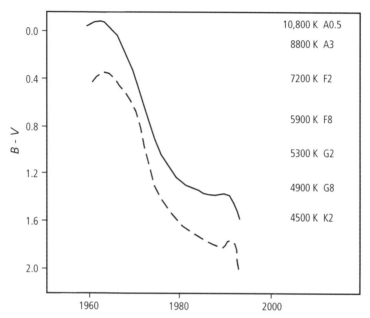

Figure 3. The change in colour of FG Sagittae during the 20th century, and the associated changes in temperature and spectral class. The dashed line is the observed colour $B-V$, determined by subtracting the V magnitude (in Figure 2(b)) from the B magnitude (in Figure 2(a)). The higher the value of $B-V$, the redder the colour. The solid line represents the actual stellar colour, corrected for the effect of the dust between the observer and the star (the interstellar reddening). The spectral type and the temperature of the star are shown on the right axis. The sharp drop in the early 1990s corresponds to a pronounced reddening as the star emitted a cloud of dust, causing it to fade.

OBSERVATIONS OF VARIABILITY

Van Genderen and Gautschy showed that FG Sagittae was already variable in 1934, with a period of 5.76 days and an amplitude (from maximum to minimum brightness) of around 0.4 magnitudes. In 1943 the period was 4.48 days and the amplitude around 0.2 magnitudes. The period has been unsteadily increasing until the 1980s, when it reached around 85 to 120 days. As will be shown later, FG Sagittae had passed through the Cepheid instability strip, a region in the HR diagram occupied by stars that pulsate with regular periods. The periods determined for Cepheid variables are directly related to the total energy (their luminosity) in a completely predictable way. A relationship between the period of FG Sagittae, its radius and its luminosity can be derived using theoretical models similar to those used for the Cepheid variables, but the Cepheid relationship itself does not apply here.

Then, in 1992, the character of the variability changed dramatically as FG Sagittae faded by several magnitudes. This type of behaviour is typical of R Coronae Borealis (R CrB) variable stars, which are red supergiants, usually with a temperature between 5000 and 9000 K. The fading appears to have caused the regular, small-amplitude variations in FG Sagittae to stop (unlike the classical R CrB stars, in which the small-amplitude variations continue whenever the stars are at maximum brightness). The fading is caused by the expulsion (and dispersal) of a cloud of dust particles from the atmosphere of the star. FG Sagittae has now faded around four or five times (Figure 4). The 1996 fading, when the star dropped by about 6 magnitudes and struggled slowly back to maximum light over several months, is very characteristic of R CrB stars (as pointed out by Andrew Vanture and Guillermo Gonzalez). Observations in the near infrared and with the Infrared Space Observatory (ISO) have detected the expelled dust, which has a temperature of around 700 to 1000 K, similar to the clouds emitted by R CrB stars.

COMPOSITION OF FG SAGITTAE

One essential characteristic of the R CrB stars is that their atmospheres are very rich in the element carbon (chemical symbol C). Thomas Blöcker and Detlef Schönberner have stated that FG Sagittae can be said to have been carbon-rich since 1981. There are features called the Swan bands due to carbon molecules (C_2) in the spectrum, showing that there is a lot of carbon in the star's atmosphere, but these particular features are not normally found in R CrB stars. However, the other characteristic feature of the composition of an R CrB star is that it is 'hydrogen-deficient', and this does not appear to be the case for FG Sagittae (yet). In 1974 Robert Kraft pointed out that in spectra of FG Sagittae obtained in 1960 the hydrogen lines were strong, showing that the star was still rich in hydrogen, but the lines now appeared to be get-

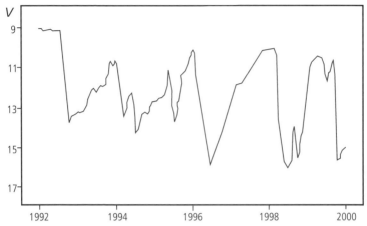

Figure 4. The light curve of FG Sagittae from 1992 to 1999, as measured in the V magnitude. The curve is the result of thousands of observations by amateur astronomers around the world. Four fading episodes are apparent, and the start of a fifth towards the end of 1999.

ting weaker. The spectrum obtained by T. Kipper and V. Klochkova in 1998 shows strong hydrogen lines (in emission) from FG Sagittae. They commented that spectral lines from some elements characteristic of R CrB stars were not present. Robert Kraft showed that lines from ionized iron and titanium (Fe II and Ti II lines) had become stronger over a five-year period.

After 1967, lines of ionized elements such as yttrium, zirconium, cerium and lanthanum (Y II, Zr II, Ce II, La II) appeared in the spectrum of FG Sagittae, and by 1972 these elements had become 25 times more abundant than in the Sun's atmosphere. These elements are known as s-process elements, created deep in the central core of a star by the slow-neutron capture process. (The process involves neutrons being released by ^{13}C when it combines with an alpha particle to become oxygen (^{16}O), which are absorbed by iron atoms to create heavier elements.) In the 1990s the abundances of the s-process elements in FG Sagittae again increased, on this occasion to a level several hundred times higher than their original values. The enhancement occurred as convection currents brought material from deep within the star up to its atmosphere.

IS FG SAGITTAE UNIQUE?

FG Sagittae is almost, but not quite, unique. There is a very small hand-ful of peculiar stars which may be similar, including one that could be performing a similar dash across the HR diagram. When FG Sagittae was first recognized as being unusual, it was classified as a nova because of its increase in brightness, until George Herbig and Alexander Boyarchuk noted that the spectrum was not 'nova-like'. More recently a Japanese amateur astronomer found a star which he thought was a nova as it brightened by several magnitudes. It was first called Sakurai's Object after its discoverer, although it now has the (not much used) designation V4334 Sgr because it has been established to be variable. Sakurai's Object has several features in common with FG Sagittae. Its sudden rise in brightness was even more dramatic than that of FG Sagittae: it has brightened by about 10 magnitudes (around 1 magni-tude per year). There are also recent observations of Sakurai's Object making an R CrB-like deep fade, and it has the hydrogen deficiency expected of an R CrB star as well as an overabundance of carbon. As with FG Sagittae, there have also been reports of enhancements of the s-process elements. However, Sakurai's Object is more massive than FG Sagittae, so its evolution will be somewhat different, and Sakurai's Object was a white dwarf before it brightened.

Another star classified as a nova because of its sudden brightening was V605 Aquilae. It underwent an outburst early in the 20th century, brightening by four magnitudes in 1919, and subsequently showed signs of the deep fading expected from an R CrB variable star. The star is carbon-rich and, as with FG Sagittae, it is the central star of a plan-etary nebula (designated A58). However, V605 Aquilae is more massive than FG Sagittae, and is now identified as an early carbon-rich Wolf–Rayet star.

V854 Centauri is an example of a recently discovered R CrB vari-able which has a mild hydrogen deficiency (hydrogen lines are visible in the spectrum) and an enhanced carbon abundance. The star is very active, showing many deep fades (around one every year) and a small-amplitude, regular variation of around 40 days caused by the pulsations in the star's atmosphere. V854 Centauri was twice 'discovered' by nova searchers, who detected its rise in brightness as it recovered from a deep fade.

WHAT HAS HAPPENED TO FG SAGITTAE?

As was stated earlier, the star FG Sagittae created a planetary nebula when it was a red giant several thousand years ago, and has now moved back to the same general region of the HR diagram. However, the track is not quite the same as before, since hydrogen is no longer the fuel, and the star is on what is called the asymptotic giant branch (AGB). This is the second time FG Sagittae has reached this area of the HR diagram, so it is really a post-AGB star – what is sometimes called a 'born-again' AGB star. As the star moved horizontally across the HR diagram, it was cooling down and the radius of the atmosphere was increasing, so the overall luminosity did not change significantly. The appearance of the carbon enrichment and the s-process elements show that the atmosphere has been stirred and mixed by enormous convection cells in the atmosphere, which drag up material from deep inside the star and bring it to the upper layers of the atmosphere. The deep fades imply that clouds of dust are being produced (occasionally) near the surface of the star, and that the star is losing material from its atmosphere.

According to van Genderen and Gautschy, a helium flash took place in FG Sagittae around 1850, when the star was near the main sequence in the HR diagram, which converted the star from burning hydrogen to burning helium in a shell around the central core. The star became bluer and dimmer at first, reaching 45,000 K (spectral type O3) in 1880 (Figure 5). The star then 'raced' across the HR diagram in around 70 years, and ended by crossing one of the Cepheid instability strips. Blöcker and Schönberner have produced theoretical models for a star such as FG Sagittae which show that it undergoes a series of thermal pulses, the helium flash occurring as part of the last thermal pulse. These models show that the star is around 0.6 times as massive as the Sun.

THE NEXT STAGE – WHERE EVERYONE CAN HELP

The discovery of the most recent example of a fast evolving star, Sakurai's Object, was made by an amateur astronomer (Yukio Sakurai). Amateur astronomers are much more likely to spot 'new' stars like this because, even though these events are rare, amateurs have the time to

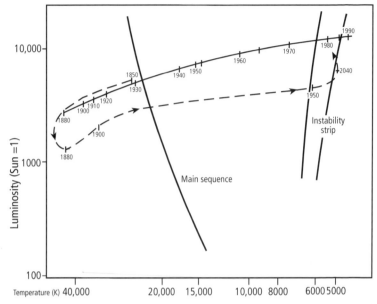

Figure 5. The track of FG Sagittae across the HR diagram, according to the compilation of data by van Genderen and Gautschy. The main sequence and the Cepheid instability strip are shown. The track is compared with results from a model produced by Icko Iben in 1984, matched so that minimum brightness in the model occurs in 1880, as it did in FG Sagittae. The model predicts a smooth fast dash across the HR diagram, slowing down when the instability strip is reached, and then a slow turn-around to higher temperatures. The data show that the speed across the diagram is variable (after 1950, tick marks are shown every five years), but FG Sagittae has slowed down significantly in the last 25 years. It has moved to slightly cooler temperatures since 1990, and the most recent estimates of the temperature suggest that it may be a little hotter than the minimum value, but this trend is not certain yet.

survey the skies for changes. Professional astronomers have always had problems explaining how R CrB stars are created, for it is difficult to explain the lack of hydrogen. The more examples we can find the better, since with stars like Sakurai's Object and FG Sagittae we may actually be able to watch the change to an R CrB star, stage by stage.

Andrew Vanture and Guillermo Gonzalez, in a 1999 review of FG Sagittae, presented a figure compiled from thousands of observations by amateur astronomers spanning three episodes of deep fading since 1992 (a fourth fading episode started in September 1999). Without the work of amateur astronomers taking measurements each night (something professional astronomers can rarely do), the picture would be incomplete, in particular the double trough in the 1994 episode, which might have a similar cause to the fading episode in 1999. We still have very little idea of how the dust that causes these fades is produced. We are not even certain where the dust is created – inside the stellar atmosphere, just outside, or a long way away from the surface of the star. Monitoring objects like FG Sagittae and V854 Centauri, which undergo frequent fading episodes, is vital for a better understanding of the mechanism.

Theory places FG Sagittae in the Cepheid instability strip, so a better estimate of the distance could result from determining the period of FG Sagittae's pulsations. Although the pulsations are not of the type that give rise to classic Cepheid variability, they can be modelled. Currently the distance is estimated to be 8150, 8800 or 12,700 light-years, depending on which research group, set of assumptions and computer model you go along with. When I was studying hotter hydrogen-deficient stars for my doctoral thesis, I observed BD +13°3224 (since known as V652 Herculis), which had a period of around 2½ hours. Some colleagues observed it about 10 years later and found a slightly shorter period, which was caused by the radius of the star decreasing (and the temperature increasing) as the star evolved away from the R CrB star region. The period decrease, just over one second per year, was consistent with the predictions based on the theoretical models, but also showed the care that was needed in making the observations. As stated earlier, the period of FG Sagittae is changing (and appears to have ceased at present), so continual, careful monitoring is needed. The British Astronomical Association Variable Star Section show a series of observations of FG Sagittae from 1984 to 1999 on their Website (http://www.telf-ast.demon.co.uk/), and the small-amplitude, regular variations in the 1980s are very obvious. Such a long series of data points is essential for finding the period of the star, and for monitoring the changes.

FG Sagittae has yet to complete its transition to an R CrB star. Currently it still has a little too much hydrogen, and it shows spectral features that indicate the presence of molecular carbon (the Swan bands), which R CrB stars do not. FG Sagittae is definitely not a nova, yet there is still a chance that it might become a carbon-rich Wolf–Rayet star – or it may do something else, so the star will be worth watching for a while yet. We may not have long to wait for something new to occur.

FURTHER READING

Descriptive articles

Marcus Chown (1997), *New Scientist* 7 June, p. 17.

Robert Kraft (1974), *Sky and Telescope* **48** (July), 17.

Andrew Vanture and Guillermo Gonzalez (1999), *Astronomy & Geophysics* **40**, 1.14.

Technical articles

T. Blöcker and D. Schönberner (1997), *Astronomy and Astrophysics* **324**, 991.

A. M. van Genderen and A. Gautschy (1995), *Astronomy and Astrophysics* **294**, 453.

G. H. Herbig and A. A. Boyarchuk (1968), *Astrophysical Journal* **153**, 397.

The Hubble Constant: Consensus at Last?

IAIN NICOLSON

When we look beyond the confines of the Local Group, the small group of galaxies to which the Milky Way Galaxy belongs, we find that all other galaxies, or clusters of galaxies, are receding from us at speeds that are proportional to their distances. That galaxies are receding in this way was first demonstrated, in 1929, by American astronomer Edwin P. Hubble. There is nothing unique about our viewpoint, however. Any observer on any galaxy would see the same general picture. Each galaxy, or cluster of galaxies, is receding from every other one because the Universe as a whole is expanding.

When the speeds at which galaxies are receding are plotted against their distances, the resulting graph (at least, in an idealized universe) is a straight line, the slope of which is known as the Hubble constant. The Hubble constant, which is denoted by the symbol H, is the constant of proportionality that relates the recessional velocity of a galaxy (v) to its distance (d), and the relationship between v, d and H, which can be written as $v = H \times d$, has come to be known as the Hubble law. The Hubble constant is usually expressed in kilometres per second per megaparsec (km/s/Mpc), where 1 megaparsec (10^6 parsecs) is equivalent to 3.26 million light years, or 3.09×10^{19} km. For example, if the value of H were 100 km/s/Mpc, a galaxy at a distance of 10 megaparsecs would be receding at a speed of 1000 km/s, a galaxy at a distance of 100 Mpc would be receding at 10,000 km/s, and so on.

In addition to defining the rate at which the Universe is expanding, the Hubble constant also gives a guide to its age. The widely accepted Big Bang theory suggests that the Universe originated a finite time ago by expanding from a hot, dense state of infinite compression. As the Universe expanded and cooled, galaxies formed from clumps of matter that were denser than their surroundings. The ongoing expansion of the Universe has continued to carry the galaxies away from one another ever since. If the Universe has been expanding at a constant rate (galaxies receding from one another at constant velocities), the time taken for any particular galaxy to recede to its present distance will be equal to its distance (d) divided by its velocity (v). Because the velocity of recession of a galaxy is proportional to its distance, all galaxies will have taken precisely the same amount of time to reach their present distances (for example, if galaxy B is 10 times farther away than galaxy A, its velocity is 10 times greater, and it will therefore have taken the same amount of time to traverse that greater distance). The time taken for the galaxies to recede to their present distances, assuming a constant rate of expansion, is known as the Hubble time, and is equal to $1/H$, the reciprocal of the Hubble constant (since $H = v/d$, $1/H = d/v$). For example, if H had a value of 100 km/s/Mpc, the value of the Hubble time would be $1/H = 1$ Mpc (3.09×10^{19} km) divided by 100 km/s = 9.8 billion years.

If the rate of expansion is slowing down, the age of the Universe will be less than the Hubble time (galaxies will have been moving apart faster in the past and so will have taken less time to reach their present distances). Conversely, if the rate of expansion were accelerating, the actual age would be greater than the Hubble time (galaxies would have been moving apart more slowly in the past and would have taken longer to reach their present distances).

The Hubble constant is one of the key cosmological parameters, its value crucial to our understanding of the scale, expansion rate and age of the Universe. Yet in most models of the Universe it is not a 'constant' in the sense of having a fixed value for all time. For example, if the Universe were expanding at a constant rate, the velocities of the galaxies would remain the same but their distances would increase. Consequently H ($= v/d$) would decrease with time. The symbol H_0 is used to denote the value of the Hubble constant at the present stage (or 'epoch') in the history of the Universe.

Establishing the value of H_0 has proved to be a daunting task, the difficulty of the challenge reflected in the fact that the measured value has changed by a factor of ten during the past seventy years. Whereas it is possible to measure the recessional velocities of galaxies to a good degree of accuracy through spectroscopic studies of the wavelengths of their spectral lines, measuring their distances has proved to be far more difficult. Furthermore, mutual gravitational attractions between neighbouring groups, clusters and superclusters of galaxies superimpose individual, or 'peculiar', motions on top of the idealized smooth general expansion of the Universe (the so-called 'Hubble flow'). Consequently it is necessary to study galaxies out to very great distances (at least several hundred million light years) before peculiar motions can be ignored and a 'genuine' value of H_0 measured.

MEASURING DISTANCES

There are two fundamental approaches to measuring the distances of galaxies: luminosity distance and diameter distance. The luminosity distance method relies on identifying objects of known luminosity – 'standard candles' – embedded within galaxies. Because, in the absence of any absorption of light by matter lying along the line of sight, the apparent brightness of a light source decreases in proportion to the square of its distance (e.g. if its distance is doubled, its apparent brightness is reduced to one-quarter of its previous value), the distance of the source, and hence the distance of the galaxy within which it is embedded, can be calculated by comparing its observed brightness with its known, or assumed, inherent luminosity. The diameter distance method relies on comparing the apparent angular diameter of a known type of object with an assumed value for its physical diameter, and working out how far away it must be in order to appear as small as it does.

Although beautifully simple in principle, these methods are very difficult to apply in practice. An ideal distance indicator would be a set of objects that are highly luminous (or very large), in order to be detectable at very great distances; very abundant, to provide plenty of examples in each galaxy; and have identical luminosities (or diameters). In practice, the objects that are used as indicators have a spread of luminosities (or diameters), and the most luminous indicators are sparsely scattered throughout the Universe. In addition to the sheer difficulty of identifying faint objects in remote galaxies and measuring their brightnesses or angular sizes, it is hard to make accurate calibrations of the various distance indicators, to allow for any absorption or scattering of light that may occur between the source and the observer, and to eliminate observational biases and selection. Little wonder, then, that measuring the distances of galaxies, and so deriving a value for the Hubble constant, has provided observational astronomers with one of their greatest challenges, a challenge that was first taken up early in the 20th century.

HUBBLE AND THE EXPANDING UNIVERSE

In 1912, Vesto M. Slipher of the Lowell Observatory, Arizona, studied about fifty galaxies (or 'spiral nebulae' as they were known at that time) and found that most of them had redshifts in their spectra: the characteristic lines in their spectra had wavelengths longer than they would have had these galaxies been at rest relative to the Earth. If it could be assumed that these displacements resulted from a Doppler effect (whereby light waves from a receding source are stretched to longer wavelengths), then these results suggested that most of the galaxies are receding from us. At that time, however, no one had measured the distance of a 'spiral nebula', and it was not known whether they were members of our own Milky Way system or separate star systems in their own right.

Four years earlier, Henrietta Leavitt of the Harvard College Observatory detected and studied Cepheid variables (pulsating stars that increase and decrease in luminosity in a periodic fashion) in the Small Magellanic Cloud (a star system that is now known to be one of our nearest neighbour galaxies). Because all these stars were at essentially the same distance from the Earth, their apparent brightnesses gave a true indication of their relative luminosities – the brighter stars really were the more luminous ones. Leavitt found that the more luminous the Cepheid, the longer its period of variation. This period–luminosity law enabled astronomers to use Cepheids as 'standard candles' for distance measurement. If Cepheids could be found in so-called spiral nebulae, and their periods of variation determined, then their inherent luminosities could be deduced from the period–luminosity law. By comparing their observed apparent brightnesses with their inherent luminosities, their distances – and hence the distance of the star system within which they were embedded – could be calculated.

Using very long exposure photography on the 100-inch (2.5-metre) reflector on Mt Wilson, California, Edwin Hubble succeeded, in 1923, in detecting and measuring a dozen Cepheids in M31 (the Andromeda Galaxy) and M33 (the Triangulum Spiral). From these data he determined that both objects lay at distances of around 900,000 light-years (an underestimate, as it subsequently turned out) – well beyond the confines of our own Milky Way system. This was the first proof that at least some of the spiral nebulae were separate star systems – galaxies in their own right.

During the rest of that decade Hubble studied some 18 spiral galaxies, and by 1929 had found that the more distant ones had larger redshifts in their spectra. He proposed that galaxies are receding from us with speeds that are proportional to their distances, and, working with his colleague Milton L. Humason, he carried out further observations that yielded a value of 550 km/s/Mpc for what is now called the Hubble constant.

A fundamental error in the distance scale was uncovered in 1952 by Walter Baade of the Mt Wilson and Palomar Observatories. Baade realized that there were two species, or populations, of Cepheid variable (now known as Type I and Type II). Both types followed a similar period–luminosity relationship, but the Type I Cepheids were inherently about five times as luminous as Type II Cepheids of the same period. Hubble had used the period–luminosity law applicable to Type II Cepheids, whereas in fact he had been observing the more luminous Type I Cepheids in the galaxies that he had been studying. To be as faint as they appeared, Hubble's Cepheids had to be about twice as far away as he had thought. This increased the distances of all galaxies by a factor of about two (the distance to the Andromeda Galaxy, for example, went up to about 2 million light years) and halved the value of H_0.

ONGOING ATTEMPTS

During the next few decades, astronomers struggled to make reliable measurements of the distances of galaxies. A degree of uncertainty remained as to the true luminosities of Cepheids, and there were disputes about the extent to which the observed brightnesses of Cepheids were affected by the absorbing effect of dust in the host galaxy, in the Milky Way and, perhaps, in intergalactic space (the effects of dust can be reduced by observing in the infrared). Crucially, despite being typically ten thousand times as luminous as the Sun, Cepheids could not, and even now cannot, be detected in galaxies sufficiently remote to be sure of eliminating the effects of locally induced motions so as to measure the true 'Hubble flow'.

Cepheids are the pre-eminent example of a *primary* distance indicator – one that has been calibrated by measuring the distances and luminosities of objects of the same kind located within our own Galaxy. In order to determine the distances of galaxies that are too far away to be measured with the aid of Cepheids (or any other kind of primary indicator), *secondary* indicators have to be used. A secondary indicator is one whose properties have been calibrated by observing objects of that kind embedded within galaxies, the distances of which have been measured by means of primary indicators. To determine the distance scale of the Universe, astronomers first have to measure the distances of as many relatively nearby galaxies as possible, using Cepheids (or some other primary indicator). Then, knowing the distances of these galaxies, they can begin to calibrate the luminosities of the various other kinds of (secondary) distance indicator these galaxies contain. Provided their luminosities are sufficiently great, secondary indicators can then be identified in more remote galaxies, and used to measure their distances.

Among the secondary indicators are bright red or blue supergiant stars, supernovae (exploding stars), globular star clusters and bright H II regions (luminous nebulae). Particularly valuable is a class of supernova known as Type Ia. A Type Ia supernova is believed to occur in a close binary system in which one star is a white dwarf very close to the maximum allowed mass for a star of this kind. If the white dwarf drags enough mass from its companion to take it over the limit, it explodes in a catastrophic nuclear detonation, and reaches a peak luminosity equivalent to about five billion Suns. Because all Type Ia supernovae reach very similar peak luminosities, and are bright enough to be seen across billions of light-years, they potentially make very good distance indicators. Unfortunately, they are very rare events (a typical large galaxy is unlikely to have more than one or two such events per century).

Other secondary indicators involve the overall properties of galaxies themselves. Of particular importance is the Tully–Fisher relation, which relates the overall luminosity of a spiral galaxy to its rotational velocity (the rotational velocity can be measured by looking at Doppler shifts in the optical, infrared or radio emissions emanating from opposite sides of its disk). Essentially, the higher the rotation speed, the more luminous the galaxy (more massive galaxies contain more stars and so are more luminous than less massive ones; and the stronger gravitational fields of massive galaxies cause the stars and gas clouds in them to orbit at higher speeds). A relationship also exists between the overall luminosity of an elliptical galaxy, the range of velocities of its constituent stars, and the radius of the circle that contains half its total luminosity. Known as the fundamental plane, this relationship can be used as a means of determining distance.

Another important technique is surface brightness fluctuations, or 'graininess', in elliptical galaxies. Because of the presence of individual high-luminosity stars, the brightness of an elliptical galaxy varies from point to point across its surface, giving the galaxy a grainy appearance. The more distant the galaxy, the less grainy it appears because most (and at large enough distances, all) of its high-luminosity stars blend together into the unresolved general background brightness.

Throughout the 1950s, 60s, 70s and 80s, several groups of astronomers spent an immense amount of time and effort, using Cepheids and a range of other indicators, in attempting to establish a firm distance scale for the Universe, and so obtain a reliable value for the Hubble constant. In particular, Alan Sandage of the Carnegie Observatories in Pasadena and Gustav Tammann of the University of Basel, Switzerland, arrived at values of the Hubble constant in the region of 50 km/s/Mpc, whereas Gerard de Vaucouleurs of the University of Texas and Sidney van den Bergh of the Dominion Astrophysical Observatories in Vancouver came up with figures in the region of 100 km/s/Mpc. This factor-of-two difference between the two distance scales persisted for decades, each camp maintaining that its results were soundly rooted in observational data. Other observers weighed in with values that supported one camp or the other, or lay between the two extremes.

The factor-of-two uncertainty in the value of the Hubble constant implied a similar degree of uncertainty in the scale of the Universe and in its age. If H had a value of 100 km/s/Mpc, the Hubble time (the age of a Universe expanding from a Big Bang at a constant rate) was about 10 billion years; if H were 50 km/s/Mpc, the Hubble time would be twice this value, 20 billion years.

THE HUBBLE SPACE TELESCOPE PLAYS A CRUCIAL ROLE

The Earth's atmosphere impeded the efforts of ground-based astronomers to detect and identify remote, faint Cepheids. When the Hubble Space Telescope was launched in 1990, one of its prime tasks, the so-called Key Projects, was to identify as many Cepheids as possible in galaxies as remote as possible with the aim of getting a much better grip on the cosmological distance scale. The international Key Project team was headed by Wendy Freedman of the Carnegie Observatories in Pasadena, Jeremy Mould of the Australian National University and Robert Kennicutt of the University of Arizona. By 1994 they had detected Cepheids in the spiral galaxy M100 in the Virgo Cluster, and had arrived at a value of 56 million light years for its distance. This led them to deduce a value of H_0 of about 80 km/s/Mpc.

A separate team led by Alan Sandage used HST observations of Cepheids to calculate the distances of several galaxies in which Type Ia supernovae had been observed, and thereby calibrate their luminosities. Assuming that all supernovae of this type peaked at closely similar maximum luminosities, Sandage used observations of more distant supernovae to derive a value of 57 km/s/Mpc, a value that was later revised to 59 km/s/Mpc.

In 1999 the HST Key Projects Team announced its final results, based on observations of more than 800 Cepheids in 25 galaxies located within the Virgo Cluster and the Fornax Group. In addition, they had succeeded in identifying nearly 50 Cepheids in the spiral galaxy NGC 4603, which lies within the massive Centaurus Cluster (a cluster that is dragging the Local Group in its direction) and had deduced its distance to be 108 million light years. They used Cepheid distances to calibrate four key secondary indicators: the Tully–Fisher relation, Type Ia supernovae, the fundamental plane for elliptical galaxies and surface brightness fluctuations. They then used these indicators to determine the distances of galaxies out to, and beyond, 150 Mpc, and, by combining these measurements with redshift data, they arrived at a value for the Hubble constant of 71 ± 6 km/s/Mpc.

ALTERNATIVE APPROACHES

Two completely independent approaches that are showing great promise, and which can be used over vast distances, are based on gravitational lensing and on a phenomenon called the Sunyaev–Zel'dovich effect.

Gravitational lensing is a phenomenon that arises from Einstein's general theory of relativity, which assumes that massive clumps of matter distort, or curve, space in their vicinity. If a ray of light from a distant source, such as a quasar, passes close to, or through, a concentration of mass such as a galaxy or a cluster of galaxies, it will be deflected. Because rays of light passing at different distances from the centre of the mass distribution are deflected by differing amounts, the gravitational field of a concentration of mass can act like a lens to produce magnified, distorted or multiple images of a more distant source. If a compact source, lens and observer lie exactly in line, the source will appear as a ring (called an 'Einstein ring') when viewed by the observer. If the alignment is not quite perfect, double or multiple images of the source will be seen. Light will have followed slightly different paths to form the different images, and so will have travelled different distances from the source to the observer. If the source undergoes a characteristic variation in brightness, the different images will vary at different times, the time differences between the observed brightness changes depending on the different paths that the various rays have followed. Observations of this kind, together with a model of the distribution of mass in the lens, allow the ray paths to be computed and the distances of the lens and source to be calculated. If the redshift of the source and the lensing galaxy or cluster can be measured, a value of the Hubble constant can then be calculated. Measurements of this kind have tended so far to produce relatively low values for the Hubble constant.

The Sunyaev–Zel'dovich effect is a slight drop in the surface brightness of the cosmic microwave background radiation (a faint background of microwave photons that fills all of space and which originated in the Big Bang) that occurs when microwave photons pass through a cloud of high-temperature plasma of the kind that is known to exist inside many major clusters of galaxies. This plasma, which consists of atomic nuclei and electrons, typically has a temperature in the region of several hundred million degrees and radiates at X-ray wavelengths. When microwaves collide with fast-moving electrons, they bounce off (scatter) in random directions, just like colliding snooker balls. In collisions of this kind, one of the 'balls' usually gains energy and the other loses energy. As microwave background radiation passes through the plasma cloud, some photons are scattered to higher energies (shorter wavelengths) and others are scattered to lower energies (longer wavelengths). Consequently, the observed intensity of the background radiation is reduced at the characteristic wavelengths of the cosmic background and redistributed into longer and shorter wavelengths.

The amount of depletion (typically about 0.05% of the microwave intensity) is proportional to the number of electrons in the line of sight through the cloud. The intensity of the X-ray emission from the hot plasma, however, is proportional to the square of the number of electrons (if the density is doubled, the X-ray emission goes up by a factor of four). Because of these different dependences, measurements of the microwave depletion and X-ray intensity can be used to calculate the diameter of the plasma cloud. When the calculated diameter is compared with the observed angular diameter, the distance of the cluster can be determined completely independently of any conventional distance indicators. This information, combined with the redshifts of the cluster galaxies, leads to a value of the Hubble constant. This technique, which is still in its infancy, has so far produced values in the range 40–100 km/s/Mpc, with a mean value in the vicinity of 60 km/s/Mpc. Improved measurements from the Chandra X-ray Observatory and ground-based radio interferometers should produce more precise results in the next few years.

SUPERNOVAE AT HIGH REDSHIFTS

Two ongoing international projects – the Supernova Cosmology project (an international collaboration headed by Saul Perlmutter of Lawrence Berkeley Laboratory) and the High-redshift Supernova Search – have produced very interesting results in the last couple of years. Each project conducts repeated surveys of a large number of regions of the sky in order to identify Type Ia supernovae. Newly discovered supernovae are then studied in detail by the Hubble Space Telescope, and large ground-based instruments such as the 10-metre Keck Telescopes, in order to determine their light curves (plots of the variation of brightness with time) and redshifts. The observed light curves of remote supernovae are then matched to templates produced from observations of nearer supernovae in order to establish their peak luminosities.

So far, more than 80 supernovae have been measured, in galaxies with redshifts of up to about 1.2 (a galaxy with a redshift of 1 is observed now as it was when the Universe was half its present size). The resulting redshift–luminosity data yield a value for the Hubble constant of 65 km/s/Mpc.

The data from these two projects appear to indicate that remote supernovae are systematically fainter than would be the case if the Universe were decelerating. These results strongly suggest that the Universe will expand for ever, and appear to rule out the possibility that the Universe may cease to expand in the distant future and then collapse in a 'Big Crunch'. More controversially, they appear to imply that the Universe is expanding at an accelerating rate.

THE AGE PROBLEM

A few years ago, the best estimates for the ages of the oldest stars in our Galaxy (stars which lie within globular clusters) were in the range 14–18 billion years. At the same time, the best estimates for the Hubble constant seemed to be in the region of 75–80 km/s/Mpc. If those values were correct, the Hubble time ($=1/H$) would be about 12–13 billion years and the actual age of the Universe, assuming (as is conventionally believed) that gravity is slowing down the rate of expansion, somewhat less than that. For example, the Einstein–de Sitter model (which assumes that the Universe is just, but only just, capable of expanding for ever at an ever-decreasing rate) yields an age equal to two-thirds of the Hubble time: 8–9 billion years, if H_0 = 75–80 km/s/Mpc. These results appeared to imply that the Universe is younger than some of the stars it contains – a paradox that is often referred to as the 'age problem'. If these results were correct, either our estimates of the ages of the stars were in error, or the standard Big Bang model of the Universe was wrong (interestingly, the conflict could be resolved if it were assumed that the Universe was accelerating and, therefore, older than the Hubble time).

Results obtained by the Hipparcos satellite (a European satellite that undertook a programme of precise parallax measurements) and published in the late 1990s went some way towards resolving the conflict. For the first time, Hipparcos was able to obtain good trigonometrical parallax measurements for a number of Cepheids. The results indicated that Cepheids were about 10% farther away than had previously been thought. This implied that galaxies were about 10% farther away than had previously been estimated, and that the Hubble constant was about 10% less, and the Hubble time 10% greater, than previous determinations had indicated. Furthermore, Hipparcos measurements indicated that globular clusters were farther away than had been thought. Therefore their brightest stars were about 20% more luminous than had previously been believed and, because more luminous stars have shorter lifetimes, the ages of the globular clusters had to be lower than had previously been thought – possibly as low as 11–12 billion years.

As the year 1999 drew to a close, it appeared that most measured values of H were converging towards the range 60–70 km/s/Mpc. Values in this range imply Hubble times in the region of 14–16 billion years, and Einstein–de Sitter ages in the range 9–11 billion years. Given the uncertainties in the measurements and in the estimates of stellar ages, it looks as if the age problem is no longer a problem, provided the Universe is an ever-expanding one that is not decelerating too rapidly.

JUST WHEN YOU THOUGHT IT WAS SAFE . . .

Just as a consensus on the value of H_0 seemed to be emerging, new results have again sown seeds of doubt about the accuracy of the Cepheid distance scale. Astronomers have been looking for alternative primary indicators. One promising candidate is a class of stars known as 'red clumps'. These are reddish stars which are similar in mass to the Sun, but older and more highly evolved, and less luminous than the better-known red giants. They all have very similar luminosities and temperatures and, because distances to about a thousand of them have been measured by the Hipparcos satellite, their luminosities are very well known. Although less luminous than Cepheids, they are much more numerous, and are bright enough to be seen in globular clusters and nearby galaxies. Krzysztov Stanek, Peter Garnavich and Andrzej Udalski have used red clumps to measure the distances of the Large and Small Magellanic Clouds and the Andromeda Galaxy. Udalski's data imply that the Large Magellanic Cloud is about 12% closer to us than is indicated by Cepheid measurements, a result that is in line with similar discrepancies revealed by other observers using different techniques. These results raise the possibility that galaxies in general may be about 12% nearer than the Cepheid measurements suggest, and imply that the value of the Hubble constant may be about 12% higher, and the age of the Universe 12% lower, than the values mentioned above. Perhaps the 'age problem' is still a problem after all.

SUMMARY

At the time of writing (January 2000), it is too early to say whether or not the red clump data will have any material impact on the accepted value for H_0. For the moment, though, a degree of consensus appears to have emerged, with most measured values lying between 60 and 70 km/s/Mpc, and some of the strongest results clustering in the range 65–70 km/s/Mpc. Advances in instruments and techniques, ongoing refinements of the Cepheid distance scale, the emergence of new primary distance indicators, and the further development of alternative approaches such as gravitational lensing and the Sunyaev–Zel'dovich effect, should enable astronomers to home in ever closer to the 'correct' value of H_0.

Choosing that First Telescope

MARTIN MOBBERLEY

A perennial problem for the budding young astronomer is the cost of astronomical equipment. For many, the first awakening of an interest in astronomy occurs around the age of ten, when children can be somewhat fickle about hobbies, and rarely have hundreds of pounds to spend. For the young observer there are a number of pitfalls even once equipment has been acquired. Most nights (in the UK at least!) are cloudy and frequently cold, objects in the night sky always seem fainter and harder to find than one is led to believe, and auxiliary equipment (star charts, torches, thermal clothing, etc.) just add to the cost. But the subtle pleasures of astronomy will reward the patient beginner, whatever equipment he or she uses. However, patience alone will not cause a telescope to materialize out of thin air, and a telescope is what most beginners really want.

BINOCULARS

So is there a low-budget solution? The answer is, 'Yes'. Binoculars are often dismissed by beginners simply because they do not provide enough magnification to see fine detail on the Moon and planets, but they do have several advantages. Our leading visual discoverer, George Alcock (Figure 1), has used binoculars with apertures from 50 to 105 mm to discover five comets and five novae (Table 1). His last two discoveries were made from indoors while observing through a double-glazed window! He is undoubtedly a man of extraordinary patience and single-mindedness, but for those who do not possess these qualities in so great an abundance, his discoveries still show what can be achieved.

In the British climate, binoculars come into their own. Gaps in the cloud are often all you get, so equipment with a quick set-up time offers a distinct advantage, and there is no set-up time at all with binoculars – you simply pick them up and go outside. But not all binoculars are

Figure 1. The legendary George Alcock of Peterborough and his 25 × 105 (tripod-mounted) and 15 × 80 binoculars. [Courtesy of Richard McKim and the BAA Mars Section Archives]

Table 1. Binocular discoveries by George Alcock

Object	Discovery date
1959 Comet C/1959 Q1 (Comet Alcock 1959e)	August 24
1959 Comet C/1959 Q2 (Comet Alcock 1959f)	August 30
1963 Comet C/1963 F1 (Comet Alcock 1963b)	March 1
1965 Comet C/1965 S2 (Comet Alcock 1965h)	September 26
1967 HR Delphini (=Nova Delphini 1967)	July 8
1968 LV Vulpeculae (=Nova Vulpeculae 1968 No 1)	April 15
1970 V368 Scuti (=Nova Scuti 1970)	July 31
1976 NQ Vulpeculae (=Nova Vulpeculae 1976)	October 21
1983 Comet C/1983 H1 (Comet IRAS–Araki–Alcock 1983 d)	May 3
1991 Nova Herculis 1991	March 25

suitable for astronomy. What is required is maximum aperture with a magnification that is tolerable for a hand-held instrument. An excellent starting point is a pair of Russian 10 × 50s such as those manufactured by Helios, a company long associated with the making of affordable binoculars for astronomy. The '10 × 50' means that the magnification is ×10, and the aperture of each lens is 50 mm; the field of view is about 5°. Helios 10 × 50 binoculars cost around £100 – a far more worthwhile purchase, in my opinion, than an 60-mm refractor or a 100-mm reflector. (All prices in this article are for the beginning of the year 2000.)

At this point it is worth digressing to explain the minimum magnification that can be used with a telescope or binoculars. At night the pupil of the human eye dilates (expands) to compensate for the reduced light level. In a young person this dilation may extend to as much as 7 or 8 mm, but in older people 5 mm is more normal. Unfortunately, as we reduce the magnification of a telescope or binoculars the diameter of the bundle of rays leaving the eyepiece (known as the exit pupil) expands. If the exit pupil is larger than the eye's pupil, light will be wasted – not what we want for astronomy. The exit pupil is calculated by dividing the aperture by the magnification. Thus for 10 × 50 binoculars it is 50 mm/10 = 5 mm, so these binoculars will suit anyone whose pupil can dilate to 5 mm or more. Changing the formula around, dividing the aperture of any pair of binoculars by 5 mm gives a sensible minimum magnification for any aperture and for all ages. Suitable specifications for astronomy are therefore 10 × 50, 14 × 70 and 20 × 100. If the budget allows, always go for the largest aperture you can afford. Russian 15 × 70s can be acquired for about £150, and 20 ×80s for about £250. Tripod-mounted 20 × 80 binoculars have more than a hundred times the light-grasp of the naked eye, and stars of 11th magnitude can be seen. Whatever telescope you are using, you will rarely benefit from magnifications of more than ×200 because of the limitations of seeing. For small telescopes (150 mm or less) a maximum magnification equal to the aperture in millimetres is a sensible upper limit, although a lot depends on telescope quality and your own eyesight.

Another consideration is how easily binoculars can be hand-held. Most beginners will find that ×10 is a sensible magnification for shaky hands, and for higher magnifications a tripod mount is preferable. However, with experience, higher hand-held magnifications can be tolerated. George Alcock's favourite hand-held instrument is a pair of

20 × 60 Russian binoculars – despite being in his late eighties, he can cope with a magnification of ×20! In the last few years there have appeared image-stabilized binoculars, which compensate for the shaky hands of the observer. Canon were the first company to introduce these, in 1998, followed by Fujinon in 1999. These are amazing to use – simply press a button on the top of the binoculars and the rapid jiggling of the stars converts into a smooth gliding motion. Predictably, this technology is not cheap – around £800 for 15 × 45s.

Binocular astronomy can be most rewarding; an excellent article on observing variable stars with binoculars by Terry Moseley appeared in the *1997 Yearbook of Astronomy*. But even if serious observing is not your aim, using binoculars for sweeping the Milky Way and finding the brighter Messier and Caldwell objects is highly rewarding. Given the choice of spending £150 to £200 on a cheap 60-mm refractor, a 100-mm reflector or a decent pair of binoculars, I would always recommend the binoculars.

SMALL TELESCOPES

Having said that, beginners crave magnification. They want to see Saturn's rings, Jupiter's moons, the phases of Venus and fine details of the lunar surface. For observing these objects a telescope is required, but good telescopes are not cheap. For the beginner with £100 to £150 to spend, a 60-mm refractor will be the first choice. It certainly was for me – this was the largest refractor I could afford at the age of thirteen!

Some care is needed when deciding where to purchase a telescope. I would recommend steering clear of the high-street camera shop – instead, seek out your nearest specialist telescope dealer. Their where-abouts are readily available from advertisements in UK astronomy magazines. A list of UK and US dealers (by no means exhaustive) that I would highly recommend appears at the end of this article.

There is no doubt that a quality 60-mm refractor, such as those manufactured by Celestron and Meade, will give great pleasure to the beginner. Even low magnifications of ×30 or ×40 will clearly show the main wonders of the Solar System: the aforementioned phases of Venus, Jupiter's moons and main belts, Saturn's rings, and craters on the Moon. However, fine detail on the Moon and planets will require a larger aperture. A decent pair of binoculars will give greater rewards provided the observer exercises patience in hunting down the myriad subtle targets in the night sky – bright binocular variables, double stars like Albireo in Cygnus, and the brighter Messier and Caldwell objects. But understandably, young enthusiastic beginners will almost certainly put the Moon and planets high on their list of priorities.

At this point a word of warning is appropriate. *Never point a telescope or binoculars at the Sun.* For most people this is common sense; even staring directly at the Sun with the naked eye can cause permanent damage. However, the big danger is that some cheap telescopes come with unsafe 'dark glass' filters, advertised as suitable for solar viewing. These filters are far from suitable, as they fit into the eyepiece barrel where the concentrated heat can reach the filter. In addition, the worst type dim the visual image but let through the lethal infrared and ultraviolet rays, lulling the observer into a false sense of security. There are highly experienced observers who use expensive specialist equipment for observing the Sun (see Don Trombino's article in the *1994 Yearbook of Astronomy*), but they know precisely what they are doing. Every year someone permanently damages their eyesight by looking at the Sun – don't be next year's statistic!

Although the 60-mm refractor will reveal exciting views to the beginner, a larger-aperture instrument will show much more. Larger apertures mean a brighter image and more resolution. Table 2 shows how the theoretical resolution and magnitude limit improve for increasing aperture, whereas the field of view decreases (making fields harder to find). If finances allow, an 80-mm refractor (£300 to £400) will really open up the Universe. It should be stressed, however, that whatever the instrument, effort is required on the part of the observer. The patient and systematic tracking down of fainter and fainter targets, and notching up little observing successes, is the key to the rewards that astronomy offers; nothing succeeds like success, and little successes can be the stepping stones to bigger things. If you fail to locate that faint moon of Saturn or obscure star cluster, try again on the next clear night. Drawing clear, simple charts which you can easily use outside, a dim red torch so as not to ruin you night vision, and warm outer clothing are all important to success in astronomy. Thorough, methodical preparation combined with a patient tolerance of cloudy weather is essential!

The resolution of a telescope is simply the smallest angle that the telescope will resolve, and it is measured in arcseconds ($''$). Sixty arcseconds make one arcminute, and sixty arcminutes make one degree.

Table 2. Aperture, resolution and magnitude

Aperture, mm (inches)	Maximum resolution (arcseconds) at stated magnification	Maximum field of view at low (degrees)	Faintest stars visible (mag)
400 (16)	0.3 at >×240	1	16.5
300 (12)	0.4 at ×180	1.3	16
200 (8)	0.5 at >×120	2	15
100 (4)	1 at >×60	4	13.5
50 (2)	2 at >×30	8	12
7 (naked eye)	60	160	6

To give examples of what this means in practice, the full moon spans ½° or 1800″. Jupiter at its closest spans 50″, and its largest moon, Ganymede, spans 1″.8. One kilometre on the lunar surface spans about 0″.6. The theoretical best resolution of a telescope, or binoculars, can be calculated from the formula

Resolution (in arcseconds) = 116/Aperture (in millimetres)

Thus, for a telescope with an aperture of 116 mm, the resolution is 116/116 = 1″, while for a telescope with an aperture of 232 mm the resolution is 116/232 = 0″.5.

In theory, then, even a small amateur telescope can resolve impressive detail on the Moon and planets. If only life were that simple! Unfortunately we have the Earth's turbulent atmosphere to contend with. On a typical night stars will be seen to dance around, moving back and forth by several arcseconds. Observing the Moon at high power, you often feel as though you are looking at the bottom of a swimming pool. Lunar and planetary observers are constantly waiting for those fleeting moments when the atmosphere is stable and fine detail can be glimpsed, photographed or imaged. Because of this, large apertures are highly desirable – it is far easier to capture that fleeting glimpse of the fine detail when you have a lot of light available than when you don't.

In this regard, reflectors (telescopes that use a mirror to focus light) are far better value for money than refractors (telescopes that use a lens to focus light). To most non-astronomers a telescope is a refractor – something with a lens at one end. However, all the world's professional astronomers use reflectors, because they are far easier to manufacture with large apertures.

A single lens acts like a series of prisms, splitting the light into its component colours. In a single-lens refractor if you focus for the blue light, stars will be surrounded by a red halo, and you get a blue halo if you focus for the red. This characteristic is called chromatic aberration. Fortunately, if you buy a refractor from a reputable manufacturer such as Celestron or Meade, you will get a quality achromatic doublet lens – i.e. a second lens is used to correct the colour dispersion of the first. With this arrangement, red and blue light focus at precisely the same point, but other colours may produce halos or colour fringes around very bright stars or around the limb of the Moon. The apochromat is the ultimate refractor, usually featuring a lens with three components, and the colour correction is virtually perfect. However, you will need to spend £2000 for 100 mm of aperture – apochromats are for the connoisseur, or the wealthy amateur (Figure 2).

The reflector does not suffer from chromatic aberration, and it is cheaper than an equivalent aperture refractor. So why doesn't everyone go for a reflector? Well, most advanced amateurs and all professionals do, so I suspect that the following concerns are paramount in the mind of the beginner when choosing that first telescope:

1. Surely the secondary mirror partially blocking the light path must cause problems?
2. I've heard that refractors are as good as larger reflectors.
3. The mirrors look fragile to me – are they easily broken or knocked out of alignment?
4. I've heard that mirrors need re-aluminizing regularly as they easily tarnish – I don't want any hassle like that.

To answer these questions one at a time:

1. The effects of the secondary mirror are insignificant when you consider the extra aperture you get for your money with reflectors.
2. A good-quality 100-mm reflector and an 80-mm refractor will give very similar views of the Moon and planets, but the reflector will typically cost two-thirds as much as the refractor, despite having a larger aperture.
3. This is a valid point, especially if the telescope is to be transported in and out of the house. Refractors are more rugged and their optical alignment is fixed. Young beginners may well lack the patience to calibrate mirrors accurately if they become misaligned.

Figure 2. An apochromatic Takahashi flourite refractor – purely for the connoisseur.

Figure 3. A modern British 300-mm Newtonian reflector made by Orion Optics.

4. A properly aluminized mirror should last for years before re-aluminizing is necessary. If the telescope is stored indoors, the aluminium coating may last for 10 years or more.

All things considered, a reflector is excellent value for money and, if finances allow, the purchase of a 150-mm instrument will provide enough light-grasp to satisfy even the greediest beginner. With 150 mm of aperture, the shadows of Jupiter's moons can easily be seen traversing the planet's disk; and comets of 8th or 9th magnitude can be tracked down by the patient beginner. A large Newtonian reflector is shown in Figure 3.

DOBSONIANS VERSUS EQUATORIAL MOUNTINGS

In terms of maximum value for money, one telescope design stands out above all others – the Dobsonian reflector, a large example of which is shown in Figure 4. The Dobsonian was invented by the Californian amateur astronomer John Dobson, who has spent a lifetime popularizing simple visual observing. The Dobsonian's strength is its simplicity – a relatively large and affordable telescope that is easy to steer around the sky. The key to the Dobsonian's design is the mounting; an altazimuth design which is simplicity itself. The azimuth bearing, at ground level, is typically just a couple of disk-shaped low-friction pads which allow rotation about a central spindle. The whole weight of the telescope is supported on the low-friction disks. The altitude bearings are typically two circular disks (sewer-pipe end caps have been used in some cases) which rest in a semicircular cut-out lined with PTFE pads. The telescope easily disassembles into tube and base, and is fairly portable up to 250 mm in aperture.

It used to be thought that a large-aperture telescope should be mounted equatorially (see below) and fitted with a motor drive to be attractive to potential users. However, this is not the case as aperture-value for money is far more attractive to purchasers. Commercial Dobsonians cost as little as £300 for a 150-mm model, and £400 for a 200-mm model. An alternative is to build the tube and mounting yourself, and buy the optics. The main disadvantage of the Dobsonian is that it cannot be used for photography as there is no motor drive to compensate for the Earth's rotation.

Telescopes that do have motor drives are mounted equatorially, and this is a good place to describe the equatorial mounting. As apertures get bigger and magnifications higher, the observer will frequently have to move the telescope to compensate for the movement of the stars and planets. This motion is, of course, caused by the Earth rotating once per day. To the beginner this may seem a trivial point, but the Moon will drift its own diameter in only two minutes of time – at high magnifications the lunar surface moves remarkably quickly. So, preferably for high-power work, and certainly for photography (or CCD imaging), a driven equatorial mounting is required.

The equatorial mounting is, in essence, an altazimuth mounting in which the azimuth bearing has been tilted away from the vertical by 90° minus the observer's latitude. Thus for London the azimuth bearing axis is tilted over by $90° - 51\frac{1}{2}° = 38\frac{1}{2}°$ (so for an observer at the north pole, a Dobsonian is an equatorial mounting!) Essentially, one axis of the telescope needs to point to the north celestial pole, which is very close to the star Polaris. Many commercial equatorial mounts feature a tiny telescope built into the polar axis so that a precise polar alignment is achieved. Unfortunately, even the best equatorial mountings cannot track with the accuracy necessary for taking unsupervised photographs through the telescope for more than a minute or two, and a human or CCD guider is required for longer exposures. However, an equatorial mounting will allow superb long-exposure photographs to be taken by piggybacking a camera with a telephoto lens (up to 200 mm focal length is usually OK) on the telescope, and this makes life a lot simpler as it removes the necessity to make continual adjustments to an undriven telescope at large magnifications. In addition, the mechanical setting circles of equatorial mountings make finding faint objects easy – you simply align the telescope on a nearby bright star, then use the setting circles to move the required angular distance, in RA and declination.

Despite these advantages of the equatorial mount, many visual observers much prefer the cheap and simple Dobsonian mounting. Dobsonians move easily, with a minimum of effort, and they stay where they are pointed. Objects directly overhead crossing from east to west can be a problem to observe with a Dobsonian, but finding objects near the pole can be an even bigger problem with an equatorial mounting. For the beginner, the altitude and azimuth motions of the Dobsonian are instinctive and easy to master – the equatorial mount is more of a challenge.

I've already mentioned the advantage of being able to use the setting circles of an equatorial mounting to find difficult-to-locate faint objects. Modern technology has an answer for the Dobsonian user in the form of digital setting circles. You can now buy kits which easily attach to more popular Dobsonian mountings and will tell you, via an LED display, where the telescope is pointing in the sky, despite the tele-scope being an altazimuth design. Bright stars can be used to calibrate the digital setting circles, and once this simple operation is performed you always know where you are. Personally, I would rate a big Dobsonian with digital setting circles as the ultimate system for visual deep-sky or comet observations. The UK's leading variable-star observer is Gary Poyner, shown in Figure 4 using a large 400-mm Dobsonian. Gary makes some 12,000 variable-star estimates per year – proof enough that Dobsonians are serious telescopes!

Many people are frustrated by not knowing their way around the night sky. Indeed, I would say that working out where you are in the sky is the single most frustrating aspect of the hobby for the beginner. Enormous confidence is generated by being 100% sure of where you are; total despair (exacerbated by clouds, cold and damp) is generated by repeated failure to recognize a starfield.

My tip here for the beginner is to make simple star charts for use at the eyepiece – this is the key to successful visual observing. The crucial point is how faint to plot the stars on a home-made star chart so that the view most resembles that seen *easily* through the lowest-power eyepiece you have. My advice may sound surprising – plot only the bright stars you can easily see as soon as you look through the eyepiece, *not* stars close to the theoretical limit. For a 60-mm refractor I would produce charts showing stars down to magnitude 6; for a 100-mm plot stars down to magnitude 7, and for a 150-mm plot stars down to magnitude 8. With practice you will be able to see stars at least a hundred times (5 magnitudes) as faint as the faintest you have plotted, but plotting all the stars you can theoretically see will just give a confusing view. Star charts plotted to these magnitudes are relatively easy to produce, as *Sky Atlas 2000.0*, for example, goes down to 8th magnitude, and *Uranometria 2000.0* goes down to magnitude 9.5. However, if your telescope budget stretches to £500 or £600, finding that elusive star-

Figure 4. Gary Poyner and his 400-mm Dobsonian at his Birmingham observatory (his smaller 200-mm Dobsonian is also shown). [Courtesy of Gary Poyner]

field may be a thing of the past. There are now (relatively) inexpensive high-tech telescopes that can do all the work for you.

INTELLIGENT TELESCOPES

Undoubtedly the telescope which started the recent hi-tech revolution is the 90-mm aperture Meade ETX-90 (Figure 5). This is the best-selling modern telescope in the world, and it is not hard to see why. It features a 90-mm aperture in a compact tube assembly which is little more than twice the aperture in length. It is highly portable and user-friendly. The basic design is altazimuth, but the mounting is easily converted to an equatorial with inexpensive accessories. An almost identical telescope in design and appearance appeared in the 1960s, namely the 3.5-inch (90-mm) Questar. Indeed, this telescope is still available today. However, the Questar is considerably more expensive and has not moved with the times. The second-generation Meade ETX-90, with its Autostar Computer Controller, is an intelligent telescope which can point itself at any one of 14,000 objects in its database, and it doesn't make mistakes. Being able to look through an eyepiece and be 100% confident that the object you want to see is somewhere in the field is an immense boost to observer morale, especially for the beginner.

To use the Meade ETX, all you do is go out on a clear night and point the telescope as close as possible to due north. You will already have told your telescope your latitude, longitude, date and local time. The first thing the telescope will do is to slew round to a bright star that it knows is above the horizon. Depending on how accurately you pointed the telescope to due north, the ETX will end up pointing either very close, or reasonably close to that bright star. Your job is then to adjust the telescope until it points precisely at the star. When this is done the ETX selects a second star, and the fine pointing procedure is repeated. Once the telescope is fixed on the second star and you confirm the alignment, it then knows exactly where it is with respect to all other stars. From this point on it can point you to any object in its database (provided the object is above the horizon, of course).

This technology will cost you around £600, but it is excellent value for money. Fortunately, access to such technology is becoming easier all the time. In late 1999 Meade introduced the DS (Digital Series) range of

Figure 5. The best-selling 90-mm Meade ETX. [Courtesy of Nick James]

refractors and reflectors, small-aperture instruments which are also able to slew themselves around the sky on demand, also using Meade's Autostar controller. While these instruments are more cumbersome than the compact ETX, they are also more affordable: the cheapest models retail at £300 to £400. Instruments in this price range that can, without fail, guarantee that the requested object is *always* in the eyepiece, time after time, can only be good for the hobby. I shudder to think of the number of potential amateur astronomers who have given up at the first hurdle, having failed to find the object they wish to observe.

The 90-mm Meade ETX-90EC with its Autostar controller is a superb, user-friendly, highly portable instrument; but for many an equally portable instrument with a larger aperture would be more attractive. Not surprisingly, Meade have catered for this requirement, and in 1999 released the ETX-125EC. This has a 125-mm aperture, and in all other respects has identical capabilities to the 90-mm model. Whereas the 90-mm instrument will show pleasing views of the Moon, the planets and the brighter Messier and Caldwell objects, the 125-mm instrument will enable really valuable scientific observing to be carried out. Needless to say, aperture comes at a cost and you will need to find £900 to purchase the ETX-125EC in the UK.

So far I have not discussed just how these instruments can be made to be so compact. I've discussed refractors and reflectors, but just what is the optical configuration of these highly portable telescopes? They come in two basic types: Schmidt–Cassegrain telescopes (commonly referred to as SCTs) and Maksutovs. The term 'Cassegrain' describes a telescope that is similar to a Newtonian reflector in that it has two main mirrors, a large primary mirror for collecting the light, and a smaller secondary mirror for directing the light to the focus. However, in the Cassegrain the second mirror is curved – it bulges outwards, in fact. This serves to increase the effective focal length of the telescope, which is good for high-power planetary or lunar work. Typically the convex secondary mirror increases the effective focal length by 4 or 5 times. In addition, the Cassegrain reflector directs the light back down the telescope tube and through a hole in the primary mirror. Thus, as in a refractor, the eyepiece is at the end of the telescope tube, not at the side, as it is in a Newtonian reflector. In an SCT the primary mirror is typically of very short focal ratio (the ratio of focal length to mirror diameter), e.g. $f/2$. But the secondary mirror typically amplifies this by a factor of 5, making the effective focal ratio about $f/10$. The result is a refractor-like focal length in a very compact tube. To compensate for optical aberrations in the SCT design, a glass corrector plate is placed across the end of the tube (such plates were originally used in Schmidt cameras, hence the name 'Schmidt–Cassegrain'). Not only does this improve the quality of the image, but it also has the great advantage of eliminating the turbulent air currents that can arise in an open tube and distort the image currents in the telescope tube.

The Maksutov design looks almost identical to the SCT, but there are subtle differences. In the Maksutov, the Schmidt corrector plate is replaced by a curved meniscus lens, and the secondary mirror is just an aluminized spot on the inside of the lens. Also, the main mirror of the modern Maksutov is highly aspheric, in contrast to the spherical primary mirror of the SCT.

It is probably true to say that the sheer compactness of the SCT and Maksutov designs is the main reason for their overwhelming popularity; they are incredibly portable instruments for their size, and even if you are building a permanent observatory they are highly attractive as the observatory can be made much smaller than for a reflector or refractor of equivalent aperture.

I think that most amateur astronomers are aware of the cut-throat, high-tech rivalry between the US telescope giants Meade and Celestron. Celestron have been around for far longer and have many very loyal followers, but in recent years Meade have caught them up and, technically at least, overtaken them in a number of key areas. But, in the field of highly portable desktop high-tech telescopes, Celestron have a worthy contender in the dramatic shape of the 125-mm NexStar telescope (Figure 6). This spectacularly styled instrument builds on Celestron's 125-mm SCT and is a direct competitor to Meade's ETX-125EC instrument. However, at £1200 it is rather more expensive, and many may be more tempted by the Meade.

LARGE SCHMIDT–CASSEGRAINS

If you are in the happy situation of being able to spend thousands of pounds on that first telescope, you may want to consider larger SCTs with even more 'intelligence'. The first commercial, fully computerized SCT was Celestron's 200-mm Compustar, which appeared on the scene

Figure 6. The portable and compact 125-mm Celestron NexStar, being demonstrated by Hazel McGee.

in the late 1980s. However, the first design to really take off and sell in large quantities was the Meade LX200 (Figure 7), introduced in 1992. The runaway success of the LX200 was largely due to highly competitive pricing, marketing, and the ability of the telescope to slew rapidly (at up to 8° per second) to within a few arcminutes of its target. This latter feature was precisely what was needed for positioning objects on the CCD detectors that appeared on the amateur scene in the 1990s. The LX200 is designed to be compatible with CCD imaging, and since its appearance various features and accessories have been introduced to make the integration of CCD and telescope as simple as possible. For example, a company called Optec specifically manufacture a field compressor which reduces the LX200's focal ratio from $f/10$ to $f/3.3$, thus tripling the CCD field of view. Also, the SBIG company (Santa Barbara Instruments Group) have built autoguiding CCD chips into their CCD cameras so that the SCT's motor drives can be adjusted by the CCD camera, if the star looks like drifting out of the field during long-exposure images.

The Meade LX200 (available as 200-mm, 250-mm, 300-mm and

Figure 7. The author and his 300-mm Meade LX200

400-mm models) and the competing Celestron Ultima 2000 (available only as a 200-mm model) can also be controlled remotely from indoors, so observing from a warm room is now a reality! Indeed, it is exactly this feature of the technology that has led to a spate of amateur supernova and asteroid discoveries in the last few years (see Ron Arbour's excellent article in the *2000 Yearbook of Astronomy*).

So, whatever your budget, from £100 to £17,000 (the cost in the UK of a 400-mm Meade LX200), astronomical equipment is out there waiting to be purchased. Potential purchasers may have noticed that in the UK telescopes generally cost the same in pounds as they do in dollars in the USA. This is an inevitable consequence of import duties, taxes, shipment and dealer handling charges. Many people save considerable amounts of money on dealer charges by buying while on holiday in the USA, or by importing direct. However, there is a significant risk: if something goes wrong with a highly technical piece of equipment, how good is your warranty, and how much hassle is there going to be in, say, shipping the telescope back to the USA? In 1997 I bought a 300-mm Meade LX200 from Broadhurst, Clarkson & Fuller of Farringdon Road, London. The telescope developed a fault in the motor-drive system, but within weeks the dealers replaced the whole telescope at no cost to myself. I could have ordered the telescope direct from the USA at a considerable financial saving, but I dread to think of what I would have had to go through had the same fault developed. When you pay a hefty dealer mark-up, you are paying for peace of mind.

ATM (AMATEUR TELESCOPE MAKING)

So far I haven't mentioned building your own telescope, something that many potential amateur astronomers consider to be well beyond their capabilities. However, I think that even the least practically minded person could attempt to make a tube and mounting for a Dobsonian (or even persuade a DIY enthusiast to help them to build one). Many people are surprised at how easily they can make a simple telescope, and fortunately the Internet is a superb source of information on the subject. I can strongly recommend the book *Amateur Telescope Making*, edited by Stephen F. Tonkin, which has a number of chapters on construction techniques for telescope and camera mountings. Stephen also runs a Website which has links to numerous telescope-making sites (see the list at the end of this article) which is well worth a look.

Many amateurs will cringe at the thought of grinding and polishing mirrors and lenses themselves, and indeed this is an area which requires a great deal of patience. However, it is remarkable what can be achieved. In Dartford, Kent, amateur telescope-maker John Wall has built 0.81-metre and 1.07-metre reflectors (Figure 8) in his back garden – including the mirrors. He is currently working on a 0.76-metre refractor.

Another option is to buy second-hand. I have frequently heard Patrick Moore comment that finding a good, cheap second-hand telescope is more difficult than finding a great auk. Certainly they are thin on the ground, but perusing the second-hand ads in astronomy magazines can sometimes turn up a bargain. Again, patience is a virtue. It may take 6 months or more before you spot what you want, and even then caution is advised – there are con-men out there, even in the field of astronomy. If in doubt, contact your local astronomical society or the British Astronomical Association for advice.

FINAL THOUGHTS

I have heard the view expressed, by more than a few amateurs, that amateur astronomy is becoming a hobby for the rich, due to the preponderance of expensive equipment available to the lucky few. There is no doubt that *in the right hands* expensive equipment can produce spectacular results, but experienced amateur astronomers will tell you that the best results are always obtained by those who have got to know all the idiosyncrasies of their equipment and know how to get the most out of it.

I well remember a coach trip to the observatory of a leading amateur astronomer in the UK. The amateur owned a huge telescope in a dome the size of a small house. One astronomer on the trip was heard to say to his friend, 'Look at this equipment and the size of this telescope, there's no point me bothering with my small reflector.' Little did the visitor know that the observatory was about to be dismantled because the telescope and dome were just too big to use easily. Don't be put off because others have bigger telescopes than you.

An enthusiastic astronomer with modest user-friendly and easily set-up equipment will always outperform an impatient astronomer with expensive equipment that is difficult to use. To succeed in astronomy

Figure 8. John Wall of Crayford Manor House Observatory and his 0.81-m and 1.07-m reflectors. [Courtsey of Arthur Cockburn]

you need to find out what you are mentally best suited to and what you like doing best, and then patiently (and single-mindedly) adjust your techniques and tweak your equipment to get the best out of it. And don't forget the enjoyment aspect and simple pleasures that astronomy can bring. I know advanced amateur astronomers who have spent tens of thousands of pounds on equipment, but still get the most pleasure from using a large pair of binoculars to scan the Milky Way. Whatever your budget and astronomical interests, there is always plenty to observe and enjoy in the Universe. You just need a bit of patience and perseverance. Good luck!

FURTHER READING

H. J. P. Arnold, P. Doherty and Patrick Moore (1999), *Photographic Atlas of the Stars*, Institute of Physics Publishing.

Stephen F. Tonkin (1999), *Amateur Telescope Making*, Springer-Verlag.

Wil Tirion and Roger W. Sinnott (1998), *Sky Atlas 2000.0*, 2nd edn, Sky Publishing Corp./Cambridge University Press.

Wil Tirion, Barry Rappaport and George Lovi (1987), *Uranometria 2000.0*, Willman-Bell.

EQUIPMENT SUPPLIERS

All the following distributors and suppliers are highly recommended by the author:

For frank and detailed reviews of astronomical accessories, take out a subscription to *Sky & Telescope*:

Sky & Telescope, PO Box 9111, Belmont, MA 02478–9111, USA; telephone (001) 617 864 7360.

For UK purchases of American-made equipment and Russian binoculars, the largest British distributor and agent for the leading US companies is:

Broadhurst, Clarkson & Fuller, Telescope House, 63 Farringdon Road, London EC1M 3JB; telephone 020 7405 2156; www.telescope-house.co.uk

The UK distributor for Celestron telescopes and accessories is:

David Hinds Ltd, Unit 34, The Silk Mill, Brook Street, Tring, Hertfordshire, HP23 5EF; telephone 01442 827768.

For world-wide mail order of filters and telescope accessories, contact:

Lumicon, 2111 Research Drive, Suites 4–5, Livermore, CA 94550, USA; telephone (001) 925 447 9570.

Pocono Mountain Optics, 104 NP 502 Plaza, Moscow, PA 18444, USA; telephone (001) 570 842 1500.

For digital setting circles, focusers and other accessories, contact:

JMI, 810 Quail Street, Unit E, Lakewood, CO 80215, USA; telephone (001) 303 233 5353.

In the UK, for Takahashi telescopes, Miyauchi binoculars and various accessories, contact:

True Technology Ltd, Woodpecker Cottage, Red Lane, Aldermaston, Berkshire, RG7 4PA; www.truetech.dircon.co.uk

SOME USEFUL INTERNET URLS

Undoubtedly the quickest way of getting up-to-date information on new astronomical products and astronomy in general is via the

Internet. Most equipment manufacturers now have their own Website, and many allow ordering via the Internet. The URLs below may well be the quickest way to find and order the product you want. They were current at the time this chapter was written.

Stephen Tonkin
http://www.aegis1.demon.co.uk/atm.htm

Meade
http://www.Meade.com

Meade User Group
http://www.austin.cc.tx.us/astro-ES/AstroDesigns/index.htm

Meade User Group
http://www.austin.cc.tx.us/astro-ES/AstroDesigns/MAPUG/ArhvList.htm

Useful Meade information
http://www.mailbag.com/users/ragreiner

Celestron
http://www.celestron.com

Sky Publishing
http://www.skypub.com/

Equipment reviews
http://www.skypub.com/testrept/testrept.shtml

True Technology
http://www.users.dircon.co.uk/truetech/

Orion Scope Center
http://www.oriontel.com

Pocono Mountain Optics
http://www.Astronomy-Mall.com

Used telescopes
http://www.StarryMessenger.com

British Astronomical Association
http://www.ast.cam.ac.uk/baa/

Part III

Miscellaneous

Some Interesting Variable Stars

JOHN ISLES

The following stars are of interest for many reasons. Of course, the periods and ranges of many variables are not constant from one cycle to another. Finder charts are given on the pages following this list for those stars marked with an asterisk.

Star	RA		Declination		Range	Type	Period	Spectrum
	h	m	°	′			(days)	
R Andromedae	00	24.0	+38	35	5.8–14.9	Mira	409	S
W Andromedae	02	17.6	+44	18	6.7–14.6	Mira	396	S
U Antliae	10	35.2	−39	34	5–6	Irregular	—	C
Theta Apodis	14	05.3	−76	48	5–7	Semi-regular	119	M
R Aquarii	23	43.8	−15	17	5.8–12.4	Symbiotic	387	M+Pec
T Aquarii	20	49.9	−05	09	7.2–14.2	Mira	202	M
R Aquilae	19	06.4	+08	14	5.5–12.0	Mira	284	M
V Aquilae	19	04.4	−05	41	6.6–8.4	Semi-regular	353	C
Eta Aquilae	19	52.5	+01	00	3.5–4.4	Cepheid	7.2	F–G
U Arae	17	53.6	−51	41	7.7–14.1	Mira	225	M
R Arietis	02	16.1	+25	03	7.4–13.7	Mira	187	M
U Arietis	03	11.0	+14	48	7.2–15.2	Mira	371	M
R Aurigae	05	17.3	+53	35	6.7–13.9	Mira	458	M
Epsilon Aurigae	05	02.0	+43	49	2.9–3.8	Algol	9892	F+B
R Boötis	14	37.2	+26	44	6.2–13.1	Mira	223	M
W Boötis	14	43.4	+26	32	4.7–5.4	Semi-regular?	450?	M
X Camelopardalis	04	45.7	+75	06	7.4–14.2	Mira	144	K–M
R Cancri	08	16.6	+11	44	6.1–11.8	Mira	362	M
X Cancri	08	55.4	+17	14	5.6–7.5	Semi-regular	195?	C
*R Canis Majoris	07	19.5	−16	24	5.7–6.3	Algol	1.1	F
*VY Canis Majoris	07	23.0	−25	46	6.5–9.6	Unique	—	M
*FW Canis Majoris	07	24.7	−16	12	5.0–5.5	Gamma Cas	—	B
S Canis Minoris	07	32.7	+08	19	6.6–13.2	Mira	333	M
R Canum Ven.	13	49.0	+39	33	6.5–12.9	Mira	329	M
R Carinae	09	32.2	−62	47	3.9–10.5	Mira	309	M
S Carinae	10	09.4	−61	33	4.5–9.9	Mira	149	K–M
l Carinae	09	45.2	−62	30	3.3–4.2	Cepheid	35.5	F–K
Eta Carinae	10	45.1	−59	41	−0.8–7.9	Irregular	—	Pec

Star	RA		Declination		Range	Type	Period	Spectrum
	h	m	°	′			(days)	
R Cassiopeiae	23	58.4	+51	24	4.7–13.5	Mira	430	M
S Cassiopeiae	01	19.7	+72	37	7.9–16.1	Mira	612	S
W Cassiopeiae	00	54.9	+58	34	7.8–12.5	Mira	406	C
Gamma Cas.	00	56.7	+60	43	1.6–3.0	Irregular	—	B
Rho Cassiopeiae	23	54.4	+57	30	4.1–6.2	Semi-regular	—	F–K
R Centauri	14	16.6	−59	55	5.3–11.8	Mira	546	M
S Centauri	12	24.6	−49	26	7–8	Semi-regular	65	C
T Centauri	13	41.8	−33	36	5.5–9.0	Semi-regular	90	K–M
S Cephei	21	35.2	+78	37	7.4–12.9	Mira	487	C
T Cephei	21	09.5	+68	29	5.2–11.3	Mira	388	M
Delta Cephei	22	29.2	+58	25	3.5–4.4	Cepheid	5.4	F–G
Mu Cephei	21	43.5	+58	47	3.4–5.1	Semi-regular	730	M
U Ceti	02	33.7	−13	09	6.8–13.4	Mira	235	M
W Ceti	00	02.1	−14	41	7.1–14.8	Mira	351	S
*Omicron Ceti	02	19.3	−02	59	2.0–10.1	Mira	332	M
R Chamaeleontis	08	21.8	−76	21	7.5–14.2	Mira	335	M
T Columbae	05	19.3	−33	42	6.6–12.7	Mira	226	M
R Comae Ber.	12	04.3	+18	47	7.1–14.6	Mira	363	M
R Coronae Bor.	15	48.6	+28	09	5.7–14.8	R Coronae Bor.	—	C
S Coronae Bor.	15	21.4	+31	22	5.8–14.1	Mira	360	M
T Coronae Bor.	15	59.6	+25	55	2.0–10.8	Recurrent nova	—	M+Pec
V Coronae Bor.	15	49.5	+39	34	6.9–12.6	Mira	358	C
W Coronae Bor.	16	15.4	+37	48	7.8–14.3	Mira	238	M
R Corvi	12	19.6	−19	15	6.7–14.4	Mira	317	M
R Crucis	12	23.6	−61	38	6.4–7.2	Cepheid	5.8	F–G
R Cygni	19	36.8	+50	12	6.1–14.4	Mira	426	S
U Cygni	20	19.6	+47	54	5.9–12.1	Mira	463	C
W Cygni	21	36.0	+45	22	5.0–7.6	Semi-regular	131	M
RT Cygni	19	43.6	+48	47	6.0–13.1	Mira	190	M
SS Cygni	21	42.7	+43	35	7.7–12.4	Dwarf nova	50±	K+Pec
CH Cygni	19	24.5	+50	14	5.6–9.0	Symbiotic	—	M+B
Chi Cygni	19	50.6	+32	55	3.3–14.2	Mira	408	S
R Delphini	20	14.9	+09	05	7.6–13.8	Mira	285	M
U Delphini	20	45.5	+18	05	5.6–7.5	Semi-regular	110?	M
EU Delphini	20	37.9	+18	16	5.8–6.9	Semi-regular	60	M
Beta Doradus	05	33.6	−62	29	3.5–4.1	Cepheid	9.8	F–G
R Draconis	16	32.7	+66	45	6.7–13.2	Mira	246	M
T Eridani	03	55.2	−24	02	7.2–13.2	Mira	252	M
R Fornacis	02	29.3	−26	06	7.5–13.0	Mira	389	C
R Geminorum	07	07.4	+22	42	6.0–14.0	Mira	370	S

Star	RA		Declination		Range	Type	Period (days)	Spectrum
	h	m	°	′				
U Geminorum	07	55.1	+22	00	8.2–14.9	Dwarf nova	105±	Pec+M
*Zeta Geminorum	07	04.1	+20	34	3.6–4.2	Cepheid	10.2	F–G
*Eta Geminorum	06	14.9	+22	30	3.2–3.9	Semi-regular	233	M
S Gruis	22	26.1	−48	26	6.0–15.0	Mira	402	M
S Herculis	16	51.9	+14	56	6.4–13.8	Mira	307	M
U Herculis	16	25.8	+18	54	6.4–13.4	Mira	406	M
Alpha Herculis	17	14.6	+14	23	2.7–4.0	Semi-regular	—	M
68, u Herculis	17	17.3	+33	06	4.7–5.4	Algol	2.1	B+B
R Horologii	02	53.9	−49	53	4.7–14.3	Mira	408	M
U Horologii	03	52.8	−45	50	6–14	Mira	348	M
R Hydrae	13	29.7	−23	17	3.5–10.9	Mira	389	M
U Hydrae	10	37.6	−13	23	4.3–6.5	Semi-regular	450?	C
VW Hydri	04	09.1	−71	18	8.4–14.4	Dwarf nova	27±	Pec
R Leonis	09	47.6	+11	26	4.4–11.3	Mira	310	M
R Leonis Minoris	09	45.6	+34	31	6.3–13.2	Mira	372	M
R Leporis	04	59.6	−14	48	5.5–11.7	Mira	427	C
Y Librae	15	11.7	−06	01	7.6–14.7	Mira	276	M
RS Librae	15	24.3	−22	55	7.0–13.0	Mira	218	M
Delta Librae	15	01.0	−08	31	4.9–5.9	Algol	2.3	A
R Lyncis	07	01.3	+55	20	7.2–14.3	Mira	379	S
R Lyrae	18	55.3	+43	57	3.9–5.0	Semi-regular	46?	M
RR Lyrae	19	25.5	+42	47	7.1–8.1	RR Lyrae	0.6	A–F
Beta Lyrae	18	50.1	+33	22	3.3–4.4	Eclipsing	12.9	B
U Microscopii	20	29.2	−40	25	7.0–14.4	Mira	334	M
*U Monocerotis	07	30.8	−09	47	5.9–7.8	RV Tauri	91	F–K
V Monocerotis	06	22.7	−02	12	6.0–13.9	Mira	340	M
R Normae	15	36.0	−49	30	6.5–13.9	Mira	508	M
T Normae	15	44.1	−54	59	6.2–13.6	Mira	241	M
R Octantis	05	26.1	−86	23	6.3–13.2	Mira	405	M
S Octantis	18	08.7	−86	48	7.2–14.0	Mira	259	M
V Ophiuchi	16	26.7	−12	26	7.3–11.6	Mira	297	C
X Ophiuchi	18	38.3	+08	50	5.9–9.2	Mira	329	M
RS Ophiuchi	17	50.2	−06	43	4.3–12.5	Recurrent nova	—	OB+M
U Orionis	05	55.8	+20	10	4.8–13.0	Mira	368	M
W Orionis	05	05.4	+01	11	5.9–7.7	Semi-regular	212	C
Alpha Orionis	05	55.2	+07	24	0.0–1.3	Semi-regular	2335	M
S Pavonis	19	55.2	−59	12	6.6–10.4	Semi-regular	381	M
Kappa Pavonis	18	56.9	−67	14	3.9–4.8	Cepheid	9.1	G
R Pegasi	23	06.8	+10	33	6.9–13.8	Mira	378	M
Beta Pegasi	23	03.8	+28	05	2.3–2.7	Irregular	—	M

Star	RA		Declination		Range	Type	Period	Spectrum
	h	m	°	′			(days)	
X Persei	03	55.4	+31	03	6.0–7.0	Gamma Cas.	—	O9.5
Beta Persei	03	08.2	+40	57	2.1–3.4	Algol	2.9	B
Rho Persei	03	05.2	+38	50	3.3–4.0	Semi-regular	50?	M
Zeta Phoenicis	01	08.4	−55	15	3.9–4.4	Algol	1.7	B+B
R Pictoris	04	46.2	−49	15	6.4–10.1	Semi-regular	171	M
*RS Puppis	08	13.1	−34	35	6.5–7.7	Cepheid	41.4	F-G
L² Puppis	07	13.5	−44	39	2.6–6.2	Semi-regular	141	M
T Pyxidis	09	04.7	−32	23	6.5–15.3	Recurrent nova	7000±	Pec
U Sagittae	19	18.8	+19	37	6.5–9.3	Algol	3.4	B+G
WZ Sagittae	20	07.6	+17	42	7.0–15.5	Dwarf nova	1900±	A
R Sagittarii	19	16.7	−19	18	6.7–12.8	Mira	270	M
RR Sagittarii	19	55.9	−29	11	5.4–14.0	Mira	336	M
RT Sagittarii	20	17.7	−39	07	6.0–14.1	Mira	306	M
RU Sagittarii	19	58.7	−41	51	6.0–13.8	Mira	240	M
RY Sagittarii	19	16.5	−33	31	5.8–14.0	R Coronae Bor.	—	G
RR Scorpii	16	56.6	−30	35	5.0–12.4	Mira	281	M
RS Scorpii	16	55.6	−45	06	6.2–13.0	Mira	320	M
RT Scorpii	17	03.5	−36	55	7.0–15.2	Mira	449	S
S Sculptoris	00	15.4	−32	03	5.5–13.6	Mira	363	M
R Scuti	18	47.5	−05	42	4.2–8.6	RV Tauri	146	G–K
R Serpentis	15	50.7	+15	08	5.2–14.4	Mira	356	M
S Serpentis	15	21.7	+14	19	7.0–14.1	Mira	372	M
T Tauri	04	22.0	+19	32	9.3–13.5	Irregular	—	F–K
SU Tauri	05	49.1	+19	04	9.1–16.9	R Coronae Bor.	—	G
Lambda Tauri	04	00.7	+12	29	3.4–3.9	Algol	4.0	B+A
R Trianguli	02	37.0	+34	16	5.4–12.6	Mira	267	M
R Ursae Majoris	10	44.6	+68	47	6.5–13.7	Mira	302	M
T Ursae Majoris	12	36.4	+59	29	6.6–13.5	Mira	257	M
U Ursae Minoris	14	17.3	+66	48	7.1–13.0	Mira	331	M
R Virginis	12	38.5	+06	59	6.1–12.1	Mira	146	M
S Virginis	13	33.0	−07	12	6.3–13.2	Mira	375	M
SS Virginis	12	25.3	+00	48	6.0–9.6	Semi-regular	364	C
R Vulpeculae	21	04.4	+23	49	7.0–14.3	Mira	137	M
Z Vulpeculae	19	21.7	+25	34	7.3–8.9	Algol	2.5	B+A

R and FW Canis Majoris

Comparison stars:

A	= 4.96
B	= 5.45
C	= 5.46
D	= 5.78
E	= 6.05
F	= 6.09
G	= 6.6
H	= 6.77

VY Canis Majoris

Comparison stars:

C	= 7.0
D	= 7.1
E	= 8.1
F	= 8.4
G	= 8.8
H	= 9.4

**Omicron Ceti
(Mira)**

Comparison stars:

Alpha (α)	= 2.52 (off map)
Gamma (γ)	= 3.46
Delta (δ)	= 4.06
Nu (ν)	= 4.87
N	= 5.34
P	= 5.41
R	= 6.00
S	= 6.32
T	= 6.49
U	= 7.19
W	= 8.06
X	= 8.42
y	= 9.00
z	= 9.33

Eta and Zeta Geminorum

Comparison stars:

Epsilon (ε) Gem	= 2.98
Zeta (ζ) Tau	= 3.03
Xi (χ) Gem	= 3.34
Lambda (λ) Gem	= 3.59
Nu (ν) Gem	= 4.14
1 Gem	= 4.15

U Monocerotis

Comparison stars:

C	= 5.72
D	= 5.85
E	= 6.00
F	= 6.62
G	= 6.97
H	= 7.51
K	= 7.81
L	= 8.03

RS Puppis

Comparison stars:

A	= 6.4
B	= 6.4
C	= 7.0
D	= 7.4
E	= 7.6
F	= 8.2
G	= 8.3

Mira Stars: Maxima, 2001

JOHN ISLES

Below are the predicted dates of maxima for Mira stars that reach magnitude 7.5 or brighter at an average maximum. Individual maxima can in some cases be brighter or fainter than average by a magnitude or more, and all dates are only approximate. The positions, extreme ranges and mean periods of these stars can be found in the preceding list of interesting variable stars.

Star	Mean magnitude at maximum	Dates of maxima
R Andromedae	6.9	Sept. 28
W Andromedae	7.4	Nov. 3
R Aquarii	6.5	July 10
R Aquilae	6.1	July 15
R Boötis	7.2	Jan. 2, Aug. 13
R Cancri	6.8	Oct. 25
S Canis Minoris	7.5	Nov. 3
R Carinae	4.6	Sept. 6
S Carinae	5.7	Mar. 26, Aug. 23
R Cassiopeiae	7.0	Nov. 21
R Centauri	5.8	July 14
T Cephei	6.0	July 29
U Ceti	7.5	Mar. 29, Nov. 18
Omicron Ceti	3.4	Aug. 24
T Columbae	7.5	July 21
S Coronae Borealis	7.3	Oct. 20
V Coronae Borealis	7.5	May 4
R Corvi	7.5	Mar. 2
U Cygni	7.2	Feb. 25
RT Cygni	7.3	Mar. 25, Oct. 1
Chi Cygni	5.2	Jan. 24
R Geminorum	7.1	Nov. 21

Star	Mean magnitude at maximum	Dates of maxima
U Herculis	7.5	Jan. 6
R Horologii	6.0	Mar. 11
R Hydrae	4.5	July 13
R Leonis	5.8	Mar. 12
R Leonis Minoris	7.1	Oct. 5
R Leporis	6.8	July 18
RS Librae	7.5	Mar. 6, Oct. 10
V Monocerotis	7.0	Mar. 26
T Normae	7.4	July 28
V Ophiuchi	7.5	Jan. 11, Nov. 5
X Ophiuchi	6.8	June 16
U Orionis	6.3	Nov. 19
R Sagittarii	7.3	Feb. 16, Nov. 13
RR Sagittarii	6.8	Sept. 1
RT Sagittarii	7.0	Jan. 17, Nov. 19
RU Sagittarii	7.2	Mar. 30, Nov. 25
RR Scorpii	5.9	July 28
RS Scorpii	7.0	Apr. 28
S Sculptoris	6.7	Dec. 9
R Serpentis	6.9	Jan. 17
R Trianguli	6.2	Sept. 17
R Ursae Majoris	7.5	Oct. 4
R Virginis	6.9	Mar. 11, Aug. 4, Dec. 27
S Virginis	7.0	Nov. 18

Some Interesting Double Stars

R. W. ARGYLE

The positions given below correspond to epoch 2000.0.

Star	RA		Declin-ation	Magni-tudes	Separation arc seconds	PA	Cata-logue	Comments
	h	m	° ′			°		
β Tuc	00	31.5	−62 58	4.4, 4.8	27.1	169	LCL 119	Both again difficult doubles.
η Cas	00	49.1	+57 49	3.4, 7.5	12.9	317	Σ60	Easy. Creamy, bluish.
36 And	00	55.0	+23 38	6.0, 6.4	1.0	315	Σ73	Period 168 years. Both yellow. Slowly opening.
ζ Psc	01	13.7	+07 35	5.6, 6.5	23.1	63	Σ100	Yellow, reddish-white.
p Eri	01	39.8	−56 12	5.8, 5.8	11.5	190	Δ5	Period 483 years.
γ Ari	01	53.5	+19 18	4.8, 4.8	7.5	1	Σ180	Very easy. Both white.
α Psc	02	02.0	+02 46	4.2, 5.1	1.8	271	Σ202	Binary. Period 933 years.
γ And	02	03.9	+42 20	2.3, 5.0	9.6	63	Σ205	Yellow, blue. Relatively fixed.
γ² And				5.1, 6.3	0.4	103	OΣ38	BC. Needs 30 cm.
ι Cas AB	02	29.1	+67 24	4.9, 6.9	3.0	227	Σ262	AB is long-period binary. Period 840 years.
ι Cas AC				4.9, 8.4	7.2	118		
ω For	02	33.8	−28 14	5.0, 7.7	10.8	245	HJ 3506	Common proper motion.
γ Cet	02	43.3	+03 14	3.5, 7.3	2.6	298	Σ299	Not too easy.
θ Eri	02	58.3	−40 18	3.4, 4.5	8.3	90	Pz2	Both white.
ε Ari	02	59.2	+21 20	5.2, 5.5	1.5	208	Σ333	Binary. Little motion. Both white.
Σ331 Per	03	00.9	+52 21	5.3, 6.7	12.0	85	—	Fixed.
α For	03	12.1	−28 59	4.0, 7.0	5.1	299	HJ 3555	Period 314 years. B variable?
f Eri	03	48.6	−37 37	4.8, 5.3	8.2	215	Δ16	Pale yellow. Fixed.

Star	RA		Declin-ation	Magni-tudes	Separation arc seconds	PA	Cata-logue	Comments
	h	m	° ′			°		
32 Eri	03	54.3	−02 57	4.8, 6.1	6.9	348	Σ470	Fixed.
1 Cam	04	32.0	+53 55	5.7, 6.8	10.3	308	Σ550	Fixed.
ι Pic	04	50.9	−53 28	5.6, 6.4	12.4	58	Δ18	Good object for small apertures. Fixed.
κ Lep	05	13.2	−12 56	4.5, 7.4	2.2	357	Σ661	Visible in 7.5 cm.
β Ori	05	14.5	−08 12	0.1, 6.8	9.5	204	Σ668	Companion once thought to be close double.
41 Lep	05	21.8	−24 46	5.4, 6.6	3.4	93	HJ 3752	Deep yellow pair in a rich field.
η Ori	05	24.5	−02 24	3.8, 4.8	1.7	78	Da5	Slow-moving binary.
λ Ori	05	35.1	+09 56	3.6, 5.5	4.3	44	Σ738	Fixed.
θ Ori AB	05	35.3	−05 23	6.7, 7.9	8.6	32	Σ748	Trapezium in M42.
θ Ori CD				5.1, 6.7	13.4	61		
σ Ori AC	05	38.7	−02 36	4.0, 10.3	11.4	238	Σ762	Quintuple. A is a close double.
σ Ori ED				6.5, 7.5	30.1	231		
ζ Ori	05	40.7	−01 57	1.9, 4.0	2.4	164	Σ774	Can be split in 7.5 cm.
η Gem	06	14.9	+22 30	var., 6.5	1.6	256	β1008	Well seen with 20 cm. Primary orange.
12 Lyn AB	06	46.2	+59 27	5.4, 6.0	1.7	68	Σ948	AB is binary, period 706 years.
12 Lyn AC				5.4, 7.3	8.7	309		
γ Vol	07	08.7	−70 30	3.9, 5.8	14.1	298	Δ42	Very slow binary.
h3945 CMa	07	16.6	−23 19	4.8, 6.8	26.8	51	—	Contrasting colours.
δ Gem	07	20.1	+21 59	3.5, 8.2	5.7	225	Σ1066	Not too easy. Yellow, pale blue.
α Gem	07	34.6	+31 53	1.9, 2.9	3.9	64	Σ1110	Widening. Easy with 7.5 cm.
κ Pup	07	38.8	−26 48	4.5, 4.7	9.8	318	H III 27	Both white.
ζ Cnc AB	08	12.2	+17 39	5.6, 6.0	0.9	80	Σ1196	Period (AB) 60 years. C has invisible companion.
ζ Cnc AB−C				5.0, 6.2	6.0	72		
δ Vel	08	44.7	−54 43	2.1, 5.1	0.9	187	I 10	Difficult close pair. Period about 100 years.
ε Hya	08	46.8	+06 25	3.3, 6.8	2.9	299	Σ1273	PA slowly increasing. A is a very close pair.

Star	RA		Declin-ation	Magni-tudes	Separation arc seconds	PA	Cata-logue	Comments
	h	m	° ′			°		
38 Lyn	09	18.8	+36 48	3.9, 6.6	2.8	230	Σ1338	Almost fixed.
ν Car	09	47.1	−65 04	3.1, 6.1	5.0	128	Rmk 11	Fixed. Fine in small telescopes.
γ Leo	10	20.0	+19 50	2.2, 3.5	4.4	125	Σ1424	Binary. Period 619 years. Both orange.
s Vel	10	32.0	−45 04	6.2, 6.5	13.5	218	Pz3	Fixed.
μ Vel	10	46.8	−49 26	2.7, 6.4	2.5	59	R155	Period 116 years. Near widest separation.
54 Leo	10	55.6	+24 45	4.5, 6.3	6.6	111	Σ1487	Slowly widening. Pale yellow and white.
ξ UMa	11	18.2	+31 32	4.3, 4.8	1.8	269	Σ1523	Binary. Period 60 years. Opening. Needs 7.5 cm.
π Cen	11	21.0	−54 29	4.3, 5.0	0.3	146	I 879	Binary. Period 39.2 years. Very close. Needs 35 cm
ι Leo	11	23.9	+10 32	4.0, 6.7	1.7	115	Σ1536	Binary. Period 192 years.
N Hya	11	32.3	−29 16	5.8, 5.9	9.5	210	H III 96	Fixed.
D Cen	12	14.0	−45 43	5.6, 6.8	2.8	243	Rmk14	Orange and white. Closing.
α Cru	12	26.6	−63 06	1.4, 1.9	4.0	112	Δ252	Third star in a low-power field.
γ Cen	12	41.5	−48 58	2.9, 2.9	0.9	346	HJ4539	Period 84 years. Closing. Both yellow.
γ Vir	12	41.7	−01 27	3.5, 3.5	1.3	253	Σ1670	Binary. Period 168 years. Closing quickly.
β Mus	12	46.3	−68 06	3.7, 4.0	1.3	44	R207	Both white. Closing.
μ Cru	12	54.6	−57 11	4.3, 5.3	34.9	17	Δ126	Fixed. Both white.
α CVn	12	56.0	+38 19	2.9, 5.5	19.3	229	Σ1692	Easy. Yellow, bluish.
J Cen	13	22.6	−60 59	4.6, 6.5	60.0	343	Δ133	Fixed. A is a close pair.
ζ UMa	13	24.0	+54 56	2.3, 4.0	14.4	152	Σ1744	Very easy. Naked-eye pair with Alcor.
3 Cen	13	51.8	−33 00	4.5, 6.0	7.9	106	H III 101	Both white. Closing slowly.
α Cen	14	39.6	−60 50	0.0, 1.2	14.1	222	Rhd 1	Finest pair in the sky. Period 80 years. Closing.

Star	RA		Declin-ation	Magni-tudes	Separation arc seconds	PA	Cata-logue	Comments
	h	m	° ′			°		
ζ Boo	14	41.1	+13 44	4.5, 4.6	0.8	299	Σ1865	Both white. Closing, highly inclined orbit.
ε Boo	14	45.0	+27 04	2.5, 4.9	2.9	343	Σ1877	Yellow, blue. Fine pair.
54 Hya	14	46.0	−25 27	5.1, 7.1	8.3	122	H III 97	Closing slowly.
μ Lib	14	49.3	−14 09	5.8, 6.7	1.9	2	β106	Becoming wider. Fine in 7.5 cm.
ξ Boo	14	51.4	+19 06	4.7, 7.0	6.6	317	Σ1888	Fine contrast. Easy.
44 Boo	15	03.8	+47 39	5.3, 6.2	2.2	54	Σ1909	Period 246 years.
π Lup	15	05.1	−47 03	4.6, 4.7	1.7	67	HJ 4728	Widening.
μ Lup AB	15	18.5	−47 53	5.1, 5.2	1.0	308	Δ180	AB closing?
μ Lup AC				4.4, 7.2	23.2	129	HJ 4543	AC almost fixed.
γ Cir	15	23.4	−59 19	5.1, 5.5	0.9	12	HJ 4787	Closing. Needs 20 cm. Long-period binary.
η CrB	15	32.0	+32 17	5.6, 5.9	0.6	69	Σ1937	Both yellow. Period 41 years. Near widest separation.
δ Ser	15	34.8	+10 33	4.2, 5.2	4.0	175	Σ1954	Long-period binary.
γ Lup	15	35.1	−41 10	3.5, 3.6	0.7	274	HJ 4786	Period 147 years. Needs 20 cm.
ξ Lup	15	56.9	−33 58	5.3, 5.8	10.2	49	Pz4	Fixed.
σ CrB	16	14.7	+33 52	5.6, 6.6	7.1	237	Σ2032	Long-period binary. Both white.
α Sco	16	29.4	−26 26	1.2, 5.4	2.9	273	Gnt 1	Red, green. Difficult from mid-northern latitudes.
λ Oph	16	30.9	+01 59	4.2, 5.2	1.5	31	Σ2055	Period 129 years. Fairly difficult in small apertures.
ζ Her	16	41.3	+31 36	2.9, 5.5	0.6	345	Σ2084	Period 34 years. Closing rapidly.
μ Dra	17	05.3	+54 28	5.7, 5.7	2.2	17	Σ2130	Long-period binary.
α Her	17	14.6	+14 24	var., 5.4	4.6	105	Σ2140	Red, green. Binary.
36 Oph	17	15.3	−26 35	5.1, 5.1	4.8	327	SHJ 243	Period 549 years.
ρ Her	17	23.7	+37 08	4.6, 5.6	4.1	318	Σ2161	Slowly widening.
95 Her	18	01.5	+21 36	5.0, 5.1	6.4	257	Σ2264	Colours thought variable in C19.
70 Oph	18	05.5	+02 30	4.2, 6.0	4.0	145	Σ2272	Opening. Easy in 7.5 cm.

Star	RA		Declin-ation	Magni-tudes	Separation arc seconds	PA	Cata-logue	Comments
	h	m	° ′			°		
h5014 CrA	18	06.8	−43 25	5.7, 5.7	1.7	346	—	Closing slowly. Orbit poorly known. Needs 10 cm.
OΣ358 Her	18	35.9	+16 58	6.8, 7.0	1.6	154	—	Period 292 years.
ε¹ Lyr	18	44.3	+39 40	5.0, 6.1	2.6	350	Σ2382	Quadruple system with ε². Both pairs visible in 7.5 cm.
ε² Lyr	18	44.3	+39 40	5.2, 5.5	2.3	82	Σ2383	
θ Ser	18	56.2	+04 12	4.5, 5.4	22.4	104	Σ2417	Fixed. Very easy.
γ CrA	19	06.4	−37 04	4.8, 5.1	1.3	50	HJ 5084	Beautiful pair. Period 122 years.
β Cyg AB	19	30.7	+27 58	3.1,5.1	34.3	54	ΣI 43	Glorious. Yellow, blue-greenish.
β Cyg Aa				3.1, 4.0	0.4	132	MCA 55	Discovered in 1976. Closing slowly.
δ Cyg	19	45.0	+45 08	2.9, 6.3	2.6	224	Σ2579	Slowly widening.
ε Dra	19	48.2	+70 16	3.8, 7.4	3.2	17	Σ2603	Slow binary.
γ Del	20	46.7	+16 07	4.5, 5.5	9.2	266	Σ2727	Easy. Yellowish.
λ Cyg	20	47.4	+36 29	4.8, 6.1	0.9	10	OΣ413	Difficult binary in small apertures.
ε Equ AB	20	59.1	+04 18	6.0, 6.3	0.8	285	Σ2737	Fine triple. AB is closing.
ε Equ AC				6.0, 7.1	10.3	66		
61 Cyg	21	06.9	+38 45	5.2, 6.0	30.6	150	Σ2758	Nearby binary. Both orange. Period 722 years.
θ Ind	21	19.9	−53 27	4.5, 7.0	6.8	271	HJ 5258	Pale yellow and reddish. Long-period binary.
μ Cyg	21	44.1	+28 45	4.8, 6.1	1.8	308	Σ2822	Period 713 years.
ξ Cep	22	03.8	+64 37	4.4, 6.5	8.2	275	Σ2863	White and blue. Long-period binary.
53 Aqr	22	26.6	−16 45	6.4, 6.6	1.8	15	SHJ 345	Long-period binary. Near periastron?
ζ Aqr	22	28.8	−00 01	4.3, 4.5	2.2	188	Σ2909	Slowly widening.
Σ3050 And	23	59.4	+33 43	6.6, 6.6	1.9	332	—	Period 350 years.

Some Interesting Nebulae, Clusters and Galaxies

Object	RA		Declina-tion		Remarks
	h	m	°	′	
M31 Andromedae	00	40.7	+41	05	Andromeda Galaxy, visible to naked eye.
H VIII 78 Cassiopeiae	00	41.3	+61	36	Fine cluster, between Gamma and Kappa Cassiopeiae.
M33 Trianguli	01	31.8	+30	28	Spiral. Difficult with small apertures.
H VI 33–4 Persei	02	18.3	+56	59	Double Cluster; Sword-handle.
Δ142 Doradus	05	39.1	−69	09	Looped nebula round 30 Doradus. Naked-eye. In Large Magellanic Cloud.
M1 Tauri	05	32.3	+22	00	Crab Nebula, near Zeta Tauri.
M42 Orionis	05	33.4	−05	24	Orion Nebula. Contains the famous Trapezium, Theta Orionis.
M35 Geminorum	06	06.5	+24	21	Open cluster near Eta Geminorum.
H VII 2 Monocerotis	06	30.7	+04	53	Open cluster, just visible to naked eye.
M41 Canis Majoris	06	45.5	−20	42	Open cluster, just visible to naked eye.
M47 Puppis	07	34.3	−14	22	Mag. 5.2. Loose cluster.
H IV 64 Puppis	07	39.6	−18	05	Bright planetary in rich neighbourhood.
M46 Puppis	07	39.5	−14	42	Open cluster.
M44 Cancri	08	38	+20	07	Praesepe. Open cluster near Delta Cancri. Visible to naked eye.
M97 Ursae Majoris	11	12.6	+55	13	Owl Nebula, diameter 3′. Planetary.
Kappa Crucis	12	50.7	−60	05	'Jewel Box'; open cluster, with stars of contrasting colours.
M3 Can. Ven.	13	40.6	+28	34	Bright globular.
Omega Centauri	13	23.7	−47	03	Finest of all globulars. Easy with naked eye.
M80 Scorpii	16	14.9	−22	53	Globular, between Antares and Beta Scorpii.
M4 Scorpii	16	21.5	−26	26	Open cluster close to Antares.
M13 Herculis	16	40	+36	31	Globular. Just visible to naked eye.

Object	RA		Declina-tion		Remarks
	h	m	°	′	
M92 Herculis	16	16.1	+43	11	Globular. Between Iota and Eta Herculis.
M6 Scorpii	17	36.8	−32	11	Open cluster; naked eye.
M7 Scorpii	17	50.6	−34	48	Very bright open cluster; naked eye.
M23 Sagittarii	17	54.8	−19	01	Open cluster nearly 50′ in diameter.
H IV 37 Draconis	17	58.6	+66	38	Bright planetary.
M8 Sagittarii	18	01.4	−24	23	Lagoon Nebula. Gaseous. Just visible with naked eye.
NGC 6572 Ophiuchi	18	10.9	+06	50	Bright planetary, between Beta Ophiuchi and Zeta Aquilae.
M17 Sagittarii	18	18.8	−16	12	Omega Nebula. Gaseous. Large and bright.
M11 Scuti	18	49.0	−06	19	Wild Duck. Bright open cluster.
M57 Lyrae	18	52.6	+32	59	Ring Nebula. Brightest of planetaries.
M27 Vulpeculae	19	58.1	+22	37	Dumbbell Nebula, near Gamma Sagittae.
H IV 1 Aquarii	21	02.1	−11	31	Bright planetary, near Nu Aquarii.
M15 Pegasi	21	28.3	+12	01	Bright globular, near Epsilon Pegasi.
M39 Cygni	21	31.0	+48	17	Open cluster between Deneb and Alpha Lacertae. Well seen with low powers.

Our Contributors

Dr Paul Murdin is Head of Astronomy at the Particle Physics and Astronomy Research Council (PPARC) and Director of Science at the British National Space Centre. He is, of course, one of our most regular and valued contributors.

Dr Colin Taylor is first and foremost an astronomer, but has a lifelong interest in the Plains Indians, and is a recognized authority on the subject.

Dr Fred Watson is Astronomer-in-Charge of the Anglo-Australian Observatory near Coonabarabran, New South Wales. When he observes with the Anglo-Australian Telescope or the UK Schmidt Telescope, binoculars are seldom far out of reach.

Bob Turner is an amateur astronomer with a special interest in the Sun. He has his observatory at Worthing in Sussex.

David Hawksett is a specialist in Solar System studies, and has a particular interest in the satellites of Jupiter; Io is at present the main subject of his research.

Dr Joe McCall, one of the world's leading specialists in the study of meteorites, spent some time in Western Australia, but now lives in England.

Chris Lintott, now at Cambridge University, has been an active member of the British Astronomical Association for several years, and has been co-editor of the Association's Student Newsletter. He serves on the BAA Council.

Dr Helen Walker carries out her research at the Rutherford-Appleton Laboratory in Oxfordshire, and has been paying special attention to infrared astronomy.

Iain Nicolson is one of our most regular contributors. He was for many years Senior Lecturer in Astronomy at the University of Hertfordshire, but now devotes his time to writing and broadcasting – from his island home off Oban in Scotland.

Martin Mobberly is a leading amateur astronomer; he is immediate Past Present of the British Astronomical Association.

The William Herschel Society maintains the museum established at 19 New King Street, Bath BA1 2BL – the only surviving Herschel House. It also undertakes activities of various kinds. New members would be welcome; those interested are asked to contact the MembershipSecretary at the museum.

Astronomical Societies in the British Isles

British Astronomical Association
Assistant Secretary: Burlington House, Piccadilly, London WIV 9AG.
Meetings: Lecture Hall of Scientific Societies, Civil Service Commission Building, 23 Savile Row, London W1. Last Wednesday each month (Oct.–June). 5 p.m. and some Saturday afternoons.

Association for Astronomy Education
Secretary: Teresa Grafton, The Association for Astronomy Education, c/o The Royal Astronomical Society, Burlington House, Piccadilly, London WIV 0NL.

Astronomy Ireland
Secretary: Tony Ryan, PO Box 2888, Dublin 1, Ireland.
Meetings: 2nd and 4th Mondays of each month. Telescope meetings, every clear Saturday.

Federation of Astronomical Societies
Secretary: Clive Down, 10 Glan-y-Llyn, North Cornelly, Bridgend County Borough, CF33 4EF.

Junior Astronomical Society of Ireland
Secretary: K. Nolan, 5 St Patrick's Crescent, Rathcoole, Co. Dublin.
Meetings: The Royal Dublin Society, Ballsbridge, Dublin 4. Monthly.

Society for Popular Astronomy (was **Junior Astronomical Society**)
Secretary: Guy Fennimore, 36 Fairway, Keyworth, Nottingham, NG12 5DU.
Meetings: Last Saturday in Jan., Apr., July, Oct., 2.30 p.m. in London.

Webb Society
Secretary: M. B. Swan, Carrowreagh, Kilshanny, Kilfenora, Co. Clare, Ireland.

Aberdeen and District Astronomical Society
Secretary: Ian C. Giddings, 95 Brentfield Circle, Ellon, Aberdeenshire AB41 9DB.
Meetings: Robert Gordon's Institute of Technology, St Andrew's Street, Aberdeen. Friday 7.30 p.m.

Abingdon Astronomical Society (was **Fitzharry's Astronomical Society**)
Secretary: Chris Holt, 9 Rutherford Close, Abingdon, Oxon OX14 2AT.
Meetings: All Saints' Methodist Church Hall, Dorchester Crescent, Abingdon, Oxon. 2nd Monday Sept.–June, 8 p.m.

Altrincham and District Astronomical Society
Secretary: Derek McComiskey, 33 Tottenhan Drive, Manchester M23 9WH.
Meetings: Timperley Village Club. 1st Friday Sept.–June, 8.00 p.m.

Andover Astronomical Society
Secretary: Mrs S. Fisher, Staddlestones, Aughton, Kingston, Marlborough, Wiltshire, SN8 3SA.
Meetings: Grately Village Hall. 3rd Thursday each month, 7.30 p.m.

Astra Astronomy Section
  Secretary: c/o Duncan Lunan, Flat 65, Dalraida House, 56 Blythswood Court, Anderston, Glasgow G2 7PE
  Meetings: Airdrie Arts Centre, Anderson Street, Airdrie. Weekly.
Astrodome Mobile School Planetarium
  Contact: Peter J. Golding, 39 Alexandra Avenue, Gillingham, Kent ME7 2LP.
Aylesbury Astronomical Society
  Secretary: Alan Smith, 182 Morley Fields, Leighton Buzzard, Bedfordshire LU7 8WN.
  Meetings: 1st Monday in Month. Details from Secretary.
Bassetlaw Astronomical Society
  Secretary: Andrew Patton, 58 Holding, Worksop, Notts S81 0TD.
  Meetings: Rhodesia Village Hall, Rhodesia, Worksop, Notts. On 2nd and 4th Tuesdays of month at 7.45 p.m.
Batley & Spenborough Astronomical Society
  Secretary: Robert Morton, 22 Links Avenue, Cleckheaton, West Yorks BD19 4EG.
  Meetings: Milner K. Ford Observatory, Wilton Park, Batley. Every Thursday, 8.00 p.m.
Bedford Astronomical Society
  Secretary: Mrs L. Harrington, 24 Swallowfield, Wyboston, Bedfordshire, MK44 3AE
  Meetings: Bedford School, Burnaby Rd, Bedford. Last Wednesday each month.
Bingham & Brookes Space Organization
  Secretary: N. Bingham, 15 Hickmore's Lane, Lindfield, W. Sussex.
Birmingham Astronomical Society
  Secretary: Peter Bolas, 4 Moat Bank, Burton-on-Trent, Staffordshire, DE15 0QJ.
  Meetings: Room 146, Aston University, last Tuesday each month, Sept. to June (except Dec., moved to 1st week in Jan.).
Blackburn Leisure Astronomy Section
  Secretary: Mr H. Murphy, 20 Princess Way, Beverley, East Yorkshire, HU17 8PD.
  Meetings: Blackburn Leisure Welfare. Mondays 8.00 p.m.
Blackpool & District Astronomical Society
  Secretary: Terry Devon, 30 Victory Road, Blackpool, Lancashire, FY1 3JT.
  Meetings: St Kentigens Social Centre, Blackpool. 1st Wednesday each month, 8.00 p.m.
Bolton Astronomical Society
  Secretary: Peter Miskiw, 9 Hedley Street, Bolton, Lancashire, BL1 3LE.
  Meetings: Ladybridge Community Centre, Bolton. 1st and 3rd Tuesdays Sept.–May, 7.30 p.m.
Border Astronomical Society
  Secretary: David Pettit, 14 Shap Grove, Carlisle, Cumbria, CA2 5QR.
  Meetings: The Observatory, Trinity School, Carlisle. Alternate Thursdays, 7.30 p.m.
Boston Astronomers
  Secretary: Mrs Lorraine Money, 18 College Park, Horncastle, Lincolnshire, LN9 6RE
  Meetings: Blackfriars Arts Centre, Boston. 2nd Monday each month, 7.30 p.m.
Bradford Astronomical Society
  Contact: Mrs J. Hilary Knaggs, 6 Meadow View, Wyke, Bradford BD12 9LA
  Meetings: Eccleshill Library, Bradford. Alternate Mondays, 7.30 p.m.
Braintree, Halstead & District Astronomical Society
  Secretary: Mr J.R. Green, 70 Dorothy Sayers Drive, Witham, Essex, CM8 2LU.
  Meetings: BT Social Club Hall, Witham Telephone Exchange. 3rd Thursday each month, 8 p.m.

Breckland Astronomical Society (was **Great Ellingham and District Astronomy Club**)
Contact: Martin Wolton, Willowbeck House, Pulham St Mary, Norfolk, IP21 4QS.
Meetings: Great Ellingham Recreation Centre, Watton Road (B1077), Great Ellingham, 2nd Friday each month, 7.15 p.m.

Bridgend Astronomical Society
Secretary: Clive Down, 10 Glan-y-Llyn, Broadlands, North Cornelly, Bridgend County, CF33 4EF.
Meetings: Bridgend Bowls Centre, Bridgend, 1st and 3rd Friday monthly, 7.30 p.m.

Bridgwater Astronomical Society
Secretary: W. L. Buckland, 104 Polden Street, Bridgwater, Somerset.
Meetings: Room D10, Bridgwater College, Bath Road Centre, Bridgwater. 2nd Wednesday each month, Sept.–June.

Bridport Astronomical Society
Secretary: Mr G. J. Lodder, 3 The Green, Walditch, Bridport, Dorset, DT6 4LB.
Meetings: Walditch Village Hall, Bridport. 1st Sunday each month, 7.30 p.m.

Brighton Astronomical and Scientific Society
Secretary: Ms T. Fearn, 38 Woodlands Close, Peacehaven, East Sussex, BN10 7SF.
Meetings: St Johns Church Hall, Hove. 1st Tuesday each month, 7.30 p.m.

Bristol Astronomical Society
Secretary: Dr John Pickard, 'Fielding', Easter Compton, Bristol BS35 5SJ.
Meetings: Frank Lecture Theatre, University of Bristol Physics Dept., alternate Fridays in term time, and Westbury Park Methodist Church Rooms, North View, other Fridays.

Cambridge Astronomical Association
Secretary: Brian Lister, 80 Ramsden Square, Cambridge CB4 2BL.
Meetings: Institute of Astronomy, Madingley Road, 3rd Friday each month.

Cardiff Astronomical Society
Secretary: D. W. S. Powell, 1 Tal-y-Bont Road, Ely, Cardiff, CF5 5EU.
Meetings: Dept. of Physics and Astronomy, University of Wales, Newport Road Cardiff. Alternate Thursdays, 8 p.m.

Castle Point Astronomy Club
Secretary: Andrew Turner, 3 Canewdon Hall Close, Canewdon, Rochford, Essex SS4 3PY.
Meetings: St Michael's Church Hall, Daws Heath. Wednesdays, 8 p.m.

Chelmsford Astronomers
Secretary: Brendan Clark, 5 Borda Close, Chelmsford, Essex.
Meetings: Once a month.

Chester Astronomical Society
Secretary: Mrs S. Brooks, 39 Halton Road, Great Sutton, South Wirral, LL66 2UF.
Meetings: All Saints Parish Church, Chester. Last Wednesday each month except Aug. and Dec., 7.30 p.m.

Chester Society of Natural Science, Literature and Art
Secretary: Paul Braid, 'White Wing', 38 Bryn Avenue, Old Colwyn, Colwyn Bay, Clwyd.
Meetings: Grosvenor Museum, Chester. Fortnightly.

Chesterfield Astronomical Society
Secretary: Mr Robert McGregor, 34 Higher Albert Street, Chesterfield, Derbyshire, S41 7QE.
Meetings: Barnet Observatory, Newbold, each Friday.

Clacton & District Astronomical Society
Secretary: C. L. Haskell, 105 London Road, Clacton-on-Sea, Essex.

Cleethorpes & District Astronomical Society
Secretary: C. Illingworth, 38 Shaw Drive, Grimsby, S. Humberside.
Meetings: Beacon Hill Observatory, Cleethorpes. 1st Wednesday each month.

Cleveland & Darlington Astronomical Society
Secretary: Dr John McCue, 40 Bradbury Road Norton, Stockton-on-Tees, TS20 1LE.
Meetings: Thorpe Thewles Parish Hall, near Stockton-on-Tees. Monthly. 2nd Friday.

Colchester Amateur Astronomers
Secretary: F. Kelly, 'Middleton', Church Road, Elmstead Market, Colchester, Essex.
Meetings: William Loveless Hall, High Street, Wivenhoe. Friday evenings. Fortnightly.

Cork Astronomy Club
Secretary: Charles Coughlan, 12 Forest Ridge Crescent, Wilton, Cork, Ireland.
Meetings: 1st Monday Sept.–May (except bank holidays).

Cornwall Astronomy Society
Secretary: J. M. Harvey, 1 Tregunna Close, Porthleven, Cornwall TR13 9LW.
Meetings: Godolphin Club, Wendron Street, Helston, Cornwall, 2nd and 4th Thursday of each month, 7.30 for 8 p.m.

Cotswold Astronomical Society
Secretary: Alan Cahill, 51 Fieldfare, Abbeydale, Gloucester GL4 4WH.
Meetings: Church House, Painswick Road, Cheltenham. 2nd Saturday each month, 8.00 p.m.

Coventry & Warwicks Astronomical Society
Secretary: V. Cooper, 5 Gisburn Close, Woodloes Park, Warwick.
Meetings: Coventry Technical College. 1st Friday each month, Sept.–June.

Crawley Astronomical Society
Secretary: Ron Gamer, 1 Pevensey Close, Pound Hill, Crawley, West Sussex RH10 7BL.
Meetings: Ifield Community Centre, Ifield Road, Crawley. 3rd Friday each month, 7.30 p.m.

Crayford Manor House Astronomical Society
Secretary: Roger Pickard, 28 Appletons, Hadlow, Kent TM1 0DT.
Meetings: Manor House Centre, Crayford. Monthly during term-time.

Croydon Astronomical Society
Secretary: John Murrell, 17 Dalmeny Road, Carshalton, Surrey.
Meetings: Lecture Theatre, Royal Russell School, Combe Lane, South Croydon. Alternate Fridays, 7.45 p.m.

Derby & District Astronomical Society
Secretary: Kevin Woodward, 3 Swiss Cottages, Chevin Road, Belper, Derbyshire.
Meetings: Friends Meeting House, Derby. 1st Friday each month, 7.30 p.m.

Doncaster Astronomical Society
Secretary: John Chapple, 5 Orchard Mews, Cusworth, Doncaster DN5 8HQ.
Meetings: Corporation Brewery Tap public house, 2nd and 4th Wednesdays each month.

Dumfries Astronomical Society
Secretary: Mr J. Sweeney, 3 Lakeview, Powfoot, Annan, DG13 5PG.
Meetings: Gracefield Arts Centre, Edinburgh Road, Dumfries. 3rd Tuesday Aug.–May, 7.30 p.m.

Dundee Astronomical Society
    Secretary: G. Young, 37 Polepark Road, Dundee, Tayside, DD1 5QT.
    Meetings: Mills Observatory, Balgay Park, Dundee. 1st Friday each month, 7.30 p.m.
    Sept.–Apr.

Easington and District Astronomical Society
    Secretary: T. Bradley, 52 Jameson Road, Hartlepool, Co. Durham.
    Meetings: Easington Comprehensive School, Easington Colliery. Every 3rd Thursday
    throughout the year, 7.30 p.m.

Eastbourne Astronomical Society
    Secretary: Peter Gill, 18 Selwyn House, Eastbourne, East Sussex, BN21 2LF.
    Meetings: St Aiden's Church Hall, 1 Whitley Road, Eastbourne. 1st Saturday each
    month, 7.30 p.m.

East Lancashire Astronomical Society
    Secretary: D. Chadwick, 16 Worston Lane, Great Harwood, Blackburn BB6 7TH.
    Meetings: As arranged. Monthly.

East Riding Astronomers
    Secretary: Tony Scaife, 15 Beech Road, Elloughton, Brough, North Humberside,
    HU15 1JX.
    Meetings: As arranged.

Astronomical Society of Edinburgh
    Secretary: Graham Rule, 105/19 Causewayside, Edinburgh EH9 1QG.
    Meetings: City Observatory, Calton Hill, Edinburgh. 1st Friday each month, 8.00 p.m.

Edinburgh University Astronomical Society
    Secretary: c/o Dept. of Astronomy, Royal Observatory, Blackford Hill, Edinburgh.

Ewell Astronomical Society
    Secretary: G. O'Mara, 46 Stanton Close, Epsom KT19 9NP.
    Meetings: Minor Hall, Bourne Hall, Spring Street, Ewell. 1st Friday of each month
    except August, 7.45 p.m.

Exeter Astronomical Society
    Secretary: Tim Sedgwick, Old Dower House, Half Moon, Newton St Cyres, Exeter,
    Devon, EX5 5AE.
    Meetings: The Meeting Room, Wynards, Magdalen Street, Exeter. 1st Thursday of
    month.

Farnham Astronomical Society
    Secretary: Laurence Anslow, 'Asterion', 18 Wellington Lane, Farnham, Surrey,
    GU9 9BA.
    Meetings: Church House, Union Road, Farnham. 2nd Monday each month, 7.45 p.m.

Foredown Tower Astronomy Group
    Secretary: M. Feist, Foredown Tower Camera Obscura, Foredown Road, Portslade,
    East Sussex BN4 2EW.
    Meetings: At the above address, 3rd Tuesday each month.

Fylde Astronomical Society
    Secretary: 28 Belvedere Road, Thornton, Lancs.
    Meetings: Stanley Hall, Rossendale Avenue South. 1st Wednesday each month.

Astronomical Society of Glasgow
    Secretary: Mr Robert Hughes, Apartment 8/4, 75 Plean Street, Glasgow G14 0YW.
    Meetings: University of Strathclyde, George St, Glasgow. 3rd Thursday each month,
    Sep.–Apr., 7.30 p.m.

Greenock Astronomical Society
Secretary: Carl Hempsey, 49 Brisbane Street, Greenock.
Meetings: Greenock Arts Guild, 3 Campbell Street, Greenock.

Grimsby Astronomical Society
Secretary: R. Williams, 14 Richmond Close, Grimsby, South Humberside.
Meetings: Secretary's home. 2nd Thursday each month, 7.30 p.m.

Guernsey: La Société Guernesiaise Astronomy Section
Secretary: Ken Staples, 4 Le Felconte, St Peters, Guernsey GY7 9QB.
Meetings: The Observatory, St Peters, Tuesdays, 8 p.m.

Guildford Astronomical Society
Secretary: A. Langmaid, 22 West Mount, The Mount, Guildford, Surrey, GU2 5HL.
Meetings: Guildford Institute, Ward Street, Guildford. 1st Thursday each month, except Aug., 7.30 p.m.

Gwynedd Astronomical Society
Secretary: Mr Ernie Greenwood, 18 Twrcelyn Street, Llanerchymedd, Anglesey LL74 8TL.
Meetings: Dept. of Electronic Engineering, Bangor University. 1st Thursday each month except August, 7.30 p.m.

The Hampshire Astronomical Group
Secretary: Geoff Mann, 11 Fir Tree Gardens, Horndean, Waterlooville, Hampshire PO8 9HF.
Meetings: Clanfield Memorial Hall. Each Friday, 7.30 p.m.

Hanney & District Astronomical Society
Secretary: Bob Church, 47 Upthorpe Drive, Wantage, Oxfordshire, OX12 7DG.
Meetings: Last Thursday each month, 8.00 p.m.

Astronomical Society of Haringey
Secretary: Jerry Workman, 91 Greenslade Road, Barking, Essex, IG11 9XF.
Meetings: Palm Court, Alexandra Palace. 3rd Wednesday each month, 8 p.m.

Harrogate Astronomical Society
Secretary: Brian Bonser, 114 Main Street, Little Ouseburn, TO5 9TG.
Meetings: National Power HQ, Beckwith Knowle, Harrogate. Last Friday each month.

Hastings and Battle Astronomical Society
Secretary: K. A. Woodcock, 24 Ennabuek Road, Hastings, East Sussex, TN34 3LB.
Meetings: As arranged.

Havering Astronomical Society
Secretary: Frances Ridgley, 133 Severn Drive, Upminster, Essex RM14 1PP.
Meetings: Cranham Community Centre, Marlborough Gardens, Upminster, Essex. 3rd Wednesday each month (except July and Aug.), 7.30 p.m.

Heart of England Astronomical Society
Secretary: John Williams, 100 Stanway Road, Shirley, Solihull, B90 3JG.
Meetings: Furnace End Village, every Thursday.

Hebden Bridge Literary & Scientific Society, Astronomical Section
Secretary: Peter Jackson, 44 Gilstead Lane, Bingley, West Yorkshire, BD16 3NP.
Meetings: Hebden Bridge Information Centre, Last Wednesday, Sept.–May.

Herschel Astronomy Society
Secretary: Kevin Bishop, 106 Holmsdale, Crown Wood, Bracknell, Berkshire, RG12 3TB.
Meetings: Eton College, 2nd Friday each month, 7.30 p.m.

Highlands Astronomical Society
 Secretary: Richard Green, 11 Drumossie Avenue, Culcabock, Inverness IV2 3SJ.
 Meetings: The Spectrum Centre, Inverness. 1st Tuesday each month, 7.30 p.m.

Hinckley & District Astronomical Society
 Secretary: Mr S. Albrighton, 4 Walnut Close, The Bridleways, Hartshill, Nuneaton, Warwickshire, CV10 0XH.
 Meetings: Burbage Common Visitors Centre, Hinckley. 1st Tuesday Sept.–May, 7.30 p.m.

Horsham Astronomy Group (was **Forest Astronomical Society**)
 Secretary: Mr A. R. Clarke, 93 Clarence Road, Horsham, West Sussex, RH13 5SL.
 Meetings: 1st Wednesday each month.

Howards Astronomy Club
 Secretary: H. Ilett, 22 St Georges Avenue, Warblington, Havant, Hants.
 Meetings: To be notified.

Huddersfield Astronomical and Philosophical Society
 Secretary: R. A. Williams, 43 Oaklands Drive, Dalton, Huddersfield HD5 8PR.
 Meetings: 4a Railway Street, Huddersfield. Every Friday, 7.30 p.m.

Hull and East Riding Astronomical Society
 Secretary: Tony Scaife, 15 Beech Road, Elloughton, Brough, North Humberside, HU15 1JX.
 Meetings: Wyke 6th Form College, Bricknell Avenue, Hull. 2nd Tuesday each month, Oct.–Apr., 7.30 p.m.

Ilkeston & District Astronomical Society
 Secretary: Mark Thomas, 2 Elm Avenue, Sandiacre, Nottingham NG10 5EJ.
 Meetings: The Function Room, Erewash Museum, Anchor Row, Ilkeston. 2nd Tuesday monthly, 7.30 p.m.

Ipswich, Orwell Astronomical Society
 Secretary: R. Gooding, 168 Ashcroft Road, Ipswich.
 Meetings: Orwell Park Observatory, Nacton, Ipswich. Wednesdays 8 p.m.

Irish Astronomical Association
 Secretary: Barry Loane, 4 Belfast Road, Newtownards, Co. Down, NG10 5EJ.
 Meetings: Ashby Building, Stranmillis Road, Belfast. Alternate Wednesdays, 7.30 p.m.

Irish Astronomical Society
 Secretary: James O'Connor, PO Box 2547, Dublin 15, Ireland.
 Meetings: Ely House, 8 Ely Place, Dublin 2. 1st and 3rd Monday each month.

Isle of Man Astronomical Society
 Secretary: James Martin, Ballaterson Farm, Peel, Isle of Man IM5 3AB.
 Meetings: The Manx Automobile Club, Hill Street, Douglas. 1st Thursday of each month, 8.00 p.m.

Isle of Wight Astronomical Society
 Secretary: J. W. Feakins, 1 Hilltop Cottages, High Street, Freshwater, Isle of Wight.
 Meetings: Unitarian Church Hall, Newport, Isle of Wight. Monthly.

Keele Astronomical Society
 Secretary: Natalie Webb, Department of Physics, University of Keele, Keele, Staffordshire, ST5 5BG.
 Meetings: As arranged during term time.

Kettering and District Astronomical Society
Asst. Secretary: Steve Williams, 120 Brickhill Road, Wellingborough, Northants.
Meetings: Quaker Meeting Hall, Northall Street, Kettering, Northants. 1st Tuesday each month. 7.45 p.m.

King's Lynn Amateur Astronomical Association
Secretary: P. Twynman, 17 Poplar Avenue, RAF Marham, King's Lynn.
Meetings: As arranged.

Lancaster and Morecambe Astronomical Society
Secretary: Miss E. Haygarth, 27 Coulston Road, Bowerham, Lancaster.
Meetings: Midland Hotel, Morecambe. 1st Wednesday each month except Jan. 7.30 p.m.

Lancaster University Astronomical Society
Secretary: c/o Students Union, Alexandra Square, University of Lancaster.
Meetings: As arranged.

Laymans Astronomical Society
Secretary: John Evans, 10 Arkwright Walk, The Meadows, Nottingham.
Meetings: The Popular, Bath Street, Ilkeston, Derbyshire. Monthly.

Leeds Astronomical Society
Secretary: Ray Emery, 39 Churchfield Lane, Rothwell, Leeds LS26 0NA.
Meetings: Centenary House, North Street. 2nd Wednesday each month, 7.30 p.m.

Leicester Astronomical Society
Secretary: Dr P. J. Scott, 21 Rembridge Close, Leicester LE3 9AP.
Meetings: Judgemeadow Community College, Marydene Drive, Evington, Leicester. 2nd and 4th Tuesdays each month, 7.30 p.m.

Letchworth and District Astronomical Society
Secretary: Eric Hutton, 14 Folly Close, Hitchin, Herts.
Meetings: As arranged.

Lewes Amateur Astronomers
Secretary: Christa Sutton, 8 Tower Road, Lancing, West Sussex, BN15 9HT.
Meetings: The Bakehouse Studio, Lewes. Last Wednesday each month.

Limerick Astronomy Club
Secretary: Tony O'Hanlon, 26 Ballycannon Heights, Meelick, Co. Clare, Ireland.
Meetings: Limerick Senior College, Limerick, Ireland. Monthly (except June and Aug.), 8 p.m.

Lincoln Astronomical Society
Secretary: David Swaey, 'Everglades', 13 Beaufort Close, Lincoln LN2 4SF.
Meetings: The Lecture Hall, off Westcliffe Street, Lincoln. 1st Tuesday each month.

Liverpool Astronomical Society
Secretary: Mr K. Clark, 31 Sandymount Drive, Wallasey, Merseyside L45 0LJ.
Meetings: Lecture Theatre, Liverpool Museum, 3rd Friday each month, 7.00 p.m.

Norman Lockyer Observatory Society
Secretary: Mr G. E. White, 6 Burrow Close, Newton Poppleford, Sidmouth, Devon, EX10 0BS.
Meetings: Norman Lockyer Observatory, Sidmouth, Fridays and 2nd Monday each month, 7.30 p.m.

Loughton Astronomical Society
Secretary: Charles Munton, 14a Manor Road, Wood Green, London N22 4YJ
Meetings: 1st Theydon Bois Scout Hall, Loughton Lane, Theydon Bois. Weekly.

Lowestoft and Great Yarmouth Regional Astronomers (LYRA) Society
Secretary: Simon Briggs, 28 Sussex Road, Lowestoft, Suffolk.
Meetings: Community Wing, Kirkley High School, Kirkley Run, Lowestoft. 3rd Thursday each month, 7.30 p.m.

Luton Astronomical Society
Secretary: Mr G. Mitchell, 47 Rossfold Road, Luton LU3 3HJ.
Meetings: Putteridge Bury, Luton. Last Friday each month, 7.30 p.m.

Lytham St Annes Astronomical Association
Secretary: K. J. Porter, 141 Blackpool Road, Ansdell, Lytham St Annes, Lancs.
Meetings: College of Further Education, Clifton Drive South, Lytham St Annes. 2nd Wednesday monthly Oct.–June.

Macclesfield Astronomical Society
Secretary: Mrs Cherry Moss, 164a Chester Road, Macclesfield, Cheshire, SK11 8PT.
Meetings: Jodrell Bank Science Centre, 1st Tuesday each month.

Maidenhead Astronomical Society
Secretary: Tim Haymes, Hill Rise, Knowl Hill Common, Knowl Hill, Reading RG10 9YD.
Meetings: Stubbings Church Hall, near Maidenhead, 1st Friday Sept.–June.

Maidstone Astronomical Society
Secretary: Stephen James, 4 The Cherry Orchard, Haddow, Tonbridge, Kent.
Meetings: Nettlestead Village Hall, 1st Tuesday in month except July and Aug. 7.30 p.m.

Manchester Astronomical Society
Secretary: Mr J. H. W. Davidson, Godlee Observatory, UMIST, Sackville Street, Manchester M60 1QD.
Meetings: At the Observatory, Thursdays, 7.00 p.m.

Mansfield and Sutton Astronomical Society
Secretary: Angus Wright, Sherwood Observatory, Coxmoor Road, Sutton-in-Ashfield, Nottinghamshire NG17 5LF.
Meetings: Sherwood Observatory, Coxmoor Road. Last Tuesday each month, 7.30 p.m.

Mexborough and Swinton Astronomical Society
Secretary: Mark R. Benton, 14 Sandalwood Rise, Swinton, Mexborough, South Yorkshire, S64 8PN.
Meetings: Swinton WMC, Thursdays, 7.30 p.m.

Mid-Kent Astronomical Society
Secretary: Peter Bassett, 167 Shakespeare Road, Gillingham, Kent, ME7 5QB.
Meetings: Riverside Country Park, Lower Rainham Road, Gillingham. 2nd and last Fridays each month, 7.45 p.m.

Milton Keynes Astronomical Society
Secretary: Mark Hurn, 23 Wallread Gardens, Loughton, Milton Keynes.
Meetings: Rectory Cottage, Bletchley. Alternate Tuesdays.

Moray Astronomical Society
Secretary: Richard Pearce, 1 Forsyth Street, Hopeman, Elgin, Moray, Scotland.
Meetings: Village Hall Close, Co. Elgin.

Newbury Amateur Astronomical Society
Secretary: Miss Nicola Evans, 'Romaron', Bunces Lane, Burghfield Common, Reading RG7 3DG.
Meetings: United Reformed Church Hall, Cromwell Place, Newbury. 2nd Friday of month, Sept.–June.

Newcastle-on-Tyne Astronomical Society
Secretary: C. E. Willits, 24 Acomb Avenue, Seaton Delaval, Tyne and Wear.
Meetings: Zoology Lecture Theatre, Newcastle University, Monthly.

North Aston Space & Astronomical Club
Secretary: W. R. Chadburn, 14 Oakdale Road, North Aston, Sheffield.
Meetings: To be notified.

Northamptonshire Natural History Society (Astronomy Section)
Secretary: Dr Nick Hewitt, 4 Daimler Close, Northampton NN3 5JT
Meetings: Humfrey Rooms, Castilian Terrace, Northampton, 2nd and 4th Mondays, most months, 7.30 p.m.

Northants Amateur Astronomers
Secretary: Mervyn Lloyd, 76 Havelock Street, Kettering, Northamptonshire.
Meetings: 1st and 3rd Tuesday each month, 7.30 p.m.

North Devon Astronomical Society
Secretary: P. G. Vickery, 12 Broad Park Crescent, Ilfracombe, Devon EX34 8DX.
Meetings: Methodist Hall, Rhododendron Avenue, Sticklepath, Barnstaple. 1st Wednesday each month, 7.15 p.m.

North Dorset Astronomical Society
Secretary: J. E. M. Coward, The Pharmacy, Stalbridge, Dorset.
Meetings: Charterhay, Stourton, Caundle, Dorset. 2nd Wednesday each month.

North Downs Astronomical Society
Secretary: Martin Akers, 36 Timber Tops, Lordswood, Chatham, Kent, ME5 8XQ.
Meetings: Vigo Village Hall. 3rd Thursday each month. 7.30 p.m.

North-East London Astronomical Society
Secretary: Mr B. Beeston, 38 Abbey Road, Bush Hill Park, Enfield EN1 2QN.
Meetings: Wanstead House, The Green, Wanstead. 3rd Sunday each month (except Aug.), 3.00 p.m.

North Gwent Astronomical Society
Secretary: J. Powell, 14 Lancaster Drive, Gilwern, nr Abergavenny, Gwent NP7 0AA.
Meetings: Gilwern Community Centre, 15th of each month, 7.30 p.m.

North Staffordshire Astronomical Society
Secretary: Duncan Richardson, Halmerend Farm, Halmerend, Stoke-on-Trent, Staffordshire, ST7 8AW.
Meetings: 21st Hartshill Scout Group HQ, Mount Pleasant, Newcastle-under-Lyme. 1st Tuesday each month (except July and Aug.).

North Western Association of Variable Star Observers
Secretary: Jeremy Bullivant, 2 Beaminster Road, Heaton Mersey, Stockport, Cheshire.
Meetings: Four annually.

Norwich Astronomical Society
Secretary: Frank Lawlor, 'Farnworth', Poringland Road, Upper Stoke Holy Cross, Norwich NR14 8NW
Meetings: Seething Observatory, Toad Lane, Thwaite St Mary, Norfolk. Every Friday, 7.30 p.m.

Nottingham Astronomical Society
Secretary: C. Brennan, 40 Swindon Close, The Vale, Giltbrook, Nottingham NG16 2WD.
Meetings: Djanogly City Technology College, Sherwood Rise (B682). 1st and 3rd Thursdays each month, 7.30 p.m.

Oldham Astronomical Society
Secretary: P. J. Collins, 25 Park Crescent, Chadderton, Oldham.
Meetings: Werneth Park Study Centre, Frederick Street, Oldham. Fortnightly, Friday.

Open University Astronomical Society
Secretary: Jim Lee, c/o above, Milton Keynes.
Meetings: Open University, Walton Hall, Milton Keynes. As arranged.

Orpington Astronomical Society
Secretary: Dr Ian Carstairs, 38 Brabourne Rise, Beckenham, Kent BR3 2SG.
Meetings: High Elms Nature Centre, High Elms Country Park, High Elms Road, Farnborough, Kent. 4th Thursday each month, Sept.–July, 7.30. p.m.

Papworth Astronomy Club
Secretary: Keith Tritton, Magpie Cottage, Fox Street, Great Gransden, Sandy, Bedfordshire, SG19 3AA.
Meetings: Bradbury Progression Centre, Church Lane, Papworth Everard, near Huntingdon. 1st Wednesday each month, 7.00 p.m.

Pendle Astronomical Society
Secretary: Kevin Pickup, 25 Lancaster Street, Colne, Lancashire.
Meetings: Parish Hall, Sacred Heart, Colne. 1st Tuesday each month, 7.30 p.m.

Peterborough Astronomical Society
Secretary: Sheila Thorpe, 6 Cypress Close, Longthorpe, Peterborough.
Meetings: 1st Thursday every month at 7.30 p.m.

Plymouth Astronomical Society
Secretary: Alan G. Penman, 12 St Maurice View, Plympton, Plymouth, Devon, PL7 1FQ.
Meetings: Glynis Kingham Centre, YMCA Annex, Lockyer Street, Plymouth, 2nd Friday each month, 7.30 p.m.

PONLAF
Secretary: Matthew Hepburn, 6 Court Road, Caterham, Surrey, CR3 5RD.
Meetings: Room 5, 6th Floor, Tower Block, University of North London. Last Friday each month during term time, 6.30 p.m.

Port Talbot Astronomical Society (was **Astronomical Society of Wales**)
Secretary: Mr J. Hawes, 15 Lodge Drive, Baglan, Port Talbot, West Glamorgan SA12 8UD.
Meetings: Port Talbot Arts Centre, 1st Tuesday each month, 7.15 p.m.

Portsmouth Astronomical Society
Secretary: G. B. Bryant, 81 Ringwood Road, Southsea.
Meetings: Monday, fortnightly.

Preston & District Astronomical Society
Secretary: P. Sloane, 77 Ribby Road, Wrea Green, Kirkham, Preston, Lancs.
Meetings: Moor Park (Jeremiah Horrocks) Observatory, Preston. 2nd Wednesday, last Friday each month. 7.30 p.m.

The Pulsar Group
Secretary: Barry Smith, 157 Reridge Road, Blackburn, Lancs.
Meetings: Amateur Astronomy Centre, Clough Bank, Bacup Road, Todmorden, Lancs. 1st Thursday each month.

Reading Astronomical Society
Secretary: Mrs Ruth Sumner, 22 Anson Crescent, Shinfield, Reading RG2 8JT.
Meetings: St Peter's Church Hall, Church Road, Earley. 3rd Friday each month, 7 p.m.

Renfrew District Astronomical Society (formerly **Paisley A.S.**)
Secretary: Mark Pollock, 14 Mains Wood, Erskine, PA8 7JW.
Meetings: Coats Observatory, Oakshaw Street, Paisley, Fridays, 7.30 p.m.

Richmond & Kew Astronomical Society
Secretary: Stewart McLaughlin, 41a Bruce Road, Mitcham, Surrey CR4 2BJ.
Meetings: Richmond Adult College, Parkshot, Richmond, Surrey, and the King's Observatory, Old Deer Park, Richmond, Surrey. Bimonthly.

Rower Astronomical Club
Secretary: Mary Kelly, Knockatore, The Rower, Thomastown, Co. Kilkenny, Ireland.

St Helens Amateur Astronomical Society
Secretary: Carl Dingsdale, 125 Canberra Avenue, Thatto Heath, St Helens, Merseyside WA9 5RT.
Meetings: As arranged.

Salford Astronomical Society
Secretary: Mrs Kath Redford, 2 Albermarle Road, Swinton, Manchester M27 5ST.
Meetings: The Observatory, Chaseley Road, Salford, Wednesdays.

Salisbury Astronomical Society
Secretary: Mrs R. Collins, 3 Fairview Road, Salisbury, Wiltshire, SP1 1JX.
Meetings: Glebe Hall, Winterbourne Earls, Salisbury. 1st Tuesday each month.

Sandbach Astronomical Society
Secretary: Phil Benson, 8 Gawsworth Drive, Sandbach, Cheshire.
Meetings: Sandbach School, as arranged.

Sawtry & District Astronomical Society
Secretary: Brooke Norton, 2 Newton Road, Sawtry, Huntingdon, Cambridgeshire, PE17 5UT.
Meetings: Greenfields Cricket Pavilion, Sawtry Fen. Last Friday each month.

Scarborough & District Astronomical Society
Secretary: Mrs S. Anderson, Basin House Farm, Sawdon, Scarborough, N. Yorks.
Meetings: Scarborough Public Library. Last Saturday each month, 7–9 p.m.

Scottish Astronomers Group
Secretary: Dr Ken Mackay, Hayford House, Cambusbarron, Stirling, FK7 9PR.
Meetings: North of Hadrian's Wall, twice yearly.

Sheffield Astronomical Society
Secretary: Mr Darren Swindells, 102 Sheffield Road, Sheffield S13 7EU.
Meetings: Mayfield Environmental Education Centre, David Lane, Sheffield S10. Twice monthly, 7.30–10 p.m.

Shetland Astronomical Society
Secretary: Chris McGinlay, Roselynn, Levenwick, Shetland.
Meetings: Clickimin Horizons Café. 1st Thursday of each month, Sept.–Apr., 6 p.m.

Shropshire Astronomical Society
Contact: David Woodward, 20 Station Road, Condover, Shrewsbury ST5 7BQ.
Meetings: The Gateway Arts & Education Centre, Shrewsbury. Occasional Fridays, 7.30 p.m.

Sidmouth and District Astronomical Society
Secretary: M. Grant, Salters Meadow, Sidmouth, Devon.
Meetings: Norman Lockyer Observatory, Salcombe Hill. 1st Monday in each month.

Solent Amateur Astronomers
Secretary: Ken Medway, 443 Burgess Road, Swaythling, Southampton SO16 3BL.
Meetings: Room 2, Oaklands Community School, Fairisle Road, Lordshill, Southampton. 3rd Tuesday each month, 7.30 p.m.

Southampton Astronomical Society
Secretary: John Thompson, 4 Heathfield, Hythe, Southampton.
Meetings: Conference Room 3, the Civic Centre, Southampton, 2nd Thursday each month (except August), 7.30 p.m.

South Downs Astronomical Society
Secretary: J. Green, 46 Central Avenue, Bognor Regis, West Sussex.
Meetings: Assembly Rooms, Chichester. 1st Friday in each month.

South-East Essex Astronomical Society
Secretary: C. P. Jones, 92 Long Riding, Basildon, Essex.
Meetings: Lecture Theatre, Central Library, Victoria Avenue, Southend-on-Sea. Generally 1st Thursday in month, Sept.–May, 7.30 p.m.

South-East Kent Astronomical Society
Secretary: Andrew McCarthy, 25 St Paul's Way, Sandgate, near Folkestone, Kent, CT20 3NT.
Meetings: Monthly.

South Lincolnshire Astronomical & Geophysical Society
Secretary: Ian Farley, 12 West Road, Bourne, Lincolnshire, PE10 9PS.
Meetings: Adult Education Study Centre, Pinchbeck. 3rd Wednesday each month, 7.30 p.m.

Southport Astronomical Society
Secretary: Patrick Brannon, Willow Cottage, 90 Jacksmere Lane, Scarisbrick, Ormskirk, Lancashire, L40 9RS.
Meetings: Monthly Sept.–May, plus observing sessions.

Southport, Ormskirk and District Astronomical Society
Secretary: J. T. Harrison, 92 Cottage Lane, Ormskirk, Lancs L39 3NJ.
Meetings: Saturday evenings, monthly as arranged.

South Shields Astronomical Society
Secretary: c/o South Tyneside College, St George's Avenue, South Shields.
Meetings: Marine and Technical College. Each Thursday, 7.30 p.m.

South Somerset Astronomical Society
Secretary: G. McNelly, 11 Laxton Close, Taunton, Somerset.
Meetings: Victoria Inn, Skittle Alley, East Reach, Taunton. Last Saturday each month, 7.30 p.m.

South-West Cotswolds Astronomical Society
Secretary: C. R. Wiles, Old Castle House, The Triangle, Malmesbury, Wilts.
Meetings: 2nd Friday each month, 8 p.m. (Sept.–June).

South-West Hertfordshire Astronomical Society
Secretary: Tom Walsh, 'Finches', Coleshill Lane, Winchmore Hill, Amersham, Buckinghamshire, HP7 0NP.
Meetings: Rickmansworth. Last Friday each month, Sept.–May.

Stafford and District Astronomical Society
Secretary: Miss L. Hodkinson, 6 Elm Walk, Penkridge, Staffordshire, ST19 5NL.
Meetings: Weston Road High School, Stafford. Every 3rd Thursday, Sept.–May, 7.15 p.m.

Stirling Astronomical Society
Secretary: Hamish MacPhee, 10 Causewayhead Road, Stirling FK9 5ER
Meetings: Smith Museum & Art Gallery, Dumbarton Road, Stirling. 2nd Friday each month, 7.30 p.m.

Stoke-on-Trent Astronomical Society
Secretary: M. Pace, Sundale, Dunnocksfold Road, Alsager, Stoke-on-Trent.
Meetings: Cartwright House, Broad Street, Hanley. Monthly.

Stratford-upon-Avon Astronomical Society
Secretary: Robin Swinbourne, 18 Old Milverton, Leamington Spa, Warwickshire, CV32 6SA.
Meetings: Tiddington Home Guard Club. 4th Tuesday each month, 7.30 p.m.

Sunderland Astronomical Society
Contact: Don Simpson, 78 Stratford Avenue, Grangetown, Sunderland SR2 8RZ.
Meetings: Friends Meeting House, Roker. 1st, 2nd and 3rd Sundays each month.

Sussex Astronomical Society
Secretary: Mrs C. G. Sutton, 75 Vale Road, Portslade, Sussex.
Meetings: English Language Centre, Third Avenue, Hove. Every Wednesday, 7.30–9.30 p.m. Sept.–May.

Swansea Astronomical Society
Secretary: Maurice Convey, 132 Eaton Crescent, Uplands, Swansea SA1 4QR.
Meetings: Lecture Room C, Mathematics and Physics Building, University of Swansea. 2nd and 4th Thursdays each month, 7.00 p.m.

Tavistock Astronomical Society
Secretary: Mrs Ellie Coombes, Rosemount, Under Road, Gunnislake, Cornwall PL18 9JL.
Meetings: Science Laboratory, Kelly College, Tavistock. 1st Wednesday each month, 7.30 p.m.

Thames Valley Astronomical Group
Secretary: K. J. Pallet, 82a Tennyson Street, South Lambeth, London SW8 3TH.
Meetings: As arranged.

Thanet Amateur Astronomical Society
Secretary: P.F. Jordan, 85 Crescent Road, Ramsgate.
Meetings: Hilderstone House, Broadstairs, Kent. Monthly.

Torbay Astronomical Society
Secretary: Tim Moffatt, 31 Netley Road, Newton Abbot, Devon, TQ12 2LL.
Meetings: Torquay Boys' Grammar School, 1st Thursday in month; and Town Hall, Torquay, 3rd Thursday in month, Oct.–May, 7.30 p.m.

Tullamore Astronomical Society
Secretary: Sean McKenna, 145 Arden Vale, Tullamore, Co. Offaly, Ireland.
Meetings: Tullamore Vocational School. Tuesdays, Oct.–June, 8 p.m.

Tyrone Astronomical Society
Secretary: John Ryan, 105 Coolnafranky Park, Cookstown, Co. Tyrone.
Meetings: Contact Secretary.

Usk Astronomical Society
Secretary: Bob Wright, Llwyn Celyn, 75 Woodland Road, Croesyceiliog, Cwmbran, NP44 2OX.
Meetings: Usk Community Education Centre, Maryport Street. Each Thursday during school term, 7.00 p.m.

Vectis Astronomical Society
Secretary: J. W. Smith, 27 Forest Road, Winford, Sandown, Isle of Wight, PO36 0JY.
Meetings: Lord Louis Library Meeting Room, Newport. 4th Friday each month except Dec., 7.30 p.m.

Vigo Astronomical Society
Secretary: Robert Wilson, 43 Admers Wood, Vigo Village, Meopham, Kent DA13 0SP.
Meetings: Vigo Village Hall, as arranged.

Walsall Astronomical Society
Secretary: Bob Cleverley, 40 Mayfield Road, Sutton Coldfield, B74 3PZ
Meetings: Freetrade Inn, Wood Lane, Pelsall North Common.

Wellingborough District Astronomical Society
Secretary: S. M. Williams, 120 Brickhill Road, Wellingborough, Northants.
Meetings: 2nd Wednesday each month. Gloucester Hall, Church Street, Wellingborough, 7.30 p.m.

Wessex Astronomical Society
Secretary: Leslie Fry, 14 Hanhum Road, Corfe Mullen, Dorset.
Meetings: Allendale Centre, Wimborne, Dorset. 1st Tuesday of each month.

West Cornwall Astronomical Society
Secretary: Dr R. Wadding, The Pines, Penzance Road, Falmouth, Cornwall, TR11 4ED.
Meetings: Helston Football Club, 3rd Thursday each month, and St Michalls Hotel, 1st Wednesday each month, 7.30 p.m.

West of London Astronomical Society
Secretary: Tom H. Ella, 25 Boxtree Road, Harrow Weald, Harrow, Middlesex.
Meetings: Monthly, alternately at Uxbridge and North Harrow. 2nd Monday in month, except Aug.

West Midlands Astronomical Association
Secretary: Miss S. Bundy, 93 Greenridge Road, Handsworth Wood, Birmingham.
Meetings: Dr Johnson House, Bull Street, Birmingham. As arranged.

West Yorkshire Astronomical Society
Secretary: Pete Lunn, 21 Crawford Drive, Wakefield, West Yorkshire.
Meetings: Rosse Observatory, Carleton Community Centre, Carleton Road, Pontefract, each Tuesday, 7.15 p.m.

Whitby and District Astronomical Society
Secretary: Rosemary Bowman, The Cottage, Larpool Drive, Whitby, North Yorkshire, YO22 4ND.
Meetings: Mission to Seamen, Haggersgate, Whitby. 2nd Tuesday of the month, 7.30 p.m.

Whittington Astronomical Society
Secretary: Peter Williamson, The Observatory, Top Street, Whittington, Shropshire.
Meetings: The Observatory, every month.

Wiltshire Astronomical Society
Secretary: Simon Barnes, 25 Woodcombe, Melksham, Wilts SN12 6HA.
Meetings: St Andrews Church Hall, Church Lane, off Forest Road, Melksham, Wilts.

Wolverhampton Astronomical Society
Secretary: Mr M. Bryce, Iona, 16 Yellow Hammer Court, Kidderminster, Worcestershire, DY10 4RR.
Meetings: Beckminster Methodist Church Hall, Wolverhampton. Alternate Mondays, Sept.–Apr., extra dates in summer, 7.30 p.m.

Worcester Astronomical Society
Secretary: Mr S. Bateman, 12 Bozward Street, Worcester WR2 5DE.
Meetings: Room 117, Worcester College of Higher Education, Henwick Grove, Worcester. 2nd Thursday each month, 8.00 p.m.

Worthing Astronomical Society
Contact: G. Boots, 101 Ardingly Drive, Worthing, West Sussex, BN12 4TW.
Meetings: Heene Church Rooms, Heene Road, Worthing. 1st Wednesday each month (except Aug.). 7.30 p.m.

Wycombe Astronomical Society
Secretary: Mr P. Tgeherne, 34 Honeysuckle Road, Widmer End, High Wycombe, Buckinghamshire, HP15 6BW.
Meetings: Woodrow High House, Amersham. 3rd Wednesday each month, 7.45 p.m.

York Astronomical Society
Secretary: Martin Whipp, 3 Marehall Close, Clifton Moore, York YO3 4WA.
Meetings: Goodricke College, York University. 1st and 3rd Fridays each month, 7.30 p.m.

Any society wishing to be included in this list of local societies or to update details, including any website addresses, is invited to write to the Editor (c/o Macmillan, 25 Eccleston Place, London SW1W 9NF), so that the relevant information may be included in the next edition of the *Yearbook*.